# LEVINAS

# LEVINAS

## An Introduction

Colin Davis

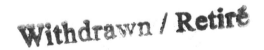

University of Notre Dame Press
Notre Dame, Indiana

Published in the United States of America in 1996 by
University of Notre Dame Press
Notre Dame, Indiana 46556
All Rights Reserved

First published in the United Kingdom in 1996 by
Polity Press, Cambridge

ISBN 0-268-01314-4 (pb.)
A CIP catalogue record for this book is available from the Library of
Congress.

The paper used in this publication meets the minimum requirements
of the American National Standard for Information Sciences—
Permanence of Paper for Printed Library Materials. ANSI Z39.48-1984.

Printed in Great Britain

# Contents

# Acknowledgements

I would like to thank all those who have helped me in innumerable ways with this book, in particular Sarah Kay, Peter Hainsworth, Edward Harcourt, Christina Howells, Gary Mole, Wes Williams, Emma Wilson, Michael Worton and Maike Bohn. I am grateful to the British Academy for granting me extended leave during which the book was completed.

# Abbreviations

References to Levinas's works are given in the text. Where a page reference is followed by slash and a second reference, the first refers to the French edition and the second to the English translation. In these cases, translations are taken from the English edition, sometimes slightly modified for consistency or clarity; titles of Levinas's works appear in English in cases where references are given to both French and English editions. Where only one reference is given, and for French texts other than those of Levinas, translations are my own. The following abbreviations have been used:

| | |
|---|---|
| AHN | A l'heure des nations |
| BV | L'Au-delà du verset / Beyond the Verse |
| DE | De l'évasion |
| DF | Difficile liberté / Difficult Freedom |
| DVI | De Dieu qui vient à l'idée |
| EDE | En découvrant l'existence avec Husserl et Heidegger |
| EE | De l'existence à l'existant / Existence and Existents |
| EI | Ethique et infini / Ethics and Infinity |
| EN | Entre nous |
| HAH | Humanisme de l'autre homme |
| MT | La Mort et le temps |
| NP | Noms propres |
| OB | Autrement qu'être ou au-delà de l'essence / Otherwise than Being or Beyond Essence |
| OS | Hors sujet / Outside the Subject |

PH     *Théorie de l'intuition dans la phénoménologie de Husserl*
QLT    *Quatre lectures talmudiques / Nine Talmudic Readings*
SS     *Du sacré au saint / Nine Talmudic Readings*
TI     *Totalité et infini / Totality and Infinity*
TO     *Le Temps et l'autre / Time and the Other*

# Introduction

The thought of Emmanuel Levinas is governed by one simple yet far-reaching idea: Western philosophy has consistently practised a suppression of the Other. Levinas has explored this idea in a publishing career which spanned over six decades. He was born in Lithuania in 1906; he moved to France in 1923, studied under Husserl and Heidegger in Germany between 1928 and 1929, and in 1930 published the first book on Husserl in French, *Théorie de l'intuition dans la phénoménologie de Husserl*. His status as one of the leading philosophers in France was confirmed with the publication of *Totality and Infinity* (*Totalité et infini*) in 1961. His considerable body of publications sought, from a variety of angles, to elaborate the ethical nature of the relation with the Other. Levinas died in 1995.

In the early part of his career, Levinas made his name as one of the earliest and most important exponents of German phenomenology in France. He began writing on Husserl and Heidegger at a time when they were largely unknown in France; and Levinas's early work played an instrumental role in making phenomenology one of the key influences on the existentialism of Jean-Paul Sartre and Maurice Merleau-Ponty in particular and post-war French philosophy in general. However, the most important phase of Levinas's philosophical career began as his dissatisfaction with the phenomenology of Husserl and Heidegger became more explicit. As early as in 1934, Levinas's essay 'Quelques réflexions sur la philosophie de l'hitlérisme' (reprinted in *Les Imprévus de l'histoire*) illustrated his concern for the ethical dimension of philosophy.

After the Second World War this concern came to dominate his work; and his distinctive contribution to ethics justifies the unique place that he has come to occupy in twentieth-century French thought.

Recent years have seen a remarkable growth of interest in Levinas's work in the French- and English-speaking worlds. Although Levinas's concerns have changed little over the last four decades, developments in French philosophy and their repercussions in British and American universities have served to make his work an almost obligatory reference point in fields as diverse as theology, sociology, anthropology, literary criticism and theory, as well as in philosophy itself. The reason for this lies in his long-standing enquiry into ethical questions. Of the major strands in post-war French thought – existentialism, Marxism, structuralism, post-structuralism – only the first two are widely seen as having a direct bearing on ethical issues; and both have long since lost much of their influence on French and international intellectual stages. Structuralism and post-structuralism seemed at least in their initial phases to have little to say on ethical matters. Structuralism characterized the subject as the intersection of linguistic, mythological or ideological forces which leave little space for individual agency and responsibility. Post-structuralist thinkers moved away from the rigid schemes and scientific claims of the structuralists, but maintained the view of the subject as an outdated humanist illusion to be demystified. Rather than the self-conscious, self-possessed source of insight and values, the subject was to be regarded as decentred and elusive, possibly no more than an effect of language or the residue of still-unliquidated and pernicious metaphysical thinking. However, the post-structuralists themselves vigorously resisted the charge that their writing was incompatible with ethical concerns. Jacques Derrida, whose work played an important role in spreading post-structuralist thought in the English-speaking world, had in fact published the first extended discussion of Levinas's philosophy in 1964; and, through the seventies and eighties, post-structuralist thinkers turned increasingly to a direct confrontation with political and ethical issues. It remains disputed whether this should be regarded as a new direction for post-structuralism or as a development of interests which were always implicit in its investigations. Whatever the case, the ethical turn of post-structuralism contributed to a climate in which contemporary philosophical debate has to a large part become dominated by Levinas's abiding concerns: what does it mean to talk of justice or responsibility when the belief systems which sustained such terms are in a state of collapse, is it possible to have an ethics without foundation, without imperatives or claim to universality?

Before all else, the contemporary importance of Levinas's ethics derives from the crucial role it accords to the problem of otherness; this ensures that Levinas's reflection has resonance in areas beyond his own circles of interest, for example in feminism, anthropology, post-colonial studies or gay and lesbian theory. Levinas pursues his investigation in the vocabulary of modern French philosophy, particularly in his use of terms such as 'Same' and 'Other'. These terms, introduced into philosophical debate by Plato, have occupied such a central position in recent French thought that Vincent Descombes uses them for the title of his study of French philosophy since 1933, *Le Même et l'autre*. Levinas's account of the relationship between Same and Other has proved to be highly influential. In Levinas's reading of the history of Western thought, the Other has generally been regarded as something provisionally separate from the Same (or the self), but ultimately reconcilable with it; otherness, or alterity, appears as a temporary interruption to be eliminated as it is incorporated into or reduced to sameness. For Levinas, on the contrary, the Other lies absolutely beyond my comprehension and should be preserved in all its irreducible strangeness; it may be revealed by other people in so far as they are not merely mirror images of myself, or (as shall be discussed in chapter 4) by religious experience or certain privileged texts. Levinas's endeavour is to protect the Other from the aggressions of the Same, to analyse the possibilities and conditions of its appearance in our lives, and to formulate the ethical significance of the encounter with it.

Levinas's conception of ethics may cause some initial confusion amongst English-speaking readers. Levinas is not interested in establishing norms or standards for moral behaviour, nor in examining the nature of ethical language or the conditions of how to live well. In most contexts, the French word used by Levinas, *l'éthique*, might just as well be translated by 'the ethical' as by 'ethics'; and the ethical, like the political (as distinct from politics in the more restricted sense), refers to a domain from which nothing human may be excluded. Levinas's ethics, as an enquiry into the nature of the ethical, analyses and attempts to maintain the possibility of a respectful, rewarding encounter with the Other; and it endeavours to discern the sources of a humane and just society in this encounter. In this book I explore some of the causes, difficulties and ramifications of Levinas's ethical enquiry.

The project of discussing the vast body of Levinas's writing (he has published around thirty books) in five short chapters seems rash, and perhaps positively brazen. A more schematic account of Levinas's work will be presented than he himself might have endorsed; and, given the disparate nature and scope of his writing, different readers will inevitably find their own interests inadequately represented in this book. I am all too aware, for example, that a great deal more could (and perhaps should) have been said about Levinas's views on history, politics and art, or about his later response to phenomenology and his influence on recent philosophy and theology. However, quite apart from the fact that such questions might have exceeded my own intellectual means, they would have gone beyond the relatively modest ambitions of this book: to give a concise, clear and readable account of the main lines of Levinas's thought and development. The question remains of whether or not a study such as this is needed. A large number of books and articles of both an introductory and a technical nature have now been published on Levinas's work. However, in my view the more technical works on Levinas's thought tend to take too much for granted, reproducing (at least for readers such as myself) many of the problems of reading posed by Levinas's texts rather than usefully elucidating them; and the introductory works, when not embarrassingly reverential, sometimes fail to explore basic difficulties raised by Levinas's key terms. For these reasons, it seemed to me worthwhile, from the position of a relative outsider and as an aid to those who like myself may feel intrigued and mystified by Levinas, to attempt to analyse in as accessible form as I could manage the coherence and obscurity of his thought.

The first chapter of the book deals with Levinas's work on phenomenology published in the thirties and forties. The chapter describes Levinas's initial enthusiasm for, and subsequent growing discontent with, the thought of Husserl and Heidegger. As Levinas comes more and more to see the work of his German teachers as replicating the suppression of alterity which he believes to be characteristic of Western thought in general, he begins to lay the foundations for his own philosophy. This chapter explores Levinas's engagement with Husserl and Heidegger in some detail in order to demonstrate the reasons for his dissatisfaction with their thought. Subsequent chapters examine the mature elaboration of his philosophy.

Chapters 2 and 3 discuss what most commentators agree are Levinas's two major philosophical texts, *Totality and Infinity* (1961) and *Otherwise than Being or Beyond Essence* (*Autrement qu'être ou au-delà de l'essence,* 1974). Although the two works have much in common, the chapters devoted to them highlight different issues which illustrate the evolution in Levinas's thought and philosophical practice. Chapter 2 concentrates on the aspect of Levinas's thought for which he is best known: his ethics, derived from an encounter with the Other which puts the self into question. In *Totality and Infinity,* however, Levinas anticipates but does not entirely effect a break with the grand traditions of Western thought: as he acknowledges, he still uses the language of ontology and, I suggest, he may not maintain the respect for the Other which he advocates. Chapter 3 shows how, partly in response to the discussion of his work by Jacques Derrida, Levinas rethinks his positions in *Otherwise than Being or Beyond Essence.* The chapter discusses how Levinas elaborates a theory of language, based on the distinction between Saying and the Said, which helps to explain his complex textual performance in that work.

Chapters 4 and 5 are more general in scope. Chapter 4 deals with Levinas's texts on religious and Judaic themes. The chapter shows how his conception of God and his understanding of Judaism have important parallels in his philosophical work, so that there is a constant and productive exchange between his different areas of interest. The final section of the chapter analyses his commentaries on the Talmud and the general theory of textuality and interpretation which underlies them. Chapter 5, entitled 'Levinas and his Readers', attempts to show how the model of textual openness discussed in the previous chapter can also be applied to Levinas's own writing. The chapter describes the difficulties that commentators have had in situating Levinas's work in the general context of contemporary French philosophy; at the same time, owing to the often enigmatic nature of Levinas's textual practice, his work has been assimilated to a wide range of different philosophical positions. The chapter attempts to explain why Levinas is at the same time so difficult to pin down and so readily adaptable to a variety of purposes.

I am aware that some readers will consult a book such as this rather than reading Levinas's notoriously difficult texts. For such readers, it is worth signalling that some of Levinas's shorter articles, such as those collected in *En découvrant l'existence avec Husserl et Heidegger* (first edition published in 1949) and *Entre nous*

(1991), give a more succinct and accessible introduction to his work than *Totality and Infinity* and *Otherwise than Being or Beyond Essence*. Finally, I should say something about spelling and capitalization. On the title pages of some of Levinas's books his name appears with an accent (Lévinas), whereas on others there is no accent. I chose not to use the accent for no better reason than that this seemed preferable in a text written in English. In the use of capitalization, notably on the word 'Other', I have attempted to reproduce Levinas's own practice as accurately as I could, even though Levinas himself is not always consistent. In some English-language editions and studies of Levinas's work, a convention has been adopted according to which *autre* (whether or not it is capitalized by Levinas) is translated by 'other' and *Autrui* by 'Other'. However, I have not followed this convention since it blurs the essential distinction made by Levinas between *autre* and *Autre* (of which *Autrui* is the personalized form), which I attempt to explain in chapter 2.

# 1

## Phenomenology

In 1932 Raymond Aron returned from Berlin to Paris and told fellow students Jean-Paul Sartre and Simone de Beauvoir about his discovery of Husserlian phenomenology. Sartre, according to de Beauvoir, 'turned pale with emotion': here was precisely what he had been looking for, a means of extracting philosophy from the most concrete, apparently most banal, experiences.[1] By this time Levinas was already intensely involved with the adventure of phenomenology. In Freiburg between 1928 and 1929 he had studied under Edmund Husserl in his final year of teaching and under Martin Heidegger in his first. In 1930 he published the first book on Husserl in French and in 1932 the first substantial article in French on Heidegger's philosophy;[2] and he collaborated on the French translation of Husserl's *Cartesian Meditations* (1931). More than Sartre, who adapted Husserl and Heidegger for his own ends, Levinas devoted much of his early philosophical career to explicating the work and significance of his German teachers. In subsequent years he has continued to insist that, despite fundamental divergences from Husserl and Heidegger, he has remained faithful to the phenomenological method that he first encountered through them.

Today, it is difficult to appreciate Sartre's emotion on first discovering Husserl. Phenomenology, out of fashion in Continental thought and never in fashion outside it, seems to belong to a quaint past where consciousness was held to be sovereign, where the reflexive, self-present subject could still assume its centrality in an intelligible world. Yet it is important to remember that phenomenology occupies a vital position in the genealogy of modern Continental thought: its influence on the existentialism of Sartre and Maurice Merleau-Ponty was crucial; it provided methods and themes for some of the most innovative literary critics of their day, such as Georges Poulet and Jean-Pierre Richard. Some of the most important recent thinkers have been preoccupied with its founding texts: Paul Ricœur has devoted a considerable part of his work to a discussion of Husserl and Heidegger; Jean-François Lyotard's first book was an introduction to phenomenology; Jacques Derrida's early reputation was established at least in part on his introduction to and translation of Husserl's *The Origin of Geometry* and his patient reading of Husserl in *La Voix et le phénomène*.[3] Phenomenology occupies a central place in the philosophical trajectory of modernity, even if its methods and aims have been rejected; and the post-structuralists might just as accurately be called post-phenomenologists.

Levinas played an important part in the dissemination of phenomenology in France; Ricœur described him as the founder of Husserl studies in France, and Sartre acknowledged that he played an important role in his discovery of phenomenology.[4] Yet Levinas's role in the dismantling of the prestige of phenomenology is no less important. The aim of this chapter is to account for Levinas's involvement with phenomenology and to explain his gradual development of a post-phenomenological ethics which characterizes itself in opposition to the philosophy of Husserl and Heidegger. The process is a slow one: in terms of published material it begins with *Théorie de l'intuition dans la phénoménologie de Husserl* in 1930 and culminates in *Totality and Infinity* in 1961.

### Husserl and Heidegger

According to his own account, Levinas discovered through Husserl 'the concrete meaning of the very possibility of "working in philosophy"' (*EI*, 19/28). Husserl offered him a method of philosophical investigation which depended neither on inflexible dogma nor on chaotic intuition. Levinas places this discovery at the very origin of his own intellectual project (see *EN*, 141). And Husserl occupies a privileged position in his writing in two senses: firstly, through the phenomenological approach which Levinas never fully renounces even though he comes to reject many of Husserl's central ideas; and, secondly, through the continuing reference to and discussion of Husserl's key texts and notions. Levinas's first book was on Husserl, and the final essay in one of his later collections, *Outside the Subject* (*Hors sujet*, 1987), is devoted to Husserl's conception of the subject. Levinas considers the principal and abiding contribution of phenomenological method to be its heightened reflexivity towards its own status; it teaches the philosopher to confront the world whilst also radically questioning the manner in which the world is presented to him or her:

> A radical, obstinate reflection about itself, a *cogito* which seeks and describes itself without being duped by a spontaneity or ready-made presence, in a major distrust toward what is thrust naturally onto knowledge, a *cogito* which constitutes the world and the object, but whose objectivity in reality occludes and encumbers the look that fixes it. [...] It is the presence of the philosopher near to things, without illusion or rhetoric, in their true status, precisely clarifying this status, the meaning of their objectivity and their being, not answering only to the question of knowing 'What is?', but to the question 'How *is* what is?', 'What does it mean that it is?' (*EI*, 20–1/30–1)

The encounter with Heidegger was, for Levinas, no less decisive than his discovery of Husserl's ideas. Already in *Théorie de l'intuition dans la phénoménologie de Husserl* Levinas presents a distinctly Heideggerian interpretation of Husserl, particularly in the emphasis on the ontological aspects of phenomenology and his criticisms of Husserl's intellectualism and neglect of historicity.[5] Yet the influence of Heidegger is more restricted: Levinas describes *Being and Time* as 'one of the greatest books in the history of philosophy' (*EN*, 255; see also *EI*, 27/37), but he rarely refers to any of Heidegger's later writings. And Levinas is cautious in his acceptance of Heidegger's influence. Although he continues to admire *Being and Time*, Levinas has difficulty separating Heidegger's later philosophy from his involvement with the Nazis in the early thirties. Like Adorno,[6] Levinas even suggests that the key notion of *Eigentlichkeit* (authenticity) already introduces into *Being and Time* the seeds of Heidegger's subsequent political disgrace (see *EN*, 255–7; *EDE*, 170). The work of Heidegger appears to Levinas as a crucial but dangerous stage in modern philosophy; to escape the limitations of his thought entails thinking through and beyond him rather than returning to the comforts of pre-Heideggerian naïvety. In the rest of this section I shall outline the significance of the work of Husserl and Heidegger as Levinas understood it in the thirties and forties; and in subsequent sections I shall describe the reasons for Levinas's increasingly critical attitude towards key aspects of their thought.

At its very simplest, phenomenology has been characterized by the slogan 'Zu den Sachen selbst' ('Back to the things themselves'). This is proclaimed by Husserl as his ambition and accepted as founding the philosophical originality of phenomenology by Heidegger at the beginning of *Being and Time*.[7] But to return to the things themselves turns out to be less simple than the slogan might have led us to hope. One of the principal ambitions of Husserlian phenomenology was to give an absolutely secure philosophical foundation to the natural sciences. This could only be provided by a stringent reflection on what science does not normally question: the role of the perceiving consciousness in the constitution of the perceived world. Husserl cannot accept as unquestionable the 'natural attitude' of scientific realism, that is the presumption that the world as we experience it exists outside and independently from consciousness. Knowledge is only entirely secure if it is, in the term used by Husserl, apodictic, that is beyond any possibility of doubt; and, at least in the initial stages of reflection, I cannot be certain that the world as I experience it really exists. As Descartes suggested, the evidence of the senses can be misleading: I might be dreaming, or I might be mad, or I might simply be mistaken in my perceptions.[8] The key notion of intentionality, which Husserl took from his teacher Franz Brentano and which plays a central role in Levinas's analysis and later critique of phenomenology, asserts that all consciousness is consciousness *of* something, that all mental acts (for example perception or memory) have an object. But even intentionality does not necessarily guarantee the independent existence of intentional objects: intended by consciousness, they are also constituted by it. Intentionality implies a relationship with something outside the self, but does not yet give it apodictic certainty. As Husserl writes in his *Cartesian Meditations*, 'Whatever exists for a man like me and is accepted by him, exists for him and is accepted in his own conscious life, which, in all consciousness of a world and in all scientific doing, keeps to itself.'[9]

So, the phenomenological 'Return to the things themselves' begins by putting into doubt the very existence of the things to which it aims to return. Husserl follows a procedure which he calls phenomenological reduction, or transcendental reduction, or the *epoché*, and which he explicitly compares to the method of Cartesian doubt. Apodictic certainty can only be acquired if everything which can be doubted is provisionally bracketed off. This includes the existence of the external world, and – crucially – the existence of other consciousnesses. What this leaves, according to Husserl, is consciousness itself: when I am conscious of a tree, I may doubt the objective existence of the tree, but I cannot doubt the reality of my consciousness. The 'me' I thus discover is not my empirical self, born in such and such a year, teaching at such and such a university: these things could themselves be errors or illusions. The *epoché* reveals a transcendental Ego which is not a part of an objective natural order, but which actually constitutes the knowable world through its intentional acts. For Husserl consciousness is primary and absolute; the transcendental Ego is the first apodictic certainty from which all others must be derived.

For the phenomenologist, getting back to the things themselves inevitably involves reflecting on the ways in which the Ego perceives and experiences those things; the intentional object cannot be separated from the consciousness that intends it. Husserl was well aware of the dangers of solipsism into which this line of thinking could easily fall. In the fifth of his *Cartesian Meditations* he attempted to offset such dangers by demonstrating that a second *epoché* could reveal the apodicticity of both other egos and the external world. I shall return to this and its importance for Levinas in the final section of this chapter. In his earliest discussions of Husserl's work, *Théorie de l'intuition dans la phénoménologie de Husserl* (1930) and 'L'Œuvre d'Edmond Husserl' (originally published in 1940 and reprinted in *En découvrant l'existence avec Husserl et Heidegger* in 1949), Levinas alludes only in passing to this problem. He concentrates on what he regards as the positive contribution of Husserlian phenomenology, making no more than brief and schematic general criticisms. The issue of solipsism remains largely implicit, and Levinas concentrates on the philosophical vistas opened up by Husserl's accounts of intentionality and intuition.

Despite Husserl's ambition of giving a secure foundation to scientific knowledge, the major achievement of his work for Levinas lies in the liberation of philosophy from the stranglehold of naturalist epistemology. Husserl achieves this by rethinking the notion of the phenomenon. Proponents of scientific objectivity implicitly rely upon an unquestioned ontology according to which a stable essence lies hidden behind the flux of perceived phenomena. The phenomenon, then, is conceived as a potentially deceptive surface which we must go beyond if secure knowledge is to be acquired. Husserl boldly erases this implicit separation of essence and phenomenon. Phenomenology is not the study of phenomena *as distinct from* essences, but the study of phenomena *as the available mode of presentation* of essences. Phenomenology, then, surpasses naturalist epistemology by establishing two new areas of investigation: existence is to be studied in all its multiplicity, and not just as a fallible sign of unchanging essences; and the phenomenologist will also enquire after the *meaning* of the existence of objects, not in any grand theological sense, but as it is conferred on the world by acts of consciousness.

The link between these two areas of investigation is provided by intentionality. Levinas describes how, for Husserl, intentionality is the characteristic activity of consciousness as it constitutes itself in relation to the world (see *PH*, 69). Consciousness is directed outside itself; and since the world as experienced is *intended*, in the phenomenological sense, its meaning and intelligibility are also assured. Husserl's consciousness, characterized by its intentional acts, is not self-enclosed; on the contrary, at the very centre of consciousness is a primary openness to what lies outside it: 'The interest of the Husserlian conception [of intentionality] consists in having put, at the very heart of the being of consciousness, contact with the world' (*PH*, 73).

Levinas describes how Husserl surpasses naturalist epistemology by rethinking its fundamental distinction between subject and object. For Husserl, the relationship with the object takes place *within the subject*; the very distinction, then, presupposes and relies upon a transcendental subjectivity in which the 'objective' world is constituted as a meaningful object of experience. Intuition, in the special sense given to the word in Husserlian phenomenology, is in consequence not an unreliable, 'unobjective' form of knowledge, but rather what Levinas calls 'the primitive phenomenon which makes possible the truth itself' (*PH*, 19). Intuition is pre-objective because it is a mode of knowledge which does not presume the existence of the objective world required by scientific realism; it makes possible the direct knowledge by consciousness of its own intentional objects.

Two important strands emerge from Levinas's discussions. Firstly, Husserlian phenomenology provides a method for investigating the experience of the world freed from the search for objective essences hidden beneath phenomenal existence. Secondly, in its reliance upon the capacity of consciousness to reflect freely upon itself, it also represents what Levinas calls 'the authentic spiritual life' (*EDE*, 45). The transcendental Ego possesses itself fully as it constitutes the world through its intentional acts. Particularly in his 1940 article, 'L'Œuvre d'Edmond Husserl', written whilst Sartre was formulating his own ideas on consciousness and liberty which would culminate in L'Être et le néant (1943), Levinas repeatedly insists that phenomenology is a philosophy of freedom:

> The philosophy of Husserl is ultimately a philosophy of freedom, of a freedom which is realized as consciousness and is defined by it; of a freedom which does not only characterize the activity of a being, but which is posited before being and by relation to which being is constituted. [. . .] Man, able to coincide absolutely with himself through phenomenological reduction, thereby regains his freedom. Phenomenology does not respond only to his need for knowledge which is absolutely founded: this is subordinate to the freedom which expresses the demand to be an I and, in relation to being, an origin. (*EDE*, 49)

At this stage in his thinking Levinas does not directly confront the issue that would preoccupy Sartre during the forties: the limitations imposed on the freedom of consciousness through its relationship with the world. Levinas pays little attention to the tensions, stresses and conflicts that might arise when consciousness encounters a world potentially hostile to its intentions. In his endeavour to promote a better understanding of Husserl, Levinas seems concerned to make him as coherent and topical as possible; and in the Introduction to *Théorie de l'intuition* he openly states that he will refrain from any full-scale philosophical critique (*PH*, 15–16). Even so, this does not mean that Levinas completely suppresses any reservations he might have. He suggests two principal avenues of criticism; one has immediate importance in the context of his study, and the other will acquire greater significance with time.

Firstly, he reproaches Husserl with his intellectualism. Consciousness, as Husserl describes it, is primarily reflexive and contemplative. Revealed through phenomenological reduction, it stands outside time and the experiences it observes; historicity and temporality appear as secondary properties rather than the very conditions of the transcendental Ego: '*Philosophy seems, in this conception, as independent of the historical situation of man as theory which seeks to consider everything sub specie aeternitatis*' (*PH*, 220).

Secondly, Levinas briefly alludes to the problem of intersubjectivity and the existence of other minds posed by the theory of the transcendental Ego. *Théorie de l'intuition* was written without explicit reference to *Cartesian Meditations* and before Husserl's important late work *The Crisis of European Sciences and Transcendental Phenomenology* (1936). So in his first book Levinas only touches on a difficulty that Husserl's own later work would attempt to resolve: the *epoché* which reveals the transcendental Ego cannot on its own demonstrate the existence of other egos (see *PH*, 214–15). In his 1940 essay Levinas mentions but does not criticize Husserl's later analysis of social relations and the presence of others (see *EDE*, 48).

The issues raised in thinking through the second of these areas will lead to the most characteristic aspects of Levinas's later thinking. The criticism of Husserl's intellectualism and the abstraction of the transcendental Ego from history derives from the fact that, even in his earliest written work, Levinas is reading Husserl through the powerful lens of Heidegger's *Being and Time*. From the very beginning of *Théorie de l'intuition* Levinas acknowledges that his reading of Husserl is heavily influenced by Heidegger (see *PH*, 14). Husserl is portrayed as laying the foundations for the work of Heidegger; and what this means in practice is that Levinas will search for those traces in the writings of Husserl which anticipate the transformation of phenomenology by Heidegger, who is seen as continuing but also crucially modifying the phenomenological project (see *PH*, 15). Heidegger gives to phenomenology an ontological turn, as he accords it a privileged role in the endeavour to describe Being. According to the opening pages of *Being and Time*, the phenomenon as it is understood in phenomenology is the site where Being reveals itself (35). From this conception, the founding questions of Heideggerian phenomenology arise: what is the meaning of Being, what is the mode of its presentation, and how do finite, historical beings (ourselves) come to understand it?

These questions influence both the language and the general shape of Levinas's reading of Husserl. As Heidegger's precursor, Husserl is described as developing a new way of thinking about Being, conceived now as revealed to perception rather than residing in some atemporal domain distinct from the experience of phenomena: 'Perception gives us being; it is through reflecting on the act of perception that we must seek the origin of the very notion of being' (*PH*, 108). So, Heidegger stresses the ontological dimension of phenomenology already found in Husserl's work, and he develops it for his own purposes. The ontology of *Being and Time* rests upon Heidegger's careful distinction between what is (being, *das Seiende*, or *l'étant* in French) and the Being of what is (Being, *das Sein*, *l'être*). As Levinas frequently insists, Heidegger emphasizes the verbal form of the word *Sein* (to be): Being is not a static essence existing outside time, but an event or process. In a sense, Being does not exist; if it did it would simply be another being. Rather, Being is the mode of existence of beings; it is not fully identifiable with beings, but neither can it be abstracted from them.

Heidegger uses the term *Dasein* to name that being by and through which Being comes to be known. *Dasein* is a problematic term for Heidegger's commentators and translators. Neither in French nor in English has any translation been found which could command broad support. Heidegger's first French translator, Henri Corbin, initially translated it by *existence*, and later, controversially, by *réalité-humaine* (human reality);[10] and Derrida, whilst criticizing Corbin's translation, argues that, although *Dasein* is not man, neither is it anything other than man.[11] The English translators of *Being and Time* prefer to leave the term in German.[12] The form of the German word is certainly important to Heidegger himself. The *Da* (there) of *Dasein* (literally: being there) indicates *Dasein*'s situatedness in time and space; and this situatedness is the inescapable condition which makes it possible for the truth of Being to be revealed. Being cannot be known, indeed it does not exist, outside the moment and place from which *Dasein* understands it. So, the understanding of Being does not liberate *Dasein* from its historical existence; on the contrary, understanding belongs to historical existence, and *Dasein* can only understand Being as historical.

For Levinas, the importance of Heidegger's phenomenological ontology lies in the dislodging of the absolute primacy accorded by Husserl to consciousness. As we saw earlier, Levinas reproaches Husserl for his intellectualism and for his abstraction of consciousness from history. The transcendental Ego of Husserl gazes at the raw matter of life from a disinterested, uninvolved, ahistorical position; consciousness is sovereign, responsible only to itself, and free. Heidegger on the other hand provides Levinas with a way of understanding Being and beings as originally constituted by the fact that they are always already engaged in time and history, without recourse to the absolute self-liberation promised by phenomenological reduction:

> For Heidegger my life is not simply a game which is played in the final analysis for the benefit of thought. The manner in which I am engaged in existence has an original meaning, irreducible to the meaning which a noema has for a noesis. The concept of consciousness cannot take account of this. For Heidegger existence certainly has a meaning; and in affirming the meaning of existence which for him does not have the opacity of a

brute fact, Heidegger remains a phenomenologist; but this meaning no longer has the structure of a noema. The subject is neither free nor absolute, he is no longer entirely responsible for himself. He is dominated and overwhelmed by history, by his origins over which he has no power since he is thrown into the world and his thrown-ness [*déréliction*] marks all his projects and all his powers. (*EDE*, 48–9)

In this passage Levinas discards the Husserlian terms *noesis* and *noema* (which refer to the acts and objects of consciousness respectively) and replaces them with a Heideggerian vocabulary: *history, world, thrown-ness* (Levinas translates Heidegger's *Geworfenheit* (thrown-ness) by *déréliction*), *project*. This change of vocabulary, with an ethical potential not realized by Heidegger but already glimpsed by Levinas, brings with it a reorientation of the phenomenological enterprise. Heidegger is still a phenomenologist because he continues to believe meaning derives from human existence and is available to human enquiry; the world is the object of, in Husserl's term, an intentional *Sinngebung* (literally: giving of sense) which guarantees that what we experience has meaning *for us* because we can only experience the world as meaningful. But Heidegger has knocked consciousness off its pedestal and made the *Da* of *Dasein* the very foundation and condition of its truth.

Heidegger, then, renews the question of Being and replaces consciousness, which is free and transcendental, with *Dasein*, which is 'dominated and overwhelmed by history' (*EDE*, 49); its Being must be understood as inseparable from temporality and historicity. What Levinas finds in Heidegger is a philosophy totally immersed (despite its off-putting language) in the world, in experience, facticity (the rootedness of the human subject in contingent, physical reality) and desire. At the same time Heidegger makes it possible to pose the fundamental question of Being: phenomenology and ontology are not opposed because Being is characterized as the mode of existence of beings; Being is that which beings understand (pre-philosophically) and seek to know (philosophically). Heidegger combines the concerns of ontology with the description of experience in a bold and exhilarating synthesis.

In Levinas's early texts on Husserl and the article 'Martin Heidegger et l'ontologie' (first published in 1932, and in a shorter version in *En découvrant l'existence avec Husserl et Heidegger*, first edition 1949) Heidegger's work appears as a new departure for phenomenology. In later essays, such as 'L'Ontologie dans le temporel' (1948) and 'De la description à l'existence' (1949) (both in *En découvrant l'existence*), Levinas continues to pursue his self-assigned role as mediator of German thought in France, but he also begins to express more openly his dissatisfaction with his philosophical masters. Heidegger's work is described as a tragic testimony to an age and to a world that may need to be surpassed (see *EDE*, 89). And at the end of 'De la description à l'existence' Levinas poses a simple but resonant question. He suggests that Heidegger's ontology is in some respects strictly classical in its account of the relationship between Being and beings, and asks, 'But is the relation of man to Being uniquely ontology?' (*EDE*, 106). Does ontology exhaust the possibilities of relationship with Being, or is there something which exceeds ontology? Does the search for the meaning of Being miss something which may be even more fundamental? Levinas does not answer his own question. Even so, it is suggested that ontology, which Heidegger established as the proper domain of phenomenology, will in turn have to be displaced; and although Levinas does not yet say so, he will discover in the ethical encounter of self and Other a relationship that cannot be explained by the ontic–ontological difference between beings and Being.

## Beyond phenomenology

In the Introduction to *Existence and Existents* (*De l'existence à l'existant*), partly written whilst he was a prisoner of war and first published in 1947, Levinas acknowledges his debt to Heidegger but also asserts the need to escape the influence of the German philosopher:

> If at the beginning our reflections are in large measure inspired by the philosophy of Martin Heidegger, where we find the concept of ontology and of the relationship which man sustains with Being, they are also governed by a profound need to leave the climate of that philosophy [*le climat de cette philosophie*], and by the conviction that we cannot leave it for a philosophy that would be pre-Heideggerian. (*EE*, 19/19)

The phrase 'the climate of this philosophy' suggests that Levinas is not just talking about specific, detailed disagreements. The events of 1933 to 1945 were decisive for his disaffection with phenomenology. It would be wrong to attribute this solely to his disgust at Heidegger's involvement with the Nazis; at the same time his disappointment over his former teacher's actions and subsequent silence about the Holocaust certainly do play a role in the evolution of his views. In intellectual terms, Levinas's desire to escape the climate of Heidegger's thought entails the rejection of a philosophical style and the world view inherent in it.

In the earliest works in which he expresses his own views rather than expounding those of others – the article 'De l'évasion' (1935), *Existence and Existents* (1947) and *Time and the Other* (1947) – Levinas adopts an approach which shows clear signs of the influence of Heidegger. His accounts of need, shame and nausea in 'De l'évasion', or laziness, fatigue and effort in *Existence and Existents*, are clearly in the lineage established by Heidegger's descriptions of anxiety, fear, dereliction or care in *Being and Time*. However, important differences of emphasis can be seen. From the beginning of the early article 'De l'évasion', Levinas clearly alludes to the concerns of *Being and Time* when he describes his aim of renewing 'the ancient problem of Being as Being' (*DE*, 74). However, as Jacques Rolland has observed, the article is characterized by a latent conflict with Heidegger, even if the German philosopher's name is not quoted in the text itself.[13] In 'De l'évasion' the relationship to Being, and by extension to Heidegger's ontology, is portrayed in dramatic terms as entailing oppression and imprisonment: Being appears as 'an imprisonment from which one must try to escape', it reveals 'its nature as a restrictive bond [*enchaînement*]', leading to 'the need to leave oneself behind, that is, *to break the most radical, the most irremissible bond, the fact that the I is itself*' (*DE*, 73). Rather than *Eigentlichkeit* (authenticity), the original relationship with Being is an unwanted bind, as the self is 'tethered to itself [*rivé à soi-même*]' (*DE*, 87), trapped and longing for escape. In this context Levinas coins his first neologism, *excendance* (see *DE*, 73): not transcendence, which implies a willed ascension to the higher reaches of Being, but an *exit from* or *exceeding of* Being without direction or ultimate goal.

During the thirties and forties Levinas's critical engagement with phenomenology takes two paths: on the one hand he begins to develop his own distinctive positions which are indebted to but also depart from those of his philosophical teachers; at the same time he undertakes a patient and detailed critique of the founding notions of Husserlian phenomenology (consciousness, intentionality, representation, presence) and the premises of Heideggerian ontology. In particular Levinas returns on numerous occasions to the notion of intentionality. In 1930 Levinas could describe intentionality as ensuring the self-transcendence of consciousness though the encounter with something other than itself: as consciousness *of* something, intentionality is a mode of contact with the external world (see *PH*, 68–9). By 1940 he is not so sure. He still insists that the intentional object lies outside the subject, but also that intentionality seals the subject off from the external world, making it a kind of monad (see *EDE*, 50): closed in on itself, without door or window on to what lies outside, the only meanings it discovers in the world are meanings that it has created.

What is at stake in Levinas's discussions of intentionality is the ability of consciousness to encounter something other than itself. If meaning is entirely given by the subject rather than found in the world, then consciousness cannot experience, perceive or learn anything that it did not already contain. Yet, in its 'Return to the things themselves', phenomenology also aims to establish contact with the world outside the subject. This is implied in the notion of presentation which Husserl adapted from Franz Brentano. In the presentation, as David Bell describes it, the perceived object is present to the perceiving subject:

> [A presentation] is an episode or awareness or consciousness in which a given item, its content, is neutrally and disinterestedly 'present'. A presentation, in other words, involves no intellectual, emotional, voli-tional, aesthetic or other attitude to the presented content on the part of the subject: it is not judged, estimated, evaluated, wanted, hated or the like; it is simply and neutrally *there*.[14]

The object, then, is literally re-presented to the subject, made present again and neutrally perceived. Although Brentano did concede that a presentation might never be entirely separable from judgement or emotion, it is nevertheless a fundamental category in his taxonomy of mental phenomena.[15] However, as Levinas becomes increasingly sensitive to tensions within the phenomeno-logical project, he dwells more on the ways in which Husserlian phenomenology makes the notion of presentation problematic even whilst apparently endorsing it. Phenomenology aims to study the encounters between consciousness and the world, but it also suggests that the world is only ever encountered as already constituted by and within consciousness. The encounter promised by intentionality may be precisely what the theory of intentionality precludes: consciousness can never meet anything truly alien to itself because the external world is a product of its own activity.

Levinas isolates a further set of problems in Husserlian pheno-menology arising from the privilege it accords to presence, the present and representation (see *EN*, 143).[16] Like Derrida in *La Voix et le phénomène*,[17] Levinas submits the texts of phenomenology to thorough close examination and finds in them a fundamental contradiction: whilst predicated on the privilege of presence, they also imply that presence is originally fissured, that it is never fully possessed. The key notion of representation thus also becomes problematic: an object which is not present to itself cannot easily be re-presented to a transcendental Ego whose own self-presence is insecure. As Levinas implies in the title of his essay 'La Ruine de la représentation', first published in 1959 in a volume commemorating the one-hundredth anniversary of Husserl's birth, Husserl's work brings the sovereignty of representation into question (see *EDE*, 131). In an essay published in the same year in another volume on Husserl, Levinas is even more assertive:

> Phenomenology is a destruction of the representation of the theoretical object. It denounces the contemplation of the object – (which, however, it seems to have encouraged) – as an abstraction, as a partial vision of Being, as a *forgetting*, one might say in modern terms, *of its truth*. (*EDE*, 114)

The key to Husserlian phenomenology lies in its denial of the natural attitude; or, as Levinas puts it, 'To do phenomenology is to denounce as naïve the direct vision of the object' (*EDE*, 114). The object is never re-presented to the subject because it can never be fully and neutrally encountered *as it is*. The mode of access to the object forms part of the object itself; it is always an intentional object and so always belongs to the world given meaning by the intentionality of consciousness. Even the division between subject and object can be regarded as one of the ways in which consciousness makes the world intelligible to itself, rather than being an opposition with objective validity outside consciousness.

In his critique of phenomenology, Levinas questions both the self-presence of the transcendental Ego and its ability to experience the world external to itself. As he draws attentions to shortcomings in Husserl's thinking, he is working towards his own conception of subjectivity as radically turned outwards, maintaining an openness to the non-self which is not subsumed under the categories of representation or knowledge. In the terms which he begins to use in the forties and fifties and which will occupy a central place in his later thinking, he wants to establish a relationship between the Same and the Other which does not entail the dissolution of either. So, he attempts to resolve the apparent antinomy of intentionality as both act of consciousness and relationship with what lies outside consciousness. Intentionality, he suggests, does not *present* the world as it is in itself, but neither does it entirely replicate what consciousness already possesses. Here, Heidegger comes to his assistance: consciousness is not outside the world, but part of it; subject and object constitute and are constituted by one another in a process which denies the sovereignty and independence of either and ensures a perpetual interchange. Through intentionality, consciousness encounters the world as opaque and enigmatic, never completely known because always available to different perceptions; and it can never be fixed in the subject's knowledge of an unchanging essence (see *EDE*, 133–4). Understood in this way, intentionality no longer confirms the self-presence of consciousness; on the contrary, it forces it to encounter the world as enigmatic and thereby interrupts its self-contented possession both of itself and of what lies outside itself. So, Levinas is able crucially to modify the definition of intentionality: no longer simply consciousness of something (implying something represented, known, returned to the hegemony of the Same), but 'an exit from oneself' (*EDE*, 145), or more fundamentally 'the relationship with alterity' (*EDE*, 139).

By showing problems within the notions of intentionality, representation and presence, Levinas uses Husserl's own texts to dislodge consciousness from the privileged position Husserl accords to it. As we have seen, Levinas draws on Heidegger in support of his critique of Husserl. But increasingly Heidegger also becomes the object of explicit rebuttal. What had seemed to be Heidegger's greatest innovation – his renewal of the question of Being from the standpoint of phenomenology – turns out to demonstrate a deep and damaging attachment to the philosophical tradition. In a sense Heidegger's shortcoming is identical to Husserl's: both thinkers subsume the Other under the authority of the Same, which is understood as consciousness in Husserl and Being in Heidegger. The Heideggerian destruction of metaphysics thus appears as a conservation of the deepest ontological presumptions of Western thought: 'this supremacy of the Same over the Other seems to me to be entirely maintained in the philosophy of Heidegger. [. . .] He does not destroy, but rather he epitomizes a whole current of Western thought. / The *Dasein* that Heidegger puts in the place of the soul, of consciousness, of the Ego, retains the structure of the Same' (*EDE*, 169). In order to avoid duplicating this most fundamental presumption of Western thought, Levinas requires a way of thinking about Being which avoids the pitfalls of Heideggerian ontology and ontology in general.

For Levinas, the importance of Heideggerian ontology lies in the place that it assigns to facticity and contingency: rather than brute facts offered to understanding, these are the very modes by which *Dasein* comprehends Being. So all human behaviour may play a role in ontological enquiry: 'The comprehension of Being not only presupposes a theoretical attitude, but also the whole of human behaviour. The whole of man is ontology' (*EN*, 14). Hence the extraordinary immodesty of ontology: Being encompasses everything there is; even the forgetting or misunderstanding of Being turn out to be modes (albeit deficient) of its understanding. In 'De l'évasion' Levinas described the escape from Being as a fundamental yet doomed project. From a Heideggerian perspective the failure of escape is inevitable: if everything human is engaged in the comprehension of Being, then the human need to escape must be part of what it is trying to escape from. In this context, then, Levinas requires a more modest way of talking about Being which disturbs the stranglehold of Heideggerian ontology. A first step is provided by what he calls the *il y a*.

Developed in *Existence and Existents* and *Time and the Other*, the *il y a* is the best-known notion from Levinas's early texts; and although he rarely discusses it at length in subsequent works it remains of great importance to his later thinking. In 'De l'évasion' Levinas had described the phrase '*there is Being* [*il y a de l'être*]' as an 'elementary truth' (*DE*, 70). At the time he seems unaware of the consequences of this 'truth' and the unassuming phrase which conveys it. It might appear that *il y a* is a simple translation of Heidegger's *es gibt*. Both phrases could be translated by 'there is', but this translation overlooks the different implications of the expressions used. Indeed, Levinas carefully distinguishes *il y a* from *es gibt* (see *EE*, 10).[18] The German phrase literally means 'it gives'. Heidegger himself draws upon this meaning; in his *Letter on Humanism* he explains that *il y a* is an inaccurate translation of *es gibt* because the 'it' of 'it gives' is not an anonymous, impersonal subject: 'The "it" which here "gives" is Being itself. The "gives", however, designates the essence of Being which gives and which confers its truth.'[19] Levinas emphasizes the implications of generosity and abundance that Heidegger's account contains: Being is *given* as the object of an original and binding act of donation (see *DF*, 407/292). Levinas's *il y a* contains no such implications of generosity. What is important here is the impersonality of the expression: *il y a* is compared to phrases such as *il pleut* (it is raining), *il fait nuit* (it is dark) or *il fait chaud* (it is hot) (see *EE*, 10; *TO*, 26/47), in which the *il* refers to no identifiable subject. The *il y a* names what Levinas calls 'existing without existents [*un exister sans existant*]' (*TO*, 25/45–6): an anonymous, impersonal *existing* (the verbal form is important here) before the constitution of the individuated human subject. Attempts to identify it more closely are necessarily paradoxical. It is the presence within absence, the sound you hear when everything is silent, Being without beings, the fullness of what is empty (see *EE*, 10–11).

At this stage there is no consciousness to experience this paradoxical state of existence. In *Existence and Existents* and *Time and the Other* Levinas endeavours to describe the emergence of consciousness from the anonymity of the *il y a*. His point is that consciousness should be understood as a hypostasis, that is as an event whereby something as yet unidentifiable acquires separate existence. In this account consciousness, along with subjectivity and identity, are secondary, emerging from the *il y a* rather than pre-existing it.

It would be difficult to attempt to assess the notion of the *il y a* in terms of its truth or persuasiveness. Levinas does not offer anything that could easily be qualified as an argument for preferring the anonymity of *il y a* to the generosity of *es gibt*. Since the *il y a* precedes and presupposes anything that can be known by reason, its appeal is to intuitive recognition rather than philosophical investigation. It nevertheless plays a vital strategic role in Levinas's escape from what he calls the 'climate' of Heideggerian philosophy, since it forms the basis of his attempt to cast off the tyranny of Being. The final stage of Levinas's reflection on the *il y a* is the one which will have the most far-reaching consequences for his subsequent thought. Levinas attempts to explain how the encounter with the Other enters into the drama of consciousness. The title of *Time and the Other* alludes to Heidegger's *Being and Time*, yet the replacement of Being by *l'autre* (the other) is of the greatest significance. For Heidegger, temporality is the condition of Being, and time is the site where the drama of the comprehension of Being by *Dasein* is played out. For Levinas, however, Heidegger's *Dasein* is always solitary; and in its dialogue with Being, contrary to Heidegger's own views, it has no real need for time and the possibilities of encounter and change that it brings with it. In Levinas's interpretation of Heidegger, the fundamental encounter for humans is not with other beings, but with Being itself; temporality is the condition of the encounter, but does not represent the possibility of radically unforeseen occurrences which might fundamentally alter *Dasein*'s understanding of Being. Levinas marks out his own views in opposition to those he attributes to Heidegger: time should be understood as the condition of an encounter with something other than Being. As Levinas puts it concisely, 'The other is the future [*L'avenir, c'est l'autre*]' (*TO*, 64/77). Time ensures a relationship with that which lies outside Being and defies the sovereignty of the transcendental Ego which attempts to derive understanding of the world only from its knowledge of itself. The principal thesis of *Time and the Other* is, he says, the attempt to think of time 'not as a degradation of eternity, but as the relationship to *that* which – of itself unassimilable, absolutely other – would not allow itself to be assimilated by experience; or to *that* which – of itself infinite – would not allow itself to be comprehended' (*TO*, 9–10/32).

Levinas describes a development which leads from the anonymity of the *il y a* to the hypostasis of consciousness and finally to the subject's encounter with something utterly alien and unable to be assimilated. This account leads Levinas beyond phenomenology and ontology in so far as he rejects knowledge of the Ego or the comprehension of Being as the goals of philosophical enquiry. At a rhetorical level, this entails a rejection of the metaphor of light which, through its associations with comprehension and knowledge, he regards as playing a determining role in the development of Western thought: Levinas argues that 'Light, whether it emanates from the sensible or from the intelligible sun, is since Plato said to be a condition for all beings' (*EE*, 74/47). In particular, phenomenology relies upon light as the very condition of the appearance of phenomena.[20] Through light, what is hidden is illuminated. The Husserlian Ego finds the world made bright by its own intentional meanings; Heideggerian *Dasein* is the being for whom Being is always already illumined, always already comprehended. The world, as the phenomenologists encounter it, is lit up, understood, known and possessed. So what comes from the outside is always experienced as a property of the subject: 'What comes from the outside – illuminated – is comprehended, that is, comes from ourselves. Light makes objects into a world, that is, makes them belong to us' (*EE*, 75/48). The ultimate failure of phenomenology, for Levinas, lies in its inability to envisage an encounter with the Other which does not entail a return to the self:

Qua phenomenology, [phenomenological description] remains within the world of light, the world of the solitary ego who has no relationship with the other as other, for whom the other is another me, an *alter ego* known by empathy, that is, by a return to oneself. (*EE*, 145/85)

In a world thus illumined, possessed and understood, there is no place for anything outside the subject. In what he calls his 'phenomenology of alterity [*phénoménologie de l'altérité*]' (*TO*, 14/35) Levinas attempts to describe encounters which do not annul the otherness, the constitutive strangeness, of the Other. The imperious metaphors of possession, property and comprehension are replaced by a vocabulary which instead privileges approach, proximity, caress and fecundity. The problem for Levinas, then, is to explain how the encounter with the Other can be achieved.

## Encountering the Other

In *Théorie de l'intuition* Levinas played down the solipsistic implications of Husserl's transcendental phenomenology, noting only that 'The reduction to the Ego, the *egological reduction*, can only be a first step towards phenomenology. It is also necessary to discover the "others", the intersubjective world' (*PH*, 215). Ten years later, in 'L'Œuvre d'Edmond Husserl', Levinas acknowledges the charge of solipsism that could be made against Husserl's work whilst attempting to offset it: 'No solipsism, but the possibility of solipsism. This possibility characterizes a manner of being in which existence is its own foundation' (*EDE*, 50). By 1947, in *Time and the Other*, he is more uncompromising: 'The intentionality of consciousness allows one to distinguish the ego from things, but it does not make solipsism disappear: its element – light – renders us master of the exterior world but is incapable of discovering a peer for us there' (*TO*, 48/65). If intentionality, the cornerstone of Husserlian phenomenology, shows me a world which is always already my own possession, I cannot share that possession with anyone else; I have no equal, I am alone, there is no Other.

Husserl himself was aware that any philosophy which takes the transcendental Ego as its first apodictic certainty must necessarily face the problem of solipsism. He raises the issue in the second of his *Cartesian Meditations* and attempts to resolve it in the fifth. The difficulty arises from the primacy accorded to the transcendental Ego, which phenomenological reduction reveals to be the source of all experience. I can encounter other people as physical objects in the natural world, but I cannot presume that other transcendental Egos exist because I can have no direct experience of them. Indeed, if I could have direct experience of them, they would by definition no longer be transcendental, since they would be part of the world as presented to and constituted by my consciousness:

> Properly speaking, neither the other Ego himself, nor his subjective processes or his appearances themselves, nor anything else belonging to his own essence, becomes given in our experience originally. If it were, if what belongs to the other's own essence were directly accessible, it would be merely a moment of my own essence, and ultimately he himself and I myself would be the same. (91/108)

There can be no direct, unmediated experience of other transcendental Egos; but if I cannot experience them directly, why should I presume that they exist at all? In his attempt to overcome the charge of solipsism which might easily be made against this line of thinking, Husserl proposes a second *epoché*, which he calls a 'reduction of transcendental experience to the sphere of ownness' (77/92). This reduction is more radical than the first: having bracketed off the objective world in the first reduction, the phenomenologist now attempts to jettison all assumptions about other subjects. The point of this is to discover what is originally and indisputably *mine*. The phenomenologist thus discovers, according to Husserl, a stratum of experience that cannot be further reduced: in the sphere of ownness I find that I have an empirical self, a 'bodily organism, the psychophysical Ego, with "body and soul" and personal Ego' (82/98). So, the transcendental Ego possesses a body which interacts with the physical world. And as it becomes aware of its own empirical self, the Ego can also observe that the world contains other bodies which act and respond in ways much like its own. Discovering itself to be embodied, the Ego finds itself in a world apparently shared with similar creatures.

The realization that the world is inhabited by other bodies does not yet in itself prove the existence of other transcendental Egos. However, the 'reduction to the sphere of ownness' and the discovery of the empirical self allow an important advance in Husserl's argument. The Other cannot be presented directly to my consciousness, but his or her body and behaviour can be. Observing the changing but concordant actions of others can lead to what Husserl calls an *analogical apperception* or *appresentation* (92/108): the Other behaves in ways that I recognize as familiar from my experience of myself, so I recognize that the Ego of the Other may be, like mine, transcendental. Thus, other Egos are not *presented*, but *appresented*, revealed by analogy; what I *can* experience gives me knowledge of what I cannot encounter without mediation:

> The character of the existent 'other' has its basis in this kind of verifiable accessibility of what is not originally accessible. Whatever can become presented, and evidently verified, *originally* – is something *I* am; or else it belongs to me as peculiarly my own. Whatever, by virtue thereof, is experienced in that founded manner which characterizes a primordially unfulfillable experience – an experience that does not give something itself originally but that consistently verifies something indicated – is 'other'. (97/114–15)

The appresentation, then, depends upon real presentations, as the physical appresents the psychical. The appresentation does not reveal other transcendental Egos, but it does reveal that such Egos are there, albeit in a state of necessary concealment from me. Husserl now claims that the problem of solipsism has been avoided and knowledge both of other selves and of the natural world is assured within his own stringent criteria of apodicticity (see 128/ 150, 133/154–5).

Such a solution to the problem of other selves would seem to have a certain amount to recommend it to Levinas, since it maintains the gulf which separates myself from other Egos, and hence maintains the radical unknowability of the Other. However, setting aside the general question of how rigorous or persuasive Husserl's argument might be,[21] it is not at all certain that he has in fact preserved – or indeed that he wanted to preserve – the otherness of the Other. It is true that other Egos are not experienced directly, so in one sense they remain unknown and unknowable to me; in another sense, however, they are known even without direct experience because all Egos are presumed to be fundamentally similar. The Ego of the Other is appresented to me only because I recognize the behaviour of his or her body as *familiar*; in other words, I acknowledge the existence of the Other because he or she is basically *like me*. This conclusion is already anticipated by Husserl's description of the self as a monad and his insistence that the allusion to Leibniz is entirely deliberate (128/150). The Leibniz-ian monad is self-contained and isolated from other monads, like the transcendental Ego; but – and this is a crucial qualification – each monad mirrors all the others.[22] So, although I cannot see or touch the monadic Ego of the other, the very fact that I call it monadic implies that it is in all important respects similar to my own. Ultimately, for Husserl, the Other can be known by empathy (*Einfühlung*): not because I can cast off my own self, but because all Egos reflect each other. Despite Hursserl's attempt to demonstrate the multiplicity of transcendental Egos, there is still in a sense only one – my own – which is the model for all others. For Husserl, in the phrase *alter ego* (other self) it is the *ego*, not the *alter*, which is most important, as he explains whilst adopting the imagery of reflection which is central to Leibniz's monadology:

> there becomes constituted an ego, not as 'I myself', but as mirrored in my own Ego, in my monad. The second ego, however, is not simply there and strictly presented; rather is he constituted as 'alter ego' – the ego indicated as one moment by this expression being I myself in my ownness. (78/94)

The Other, Husserl continues, is a reflection of myself; and because each Ego is a monad, reflecting, containing and contained in all other Egos, the crucial terms of Husserlian intersubjectivity can be supported: harmony, community, communion, empathy, reciprocal recognition. The Ego is no longer a *solus ipse* (128/150); it occupies a sovereign place in an intelligible world in which the totality of experience and knowledge is available to it:

> [It is] the systematic unfolding of the *universal logos of all conceivable being*. In other words: As developed systematically and fully, transcendental phenomenology would be *ipso facto* the true and *genuine universal ontology* – not, however, just an emptily formal universal ontology, but also one that comprised in itself all regional existential possibilities, and did so in respect of all the *correlations* pertaining to them. (132/155)

From Levinas's perspective, Husserl's solution to the problem of the existence of other selves succeeds only in relocating the question: sweeping it under the carpet, as it were, rather than clearing it up. Although the Other is never fully present to me, he or she is *known* by empathy and *assimilated* because conceived as a reflection of myself. So, in Levinas's view, Husserl's attempt to demonstrate the existence of transcendental Egos other than my own in effect leaves no place for the Other as Other.

The problem of solipsism arises for Husserl because, like Descartes, he takes the subject as the first apodictic certainty: if we can be sure only of the existence of the subject, perhaps the subject is all that exists? In *Being and Time* Heidegger avoids this difficulty because he does not derive his philosophy from the apodicticity of the transcendental Ego. For him, *Dasein* always inhabits a world which is shared with others: 'In clarifying Being-in-the-world we have shown that a bare subject without a world never "is" proximally [*zunächst*, from the beginning], nor is it ever given. And so in the end an isolated "I" without Others is just as far from being proximally given' (116). By depicting *Dasein*'s world as always already shared with others, Heidegger sidesteps the problem of the solipsistic Ego. For him the issue is not to give an unquestionable foundation to knowledge of the Ego in its dealings with the world, but to analyse the ontological significance of the presence of others.

Heidegger rejects Husserl's notion of empathy (*Einfühlung*) as a key to understanding the Other; empathy implies that the Other is merely 'a duplicate of the self' (124) and therefore an inherent part of the Being of *Dasein*. So Heidegger sets out to resist the reduction of alterity brought about in his (and Levinas's) view by Husserl's phenomenology. Heidegger's account of a world shared with others is governed by his use of the word and prefix *mit* (with): 'By reason of this *with-like* [*mithaften*] Being-in-the-world, the world is always the one that I share with [*mit*] Others. The world of Dasein is a *with-world* [*Mitwelt*]. Being-in is *Being-with* [*Mitsein*] Others. Their Being-in-themselves within-the-world is *Dasein-with* [*Mitdasein*]' (118). The Being of *Dasein* must be understood as a Being *with* others; so Being is qualified by the key Heideggerian term *Mitsein* (Being-with).

Heidegger's account has attractions for Levinas because the others with whom *Dasein* shares the world are not conceived as reflections of myself. However, Heidegger's ontological concerns offset this important gain: he is interested in modes of Being rather than empirical encounters. Indeed, he makes it clear that the encounter with the Other is not at all essential for the understanding of Being as *Mitsein*. The empirical presence or absence of others may be ontically important (i.e. important to us as individuals), but it is ontologically meaningless:

> Being-with [*Mitsein*] is an existential characteristic of Dasein even when factically no Other is present-at-hand or perceived. Even Dasein's Being-alone is Being-with in the world [*Auch das Alleinsein des Daseins ist Mitsein in der Welt*]. The Other can *be missing* only *in* and *for* a Being-with. Being-alone is a deficient mode of Being-with [*Das Alleinsein ist ein defizienter Modus des Mitseins*]; its very possibility is the proof of this. (120)

*Mitsein*, then, has little to do with being with or encountering others in the everyday sense. It characterizes the relationship of *Dasein* with Being, but not of beings with one another: 'Being-with is in every case a characteristic of one's own Dasein' (121).

Levinas bases his objection to this account of being-with-others on the solitariness of *Dasein*: despite Heidegger's frequent use of the word *begegnen* (to meet or to encounter) in the pages devoted to *Mitsein*, it is not at all clear that any real encounter with the Other is entailed or required by the notion. Collectivity, communion and sociality are part of the relationship of *Dasein* to Being rather than a relationship with anything radically alien. So *Dasein* remains fundamentally solitary: 'Just as in all the philosophies of communion, sociality in Heidegger is found in the subject alone; and it is in terms of solitude that the analysis of *Dasein* in its authentic form is pursued' (*TO*, 89/93; see also *EE*, 162/95). *Mitsein* does not break the structure of *Jemeinigkeit* (mine-ness) which characterizes *Dasein*'s experience. The Other does not come from the outside to challenge the sovereignty of my possession and comprehension of the world; instead, he or she is encountered (if at all) in the intimacy of Being, and the priority of the Same is maintained. If, for Heidegger, Husserl's empathy showed the failure to conceive the Other as Other, then for Levinas Heidegger's *Mitsein* makes precisely the same mistake.

Levinas needs to find some way of showing that an encounter with what lies outside Being, or the Same, or the Ego, may be possible. From this point of view, the discussion of death in *Time and the Other* forms a pivotal moment in Levinas's thinking. As in his more recent book, *La Mort et le temps* (lectures given in 1975, first published in 1991), Levinas develops his own ideas partly through a dialogue with Heidegger. For Heidegger, in *Being and Time*, no one can die for anyone else in a genuine sense:

> No one can take the Other's dying away from him. Of course someone can 'go to his death for another'. But that always means to sacrifice oneself for the Other 'in some definite affair'. Such 'dying for' can never signify that the Other has thus had his death taken away in even the slightest degree. Dying is something that every Dasein itself must take upon itself at the time. By its very essence, death is in every case mine, in so far as it 'is' at all. (240)[23]

Death, then, is always my own death; I cannot die in the place of anyone else, nor does death entail an experience of anything outside myself. Heidegger insists that, ontologically, death is constituted by *Jemeinigkeit*: it does not disturb the relationship with Being in which is contained the sum of my possible experiences.

Levinas argues that Heidegger's description of *Sein zum Tode* (Being for death) has missed the essential point of death. If death is part of the relationship with Being, then it is always comprehended (albeit pre-philosophically) by *Dasein*; but for Levinas death is that which lies irretrievably beyond experience, it is utterly unknowable and thus it marks 'the end of the subject's virility and heroism' (*TO*, 59/72) which Heidegger's position maintains. Death is not something that can be seen, known and comprehended; it disrupts the subject's mastery of itself; it shows that an event is possible which I cannot assume as part of an intentional or existential project (see *TO*, 62/74). The approach of death shows the subject that something absolutely alien is about to happen, something that escapes the sovereignty of intentionality or the comprehension of Being:

> This approach of death indicates that we are in relation with something that is absolutely other, something bearing alterity not as a provisional determination we can assimilate through enjoyment [*jouissance*], but as something whose very existence is made of alterity. My solitude is thus not confirmed by death but broken by it. (*TO*, 63/74)

Both Husserl's transcendental Ego and Heidegger's *Dasein* are, for Levinas, essentially solitary. Death breaks this solitude by establishing the possibility of an encounter with something outside the self. This marks a crucial point of departure from Levinas's phenomenological precursors: the Other is not another self, but is constituted by alterity; it is unknowable and therefore refractory to the metaphors of light which support the phenomenologists' claims to knowledge; and it disrupts the self-enclosed totality of a world described in terms of harmony and communion:

> But this precisely indicates that the other is in no way another myself, participating with me in a common existence. The relationship with the other is not an idyllic and harmonious relationship of communion or a sympathy [*sympathie*, Levinas's translation of Husserl's *Einfühlung*] through which we put ourselves in the other's place; we recognize the other as resembling us, but exterior to us; the relationship with the other is a relationship with a Mystery. (*TO*, 63/75)

This passage indicates the crux of Levinas's dispute with phenomenology: in the phrase *alter ego* only the word *ego* has been thoroughly examined, whereas the *alter* has been suppressed.

Through his discussion of death Levinas demonstrates what he calls 'the possibility of an event' (*TO*, 65/77), that is the possibility that something might occur which is not always already intended and known by the transcendental Ego or assumed within the relationship with Being. He begins to examine such 'events' in which the alterity of the Other is maintained (sex, paternity, fecundity), and at the end of *Time and the Other* he acknowledges that his procedure can no longer be qualified as phenomenological (see *TO*, 87/92: 'I have not proceeded in a phenomenological way').

The Other is encountered as an essential mystery; it is not known or knowable. Rather than a philosophy of the phenomenon which appears in the light as an object of knowledge, in his 1965 essay 'Énigme et phénomène' Levinas begins to develop what he calls a philosophy of the enigma, a philosophy of darkness in which the Other is never fully seen, known or possessed (see *EDE*, 203–16). This raises problems which will remain central to Levinas's philosophical project for the rest of his career. How is it possible to discuss the Other whilst retaining its essential strangeness, without making it familiar and thus no longer Other? What is the status of a philosophical practice which denies that it is offering us knowledge or illumination, since these would destroy the very objects of its enquiry? Such questions in turn raise fundamental problems about how we should read Levinas's texts. His own philosophical practice is necessarily implicated in the tradition of thought which he so roundly criticizes. This becomes one of the central issues in Levinas's writing, and it will be necessary to return to it in subsequent chapters.

Initially, Husserl and Heidegger seemed to offer a new direction for philosophy, providing the philosopher with powerful techniques for analysing concrete areas of experience in relation to broader questions of meaning, subjectivity and Being. In the course of his long and patient study of their work, Levinas begins to see more and more that their innovations are accompanied by an inability to think outside the most traditional philosophical lines. So, his dissatisfaction with phenomenology develops into a critical reading of the history of Western philosophy in general:

> Western philosophy coincides with the unveiling of the other in which the Other, by manifesting itself as a being, loses its alterity. Philosophy is afflicted, from its childhood, with an insurmountable allergy: a horror of the Other which remains Other. It is for this reason that philosophy is essentially the philosophy of Being; the comprehension of Being is its final word and the fundamental structure of man. (*EDE*, 188)

Levinas's point about Western philosophy is astonishingly simple, but it will have major philosophical consequences: philosophy, he suggests, has been characterized by its failure to think of the Other as Other. The history of philosophy has been like the story of Ulysses who 'through all his wanderings only returns to his native island' (*EDE*, 188). Levinas prefers the story of Abraham: 'To the myth of Ulysses returning to Ithaca, we would like to oppose the story of Abraham leaving his country for ever to go to a still unknown land and forbidding his servant to take even his son back to this point of departure' (*EDE*, 191). Philosophy has always sought to return to familiar ground (Being, Truth, the Same). Levinas's endeavour will be to take it elsewhere, to make it susceptible to an encounter with what it has always suppressed. The problem of the Other has been misposed: rather than seeking knowledge of it (thus reducing its otherness), we should accept that we do not, cannot and should not know the Other. The rest of Levinas's philosophical career will, then, be dominated by one question: what does it mean to think of the Other as Other?

By the early fifties Levinas had spent a quarter of a century studying and explicating the texts of Husserl and Heidegger. He had laid the basis for a thorough critique of phenomenology; and in particular, although as yet he has only begun to anticipate the consequences of this insight, he has isolated the ethical lacuna entailed in its suppression of the Other. After publishing three books in the late forties, *Existence and Existents*, *Time and the Other* and *En découvrant l'existence avec Husserl et Heidegger*, he published only articles in the fifties. It would be more than a decade before the publication of his next book; but that book, *Totality and Infinity* (first published in 1961), would consolidate his standing as one of the most important French thinkers of the century, as it points a distinctive way out of the ethical impasse of phenomenology.

# 2

## Same and Other:
## Totality and Infinity

### Introduction

Twelve years separate the publication of *En découvrant l'existence avec Husserl et Heidegger* (1949) from that of *Totality and Infinity* (1961), the first of Levinas's two major philosophical works. In the fifties a series of important articles had given notice of the new direction that Levinas's thought was beginning to take.[1] His earlier work remained heavily influenced by Husserl and Heidegger, despite differences of approach and emphasis. The title of Levinas's *Existence and Existents*, for example, signalled the importance for Levinas of the Heideggerian enterprise, whilst also announcing a reversal of Heidegger's priorities.[2] Rather than progressing from beings to knowledge of Being, Levinas aimed to pursue his enquiry in the opposite direction: beings should be preserved in their specificity and isolation, and not subsumed under the general category of Being. *Totality and Infinity* represents a new departure. The central focus is no longer on the relationship between Being and beings, but on the question: what is there other than Being? And since Being under its various guises (the One, the Same, or totality) appears to be coextensive with the whole of reality itself, this question could also be posed as: what is there apart from everything?

Levinas's answer is both simple and complex. Simple, because a relatively restricted series of words, overlapping in sense and usage to the point of sometimes appearing synonymous, is used to name this something-outside-everything: transcendence, exteriority, infinity, the Other, alterity, discourse and, most crucially, ethics. The complexity of the answer arises from the very act of designating that which lies outside totality or Being. The terms that Levinas uses risk transforming what they name into objects of philosophical investigation, thereby restoring them to the tradition which they were supposed to exceed. So, by a process of recuperation which Levinas regards as typical of Western philosophy, the other-than-Being turns out to be part of Being after all, only erroneously or provisionally separate from it. Like Ulysses returning to Ithaca (to use one of Levinas's favourite analogies), Levinas returns – albeit in his case unwillingly – to the homeland of ontology from which he had departed.

Levinas frequently alludes to a passage of Plato's *Republic* in which Socrates describes the good which 'is not essence but still transcends essence in dignity and surpassing power'.[3] Levinas takes this to mean that ethical questions are separate from ontological concerns; since the good transcends essence, it does not belong to Being or totality. Levinas's problem is to find ways of maintaining the separation of ethics and ontology, when the philosophical tools at his disposal derive from a tradition which regards ethical enquiry as dependent upon ontological insights. Levinas will tussle with this problem in his two most important and challenging philosophical works, *Totality and Infinity* and *Otherwise than Being*, which I shall discuss in detail in this and the following chapter. Levinas's acute awareness of the pitfalls involved in overcoming ontology, in becoming Abraham boldly stepping out into the unknown rather than Ulysses seeking only what he had left behind, helps to explain the extraordinary difficulty of his writing. His texts are assertive and propositional, but also enigmatic, fragmented, paradoxical or perhaps just plain inconsistent. For reasons I shall attempt to explain, the encounter with the Other is an experience which is not an experience, establishing a relationship which is not a relationship; and anyway this *encounter* is not an event which can be located in time or the history of the subject.

Much of the difficulty of Levinas's writing derives from the complexity of his prose and the deceptive familiarity of his key terms. He is best known both in France and internationally as a philosopher of ethics, and the problems of comprehension that his writing raises cluster in particular around the significance of ethics in his thought. Ethics, in his use of the term, is neither a code of rules nor the study of reasoning about how we ought to act.[4] The first use of the word *éthique* in the original preface to the 1961

edition of *Totality and Infinity* informs us, in a pronouncement that
is as enigmatic as it is axiomatic, that 'ethics is an optics' (*TI*, 8/
23). The context tells us more about what this does not mean than
what it does; and the later qualification that 'Ethics is the spiritual
optics' (*TI*, 76/78) might be thought to confuse the issue even
further. Whatever ethics might be, it also entails a disturbance of
the very language in which ethical enquiry will be pursued.

The first use of the word *éthique* in the main text of *Totality and
Infinity* is perhaps the most quoted passage of the book, and one
which reveals a great deal about Levinas's approach:

> A calling into question [*mise en question*] of the Same – which cannot
> occur [*se faire*] within the egoistic spontaneity of the Same – is brought
> about [*se fait*] by the Other [*l'Autre*]. We name this calling into question
> of my spontaneity by the presence of the Other [*Autrui*] ethics. The
> strangeness of the Other, his irreducibility to the I [*Moi*], to my thoughts
> and my possessions, is precisely accomplished [*s'accomplit*] as a calling
> into question of my spontaneity, as ethics. Metaphysics, transcendence,
> the welcoming of the Other by the Same, of the Other by Me, is concretely
> produced [*se produit*] as the calling into question of the Same by the
> Other, that is, as the ethics that accomplishes [*accomplit*] the critical
> essence of knowledge. (*TI*, 33/43)

In a sense, the whole philosophy of *Totality and Infinity* is contained
in embryo in this passage, and one of the aims of the rest of this
chapter will be to explicate it further. For the moment it is worth
drawing attention to some elements of Levinas's style. At first, the
passage seems repetitive and static. Of the four sentences quoted,
the first makes a proposition, which can be summarized as 'the
Other problematizes the Same', and which the following three
sentences reiterate. The phrase *mise en question* (calling into question) is repeated four times, once in each sentence; the word *sponta-
néité* (spontaneity) occurs in each of the first three sentences, and
*éthique* (ethics) in the second, third and fourth. Even the structure of
the sentences seems curiously unvaried, as the first, third and fourth
are built around near-synonymous reflexive verbs: *se fait, s'accomplit*
(with *accomplit* repeated in the following sentence) and *se produit*.

Yet each sentence adds nuance and extends the range of the
original claim. The general terms Same and Other (*l'Autre*) are
given more concrete reference by their modification to the I (*Moi*)
and the Other (*Autrui*). The questioning of the Same is defined as
ethical, and the simple *presence of the Other* is further qualified as
his or her strangeness or irreducibility to the I. By the end of this

short passage, then, the original proposition has been modified, its scope dramatically extended to the point that the relationship between Same and Other has become the site where both ethics and knowledge are at stake. This extraordinary broadening has not been achieved by what we might readily accept as a rational, academic or philosophical argumentative procedure. Instead, Levinas perpetually returns to his starting point, reiterating, modifying and expanding his ideas as he goes.

This small passage encapsulates a vital aspect of the manner in which Levinas goes about writing philosophy. Derrida has compared his style to the movement of the sea, perpetually lapping against the same shore.[5] Derrida's comparison conveys the insistent, repetitive motions of Levinas's prose, but perhaps underplays the urgency of its intense speculative restlessness. Levinas appears anxious not to be misunderstood, yet he is also (sometimes) almost wilfully obscure and sibylline. His distrust of the potentially misleading nature of the written word is indicated by his frequent references to Plato's *Phaedrus*; in this text Socrates expresses his preference for speech over writing on the grounds that the latter, 'being unable to defend or help itself',[6] may be misinterpreted when unaided by the living presence of a speaker. At the same time, the constant modification and redefinition to which Levinas submits key notions and terms seem precisely to prevent his readers from arriving at a clear understanding of his texts. They can appear at once to be both tediously repetitive and intriguingly or irritatingly elusive.

The difficulty of reading *Totality and Infinity* is compounded by the misleading construction of the work. It appears to have a structure of exemplary clarity: a preface, a first section sketching out the general themes of Same and Other, a second section on the Same, a third on the Other, a fourth which endeavours to go a step further in the description of the relationship with alterity, and a fifth concluding section. But *Totality and Infinity* does not manifest the clear argumentative development that this structure would imply: it doubles back on itself, anticipates or repeats future or past arguments, and then seems to reassert conclusions that had earlier been discredited. From the perspective of analytic philosophy, it would be easy to dismiss Levinas's text as exhibiting a typically Continental combination of lack of intellectual rigour and hopeless confusion. In this and the following chapter I shall attempt to show that the difficulty of Levinas's writing is essential to the paradoxical attempt to think outside the philosophical history to which he also knows he belongs. Levinas acknowledges that *Totality and Infinity* continues to use the language of ontology (*TI*, preface to the German edition, I–II; not reproduced in the English translation), even though the arguments advanced in that book aspire to overturn ontology; *Otherwise than Being* attempts to go beyond the language of ontology, becoming in the process a bewildering and bold exploration of what a post-ontological textuality, a practice of thought which has accepted the linguistic consequences of its theoretical positions, might be.

*Totality and Infinity* and Levinas's later texts are engaged in an intensely paradoxical intellectual project. They are articulated around a self-challenging double movement: the texts make propositions (about Being, subjectivity, ethics and so on), but simultaneously endeavour to avoid being reducible to such propositions. The process of thought remains fluid, whilst sometimes crystallizing in the form of analysable themes and ideas. Meaning is given and withdrawn with often breathtaking rapidity. In this chapter I discuss this double movement by adopting a more sequential narrative than *Totality and Infinity* itself. The first two sections summarize the central ideas of the work with respect to subjectivity, alterity and ethics; for reasons of explanatory clarity, these are treated as if they can be separated from the complex textual network in which they are elaborated. The final sections of the chapter will return to the problem of Levinassian textuality to consider how this contributes to the meaning of the work.

### Subjectivity and alterity

According to one of the truisms of modern Continental thought, the subject is now well and truly decentred.[7] The Marxists dissolved it into historical struggles, the structuralists into vast interlocking signifying systems; Louis Althusser famously combined the two by defining history as 'a process without a subject'.[8] The post-structuralists offered no greater comfort to the depleted humanist subject, depicting it as a textual effect constantly under deconstruction. Levinas unambiguously opposes this assault on the beleaguered subject. In the preface to *Totality and Infinity* he expresses one of the central aims of his book:

> This book then does present itself as a defence of subjectivity, but it will apprehend subjectivity not at the level of its purely egoist protestation

against totality, nor in its anguish [*angoisse*] before death, but as founded
in the idea of infinity. (*TI*, 11/26)

The defence of subjectivity will not be mounted in the name of
traditional humanism, nor will it establish subjectivity on the
grounds of transcendental phenomenology or the *Angst* (*angoisse*,
anguish) of Heideggerian *Dasein*. According to Levinas, the subject
is founded in the idea of infinity; this phrase alludes to the third of
Descartes's *Méditations* (1641), a crucial point of reference for
Levinas's thought. Levinas describes Descartes's meditation on the
idea of the infinite as one of the boldest moments of Western
philosophy, even if Descartes himself misunderstood its significance. Descartes questions whether or not the subject can regard
itself as the source of all the ideas it contains. Since an effect cannot
be greater than its cause, Descartes argues that the subject cannot
be the source of ideas which are greater or more perfect than itself.
The idea of God is just such an idea which cannot have been
conceived independently by the subject: 'for, even though the idea
of substance is in me, by the very fact that I am a substance, I
would nevertheless not have the idea of an infinite substance, I
who am a finite being, if it had not been put in me by some
substance which was truly infinite.'⁹ Thus, in Descartes's view,
belief in God can be justified on the basis of the subject's certainty
in its own existence.

In discussing the Third Meditation in *Totality and Infinity*,
Levinas isolates two movements in Descartes's thought. The first
is that of the Cogito, in which the subject confirms its own existence
as beyond doubt. In the second movement the subject proves to
itself the existence of God and thus finds itself to be created by
something which transcends it. The Cartesian subject seizes itself
as subject by reference to the non-self. For Descartes the idea of the
infinite comes from God and thus justifies his own Christianity.
Levinas adapts Descartes's thought for his own purposes and in
his own vocabulary. For Levinas the significance of the Cartesian
discovery lies in the encounter with the infinite as something beyond
knowledge and utterly resistant to the solipsism of the transcendental Ego. Most importantly, this encounter does not endanger or
annihilate the subject, but on the contrary enables its constitution:
'Descartes, better than an idealist or a realist, discovers a relation
with a total alterity irreducible to interiority, which nevertheless
does not do violence to interiority – a receptivity without passivity,
a relation between freedoms' (*TI*, 233/211).

So Levinas transforms Descartes's infinite God into his own Other: 'The infinite is the absolute other' (*TI*, 41/49), 'God is the Other' (*TI*, 232/211). This allows an explanation of some of the key terms from *Totality and Infinity*: infinity, transcendence, exteriority, alterity. The infinite is the Other; its alterity is also transcendence and exteriority because it is outside, above and beyond the powers of the subject: 'The Cartesian notion of the idea of the Infinite designates a relation with a being that maintains its total exteriority with respect to him who thinks it' (*TI*, 42/50).

The terms *Same* and *Other*, which now come to occupy a central place in Levinas's writing, have been common currency in philosophy since Plato's dialogues.[10] The privileged term, Levinas argues, has always been the Same, which is conceived as incorporating, actually or potentially, that which lies outside it. Plato's *Timaeus*, for example, describes how the 'reluctant and unsociable nature' of the Other is compressed by force into the Same.[11] The Other belongs to a totality which ensures that it can be ultimately reconciled with the Same; this, Levinas argues, is the characteristic move of Western philosophy: 'Western philosophy has most often been an ontology: a reduction of the Other to the Same by interposition of a middle and neutral term that ensures the comprehension of being' (*TI*, 33–4/43).

The ontological imperialism of Western thought manifests itself in different forms, but the hidden purpose is always to find a means of offsetting the shock of alterity. The Platonic theory of knowledge as *anamnesis* (recollection) asserts that I already know what I seek to know, all knowledge is already contained within myself; Husserlian phenomenology, with its concepts of intentionality and representation, establishes the Ego as the source of all meaning and knowledge; the Heideggerian relation of beings to Being entails the exclusion of anything that might lie outside that relation. Thus, philosophy is an egology, asserting the primacy of the self, the Same, the subject or Being. The Other is acknowledged only in order to be suppressed or possessed; as in the workings of the Hegelian dialectic, the characteristic gesture of philosophy is to acknowledge the Other in order to incorporate it within the expanding circles of the Same. The totality of Being is flawless and all-encompassing; because it incorporates alterity within the empire of sameness, the Other is only other in a restricted sense. Totality has no outside, the subject receives nothing, learns nothing, that it does not or cannot possess or know.

In the first section of *Totality and Infinity*, entitled 'The Same and the Other', Levinas establishes a vocabulary to replace the categories of traditional thought: instead of totality, Being and ontology, he offers infinity, exteriority and metaphysics. But it is crucial that this revised vocabulary should not simply represent a reversal of traditional priorities, whereby the Other dislodges the primacy of the Same, or infinity abolishes totality. Levinas's book is called *Totality and Infinity*, not 'Totality *or* Infinity'. To privilege the Other rather than the Same would end up reproducing the totality-thinking from which Levinas is trying to escape: it would lead to the invasion of the Same by the Other, so ultimately suppressing one of the terms of the opposition. The break with ontology that Levinas is trying to achieve entails the preservation of both Same and Other. This is why Descartes's Third Meditation occupies such an important place in *Totality and Infinity*: it provides a model of the subject existing in relation to infinity, and founded by that relation rather than destroyed by it.

The central difficulty for Levinas is to elaborate a philosophy of self and Other in which both are preserved as independent and self-sufficient, but in some sense in relation with one another. This is more difficult than it might appear, since it is in the nature of the *relation* to bring the Other into the self's sphere of familiarity, thus making it intelligible from the perspective of the self and reducing its true otherness. Descartes observes that the infinite must necessarily remain beyond the understanding of finite beings such as myself.[12] This essential lack of intelligibility also characterizes the Other when viewed from the standpoint of the self; indeed for Levinas the failure of understanding is essential if the radical otherness of the Other is to be preserved. And the lack of intelligibility also lies at the centre of the problem of description posed by the relation between self and Other. To preserve the Other as Other, it must not become an object of knowledge or experience, because knowledge is always *my* knowledge, experience always *my* experience; the object is encountered only in so far as it exists *for me*, and immediately its alterity is diminished. Levinas endeavours to avoid this diminution of alterity. The philosophy of Same and Other, then, must confront three fundamental problems: it requires a description and defence of subjectivity, but also an account of alterity which does not reduce the Other to the Same; and finally it needs some means of accounting for the relation between Same and Other that does not effectively abolish either.

The first stage of Levinas's argument requires a description of the self as independent and self-sufficient. Levinas avoids writing in terms of difference or opposition because both these notions ultimately view self and Other from the standpoint of totality. To describe the self as *different* from the Other implies that there is some grand, objective perspective from which qualities can be viewed and compared; it also implies a knowledge of the Other which would deny its position as Other. To think in terms of *opposition* would be to conceive of self and Other as two sides of a coin, defined in relation to one another and therefore belonging to the same totality: 'If the Same were to establish its identity by simple *opposition to the Other*, it would already be part of a totality encompassing the Same and the Other' (*TI*, 27/38). So Levinas describes the self as neither different from nor opposed to the Other, but separate from it. The self is the site where the Same identifies itself as such. This does not mean that the self is unchanging and inalterable; on the contrary, it is constantly caught unawares by the world and by itself, forever finding itself to be unlike what it believed it was. But this is not a sign that it has been overwhelmed by alterity. The self is characterized by its capacity to survive change, and to identify itself as the Same even as it becomes different. As Levinas puts it, 'The I is identical in its very alterations' (*TI*, 25/36). So the self can discover itself other, but never Other; the other within the Same prompts a reidentification and forms part of the identity (the process of self-identification) which constitutes the Same.

The self is separate, its identity confirmed by its ability to recognize itself as the Same even as it changes. It has its own occupations, needs and pleasures which Levinas describes as its economy, and which he analyses in the second section of *Totality and Infinity*, entitled 'Interiority and Economy'. This is the part of the book which is the most classically phenomenological in that it analyses the self as it experiences the world and gives it meaning. At the same time, Levinas distinguishes his analyses from those of Husserl and Heidegger. The key to the self's experience of the world is neither representation nor intentionality, nor is the self's presence characterized by *Geworfenheit* or exile. In representation, that which is not the self is always determined by reference to the self: 'Intelligibility, the very occurrence of representation, is the possibility for the Other to be determined by the Same without determining the Same, without introducing alterity into it; it is a free exercise of the Same. It is the disappearance within the Same, of the I opposed to the non-I' (*TI*, 129/124). More fundamental than this recuperation of the non-self within the Same is what

Levinas calls *living from* . . . (*vivre de* . . .): 'We live from "good soup", air, light, spectacles, work, ideas, sleep, etc. . . . These are not objects of representation' (*TI*, 112/110). *Living from* . . . offers a mode of encounter with the world which confirms the identity and sovereignty of the self; the world is fully available to me, ready to meet my needs and to fulfil my desires. This situation is character-ized by what Levinas calls enjoyment (*jouissance*), the exhilaration of the self in its possession of the world. In food, for example, energy to be found in something outside the self is transformed into my own energy. This 'transmutation of the other into the Same' is, according to Levinas, 'the essence of enjoyment' (*TI*, 113/111).

The other, but not the Other, is taken into the Same as a source of *jouissance*. The distinction between other and Other (*l'Autre*, or its personalized form *Autrui*) may appear trivial, but it is neverthe-less indispensable to Levinas's thinking. The former may be incorporated into the Same whereas the latter never can be; the former confirms totality, the latter reveals infinity. The other may initially appear alien to the empirical self, but it does not funda-mentally challenge its supremacy; the Other is utterly resistant to the transcendental Ego and cannot be assimilated to the world the Ego creates for itself. Unaware of the challenge of the Other, the self finds itself in an alien environment, surrounded by objects which comply with or oppose its needs, but it is not in exile; on the contrary, it feels entirely at home. The strangeness of the world is its charm, a cause of happiness. *Jouissance* names the process by which the subject makes itself at home in an environment where otherness is not a threat to be overcome, but a pleasure to be experienced. Need, in this respect, should not be defined nega-tively; it reveals the dependence of the self on the non-self, but also the ability of the self to find satisfaction and happiness in the encounter with 'the other which the world is' (*TI*, 119/115). Need and *living from* . . . are a dependence which the self can master; they affirm its sovereignty and confirm its essentially egotistical happiness (*TI*, 118/114). Levinas paints an edenic picture of the self in its joyous possession of the world:

> The I is, to be sure, happiness, presence at home with itself. But, as sufficiency in its non-sufficiency, it remains in the non-I; it is enjoyment of 'something else', never of itself. Autochthonous, that is, enrooted in what it is not, it is nevertheless, within this enrootedness, independent and separated. (*TI*, 152/143)

The self feels at home in the world. Levinas devotes a large portion of *Totality and Infinity* to the description of the well-being of the subject at ease with itself and its surroundings. It inhabits the world, takes a home which is described as 'the utopia in which the "I" recollects itself in dwelling at home with itself' (*TI*, 167/156). In the home the self withdraws, reflects, maintains its independence and privacy, and may accept or refuse to act as host to alien presences.

In this account of the self as sovereign, characterized by *jouissance*, Levinas writes as if the subject were essentially alone in the world:

> In enjoyment I am absolutely for myself. Egoist without reference to the Other, I am alone without solitude, innocently egoist and alone. Not against the others, not 'as for me . . .' – but entirely deaf to the Other, outside of all communication and all refusal to communicate – without ears, like a hungry stomach. (*TI*, 142/134)

Even the feminine presence which shares the home (about which I shall say more later in this chapter) does not constitute a danger to the self's tranquil possession of the world. She is a *tu* rather than a *vous*, a familiar part of my world rather than an *Autrui* who might put it into question (*TI*, 164–7/154–6).[13] At the same time, however egoistical the self may be, it is not a transcendental Ego in the Husserlian sense: its separation from the world requires that the world from which it is separate should also have independent existence; that independence is indeed the source and condition of the self's *jouissance*, as the self confirms its dominance through the transmutation of the other.

The self is absolutely unique, not subsumable by a genus or a concept (*TI*, 122/118). It is not part of a totality, which requires that there be some relationship between its constituent parts. So, the separate existence of the self requires the disruption of totality, a disruption effected by the impossibility of eliminating what Levinas calls alterity from the system. Although in the second section of *Totality and Infinity* the self is described as if it were alone in the world, in fact its separate existence (its independence from totality) is possible *only because* the Other also exists. Alterity constitutes the grounds which make separation possible; the self exists because the Other is irreconcilable with it. Otherwise, both self and Other would be parts of a greater whole or totality which would invade and invalidate their separateness. So, although the self may feel that its separateness ensures both its mastery and freedom in the world, that separateness depends upon the possibility of an encounter which will put both mastery and freedom into question; and Levinas's thinking is at its most distinctive, and at the greatest remove from phenomenology, in his account of the encounter between self and Other.

The difficulty in describing the encounter with alterity lies in the constant danger of transforming the Other, however unwittingly or unwillingly, into a reflection or projection of the Same. If the Other becomes an object of knowledge or experience (*my* knowledge, *my* experience), then immediately its alterity has been overwhelmed. So Levinas must use paradoxical formulations in the attempt to avoid returning to the ontology from which he is trying to escape. Even to describe the relationship with the Other as a relationship implies a totalizing perspective from which both self and Other are seen to share a common ground, which has the consequence that the Other becomes just another version of the Same. To avoid this, the relationship with the Other is characterized paradoxically as a 'relation without relation' (*TI*, 79/80). It is a relation because an encounter does take place; but it is 'without relation' because that encounter does not establish parity or understanding, the Other remains resolutely Other. Moreover, the encounter is not an event that can be situated in time; it is rather a structural possibility that precedes and makes possible all subsequent experience.

Levinas is engaged in a struggle with the language of his own text in so far as it carries with it unwanted philosophical implications. The contortions through which his text passes, and much of the difficulty of *Totality and Infinity*, derive from the endeavour to avoid describing the encounter with the Other in terms that would implicitly restore primacy to the Same. Levinas bases his analysis on three interrelated areas: desire, what he calls *le visage* (the face), and discourse.

1 Desire. The main text of *Totality and Infinity* begins with a section on desire which picks up discussions from Levinas's earlier texts, particularly the final sections of *Time and the Other*. Desire is sharply distinguished from need. Whereas the latter might reveal a lack or an absence which can be filled, desire is insatiable. Contrary to the myth of the Platonic hermaphrodite or the Romantic yearning for fusion, Levinas's desire does not seek to restore something (fantasized as) lost. What desire desires is transcendence, alterity, the exteriority of the Other; in the aphoristic style

often adopted by Levinas, we are told that 'Desire is desire for the absolutely Other' (*TI*, 23/34). This is desire for the Other, which cannot be satisfied, rather than need for the other, which can. Its most intense form is found in erotic love, which is discussed in the final section of *Totality and Infinity*, 'Beyond the Face'. In erotic love neither self nor Other is abolished; both are in fact confirmed, since the Other is desired as Other, not as an other to be reduced to the Same. The loved one is *caressed* but not *possessed*.[14]

2 *Le visage*. Of all Levinas's terms, *visage* is perhaps the best known and the most mysterious. The role played by the term is clear enough. Levinas needs a means of describing the relationship between self and Other which does not imply that the Other is *with* me (therefore fundamentally like me) or *against* me (therefore opposed to me and dialectically part of the same totality). Instead, the Other is simply there, present to me in an originary and irreducible relation that Levinas calls *le face à face* (the face to face). But the word *visage* is problematic because it both does and does not refer to real human faces. The face is that part of the body of other people which is most readily (or most often) visible; it is also the most expressive part of the body, and the notion of the face as expression plays an important part in Levinas's thinking. But the face is not *simply* seen: to see the face would be to make of it an intentional object of the perceiving consciousness, so reducing its absolute otherness. The face, then, is not the object of 'experience in the sensible sense of the term, relative and egoist' (*TI*, 211/193). It is an epiphany or revelation rather than an object of perception or knowledge. The term *visage* encapsulates the problems raised by the paradoxical nature of the self's encounter with the infinite: it is something that is not available to vision but described as if it were, signalling an encounter which is not an event and an experience which does not occur in the consciousness of any subject.[15]

3 Discourse. Because the face (in Levinas's sense) is not an object of experience, it is not susceptible to the phenomenological *Sinngebung* by which consciousness confers meaning on the world around it. Instead, the face is *expression*, a source of meanings coming from elsewhere rather than the product of meanings given by me. This explains the relationship between face and discourse: both are modes of contact with the Other in which I receive more than I give. Indeed, in Levinas's account the face appears more like a source of language than something that can be seen: 'The face speaks. The manifestation of the face is already discourse' (*TI*, 61/66). The essential part of language, according to Levinas, is

*interpellation*, the address the Other makes to me and I make to the Other (*TI*, 65/69). The word is not a sign of a meaning which is fixed and given. The truth it contains is not *dévoilement*, the unveiling of something present from time immemorial; in Levinas's account it is a revelation, an unforeseen and unforeseeable breach within what is known and knowable. It entails the production of new, unexpected meanings rather than the communication of what was already familiar. But it is also teaching (*enseignement*): language teaches what I could not have discovered for myself and within myself, it produces meaning from beyond my experience and resources (*TI*, 65–6/69–70). Crucially also, through discourse I find that I am not the exclusive possessor of the world. What had seemed uniquely mine is revealed as shared with the Other (*TI*, 189/173).

The idea of the infinite both grounds the possibility of the self as separate and also puts into question the self's sovereign authority over the world. The next step in Levinas's argument is the one which forms the basis of his originality and repute: the relation between Same and Other is described as originally and fundamentally *ethical* in nature.

### Ethics

From the standpoint of the Anglo-American analytic tradition in philosophy, it is difficult to see why such a fuss is made of Levinas as a philosopher of ethics. His work fulfils none of the conditions by which ethical or meta-ethical philosophy might be recognized. He does not intervene in the classic debates between consequentialists and deontologists;[16] he does not answer the Socratic question 'How should one achieve happiness?'[17] or the Kantian 'What ought I do?' Although he refers to Plato, he does not explicitly engage with the work of other fathers of ethics, such as Aristotle, Kant or Hobbes. He does not provide foundations or rules for morality, nor does he discuss virtue, or rights and duties, and he offers no account of the language and logic of ethical enquiry. Indeed, like a radical non-cognitivist, he implies that such questions are beyond the scope of philosophical enquiry.[18]

Yet Levinas has established an immense, unmatched reputation as the person who almost single-handedly restored philosophical respectability to ethics in post-war French thought. So the question must be posed: in what sense is Levinas a philosopher of ethics? In fact it is by no means clear that *ethics* is the correct term to describe his work. When Levinas uses the word *éthique* it is almost always either as an adjective or, when it appears as a noun, in contexts in which it is impossible to ascertain its gender. The point may seem trivial, but it does have a bearing on the meaning of *éthique*: as a feminine noun, which would be the most common usage, it refers to ethics in the English sense; as a masculine substantivized adjective it would mean something like 'the ethical', different from ethics in the same way that 'the political' may be distinguished from 'politics'. The ethical is the broader domain, where ethical experiences and relationships occur before the foundation of ethics in the sense of philosophically established principles, rules or codes. I suggest that Levinas is more frequently concerned with the ethical than with ethics, even though the former inevitably leads into the latter.[19]

As I have described it so far, *Totality and Infinity* revolves around an encounter between self and Other. This encounter cannot be explained in exclusively ontological terms because it involves more than Being, entailing a breach which cannot be understood as part of Being's relationship with itself. The encounter is also not an empirical event (though it may be enacted in any number of empirical events); it is rather, in terms continually used by Levinas, original, essential or fundamental. This is because the encounter with the Other lies at the origin of the separateness of the self; only by discovering the irreducibility of the alterity of the Other can I understand that I am neither solipsistically alone in the world nor part of a totality to which all others also belong. This encounter is, Levinas insists, ethical; and the ethical bond with the Other is the most fundamental subject for philosophical reflection because there is nothing that precedes it or has priority over it. It characterizes human relations at their most basic level.

The reason for this is relatively simple: the Other makes me realize that I share the world, that it is not my unique possession, and I do not like this realization. My power and freedom are put into question. Such a situation is ethical because a lot depends upon how I respond. Sartre insisted, against Heidegger's notion of *Mitsein*, that the fundamental nature of human relations was conflict.[20] Levinas argues against both Sartre and Heidegger: the relationship between self and Other does not entail the absorption of the Other effected by *Mitsein*, neither is it essentially violent. The encounter with the Other, or the face to face, is originally pacific because the revelation or epiphany of the face is essentially non-violent, or non-allergic in the term used by Levinas. It occasions a calling into question but not a threat:

> The face in which the Other – the absolutely other – presents himself does not negate the Same, does not do violence to it as do opinion or authority or the thaumaturgic supernatural. It remains commensurate with him who welcomes; it remains terrestrial. This presentation is preeminently nonviolence, for instead of offending my freedom it calls it to responsibility and founds it. As nonviolence it nonetheless maintains the plurality of the Same and the Other. It is peace. (*TI*, 222/203)

The Other puts me into question by revealing to me that my powers and freedom are limited. But the face does not annihilate the self; on the contrary, it is the condition of its separateness. It instigates dialogue, teaching, and hence reason, society and ethics (*TI*, 223/203–4). It also gives a proper foundation to freedom. The transcendental Ego would like to be the sole source of its own knowledge, actions and meanings; the encounter with the Other shows such freedom to be egoistical, arbitrary and unjustified. Alluding to Sartre, Levinas denies that existence is condemned to freedom (*TI*, 83/84); freedom is rather conferred, as at an investiture, through the agency of the Other. Without the Other, freedom is without purpose or foundation. In the face to face, the Other gives my freedom meaning because I am confronted with real choices between responsibility and obligation towards the Other, or hatred and violent repudiation. The Other invests me with genuine freedom, and will be the beneficiary or victim of how I decide to exercise it.

Ethics, in the restricted sense of ethical preferences, choices and actions, derives from the original ethical moment when the self is challenged by the presence of the Other. Of course, the fact that the encounter with the Other is ethical does not mean that I will respond to it in an ethical way. Although Levinas talks in terms of obligations and responsibilities, his thought does not aspire to establish a deontological theory which might hope to provide compelling reasons for meeting one's obligations. In keeping with his phenomenological background he is descriptive rather than prescriptive, attempting to depict fundamental realities. And at this level I am just as likely to respond to the non-violence of the Other with violence as with respect.

When the face erupts into our world, its first expression is a commandment: 'you shall not commit murder' (*TI*, 217/199). This is in fact the only commandment to which Levinas refers; he takes it as the first and most fundamental of laws, from which all others derive. Fundamental, but not founded: it is not backed up by divine authority, nor justified on utilitarian grounds, nor supported by the appeal to reason of the Kantian Categorical Imperative.[21] The authority of the Other is not compelling; the Other commands from a position of absolute otherness, from a paradoxical position of majesty and misery. The Other orders me not to kill, but has no means of persuading me to obey.

So, in Levinas's account, my obligation to the Other is not enforced by any rational argument or physical coercion which compel me to respect the vulnerability of the Other. Indeed, there seems to be good reason for *not* respecting it. The Other escapes my power in the way that nothing else does. If I kill an animal for food or use an object as a tool, I am responding to my needs and appropriating the world for my own purposes. But the Other resists those purposes. The resistance offered by the Other should not be understood as a force which is superior, or even comparable, to my own. The Other is not stronger than me in any ordinary sense: to speak in such terms implies a commensurability between self and Other which would be contrary to the essence of alterity. No comparison can be made between the force with which I attack the Other and the resistance it offers. Levinas conveys this in a further paradox, referring to 'the resistance of what has no resistance – the ethical resistance' (*TI*, 217/199). This ethical resistance is not measurable in terms of force. In it lies both the strength and weakness of the Other. The Other resists my attempts at appropriation and domination; it escapes my power since I cannot possess or even understand it. My only way of suppressing it is to seek its annihilation:

> To kill is not to dominate but to annihilate; it is to renounce comprehension absolutely. Murder exercises a power over what escapes power. [. . .] I can wish to kill only an existent which is absolutely independent, which exceeds my powers infinitely, and therefore does not oppose them but paralyses the very power of power. The Other is the sole being I can wish to kill. (*TI*, 216/198)

The Other, then, is the only being that I can want to kill, to annihilate completely, because it is absolutely beyond my power. Yet Levinas does not tell us that we *should not* kill the Other; he tells us rather that the Other *cannot* be killed. Here, the distinction between the Other and others is again crucial. Of course I can kill others; murder is 'this most banal incident of human history' (*TI*,

217/198). But the Other remains inviolate and inviolable. The face appears in my world but does not belong to it; I can do it no harm. At this point Levinas's thought might appear to be at its most utopian. The apparently dismissive reference to the banality of actual murders offers little comfort to their victims and gives no moral authority to those who oppose them. When Levinas suggests that 'the extermination of living beings' (*TI*, 216/198) does not affect the face, his reference to extermination is uncomfortably reminiscent of the Holocaust and other modern atrocities. So the belief that the face, in Levinas's very specific philosophical sense, is unharmed seems disturbingly reticent about the countless people who were harmed. Bluntly, the fact that the Other survived Auschwitz unscathed seems incalculably less important than the murder of those who did not.[22]

Levinas would not disagree with this; and, although *Totality and Infinity* is not a moralizing work, a clear moral impulse underlies it. Levinas does not denounce violence as wrong; rather he attempts to show that it always fails, that it can never succeed in its true aims. When I kill, I am trying to kill the Other, that which is utterly beyond my powers; I may succeed in killing the other, or even innumerable others, but the Other survives. Violence, then, always ends or continues in failure. Conflict or war are not what Levinas calls 'the first event of the encounter' (*TI*, 218/199). Violence can only be a second or secondary response to the revelation that I cannot kill the Other. The original relationship is peace, 'the antecedent and non-allergic presence of the Other' (*TI*, 218/199). In distinguishing between the Other (the true object of hatred which I cannot kill) and others (whom I can kill, all too easily), Levinas is attempting to demonstrate the futility and ultimate failure of violence, which never attains its real targets.

One of the most distinctive aspects of Levinas's ethics is his insistence on the asymmetrical nature of the ethical relationship: the Other, which Levinas characterizes by a biblical formula as the stranger, widow or orphan,[23] does not share my powers or responsibilities. The decoupling of responsibility from reciprocity has been described as the decisive act which distinguishes Levinas's ethical theory from virtually all others.[24] It would be a mistake for me to respect the Other because I expect anything in return: my obligation and responsibility are not mirrored by the Other's reciprocal responsibility towards me. This asymmetry is consistent with Levinas's conception of the Other: to insist on symmetry or reciprocity would be to imply that I was empowered to speak for

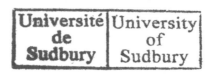

the Other, that the Other belongs to the same species or genus as myself. But for Levinas the ethical relationship entails an obligation which is incumbent on me alone; no power *forces* me to act in moral ways. Morality is not moral if it is maintained either because I have no choice in the matter or if I expect to get something in return. The ethical encounter with the Other leads to an ethics which is necessarily one-sided and not formulable in terms of rules applicable to all; and, since it is asymmetrical, the ethical relationship cannot be universalized and transformed into a moral code. As Bauman puts it, '"I am ready to die for the Other" is a moral statement; "He should be ready to die for me" is, blatantly, not.'[25]

So far, this account of Levinas's ethics has concentrated solely on the encounter between self and Other. Since the universalization of this relationship has been ruled out, it is as yet unexplained how the validity of broader issues such as justice or social equality may be established. Levinas requires some account of how, without universalization, the encounter with the Other can be at the foundation of a moral society. He attempts to respond to this problem by introducing the notion of *le tiers* (the third party), which functions as the key to social justice.[26] The face to face does not establish a cosy intimacy between myself and the Other; it shows me the existence of a whole world outside myself. So, at the same time as I discover the Other, the potential presence of innumerable others is also revealed to me. On the basis of this revelation, the ethical relation may turn into a concern for social justice:

> The third party looks at me in the eyes of the Other – language is justice. [. . .] the epiphany of the face qua face opens humanity. The face in its nakedness as a face presents to me the destitution of the poor one and the stranger; but this poverty and exile which appeal to my powers, address me, do not deliver themselves over to these powers as givens, remain the expression of the face. The poor one, the stranger, presents himself as an equal. His equality within this essential poverty consists in referring to the *third party*, thus present at the encounter, whom in the midst of his destitution the Other already serves. (*TI*, 234/213)

The Other is unlike me and so not comprehensible in terms of equality; the third party is revealed to me at the same time as the Other, but is equal to me. As Simon Critchley explains, '*the community has a double structure*; it is a commonality among equals which is at the same time based on the inegalitarian moment of the ethical relation.'[27] The simultaneous revelation of the Other and the

third party allows Levinas to combine asymmetry and equality within the social relation. Plurality does not preclude community and fraternity. The discussion of the third party remains one of the briefest and most sketchy parts of *Totality and Infinity*. Nevertheless, it occupies a crucial role in the development of Levinas's thinking as it provides a way of developing the ethical relationship with the Other into the social and political domain. The notion will be taken up again and expanded in *Otherwise than Being*, and it is discussed further in the next chapter of this book.

I began this section by listing some of the things that Levinas did not do in his ethics. It is in fact much easier to say what his ethics is not than what it is. It does not provide a code or set of principles; and it refuses the Kantian move of establishing reason as the foundation of ethics since, if reason is a source of consensus between all rational subjects, there is no dialogue in it (though there may be dialogue *about* it), it allows for no encounter with the Other and represents only the seamless monologue of the Same (*TI*, 69/72, 228–9/207–8). So Levinas's analysis of the ethical provides none of the rules or justifications that we might hope to find in an ethics. According to Bauman this is precisely the point: Levinas's work represents the best example of an attempt to think through the ethical consequences of the postmodern situation, and the condition of postmodern ethics is to be without foundation or universality.[28] The postmodern vantage point does not, as Bauman insists, make moral life any easier;[29] on the contrary it involves coming to terms with the notion of morality as aporetic, never resolved, without recourse to comforting principles which help to simplify difficult choices:

> What the postmodern mind is aware of is that there are problems in human and social life with no good solutions, twisted trajectories that cannot be straightened up, ambivalences that are more than linguistic blunders waiting to be corrected, doubts which cannot be legislated out of existence, moral agonies which no reason-dictated recipes can soothe, let alone cure. The postmodern mind does not expect any more to find the all-embracing, total and ultimate formula of life without ambiguity, risk, danger and error, and is deeply suspicious of any voice that promises otherwise. [. . .] The postmodern mind is reconciled to the idea that the messiness of the human predicament is here to stay.[30]

Levinas offers an account of the subject as ethical in its very foundations, involved in ethical relations whether it likes it or not. This does not mean that I cannot behave unethically (*TI*,

188/172–3); indeed, any compulsion within the ethical obligation would deprive it of its morality. For Levinas, the ethical is the condition of my existence whatever the worth or worthlessness of my actions. Rather than solutions to moral dilemmas or an analysis of moral terminology, Levinas provides a description of the context in which the stakes of ethics are established, a context crucially defined by the presence of the Other. It must be emphasized that, although Levinas rejects the validity of all universal principles, this does not make of his ethics a relativism.[31] On the contrary, his ethics turns out to be more demanding than any formal code. My responsibility for and obligation to the Other are absolute; they exceed my ability to fulfil them, always demand more, are never satisfied by the completion of any action or service. As a moral subject I am always found wanting, because ethics is not just a *part* of my existence, not simply one of the things I do amongst others; it defines the entire domain that I inhabit. Levinas's ethics places more stringent demands on the subject than the most rigid absolutism because I can never hope to come near to fulfilling satisfactorily my obligation to the Other. Once again, Bauman describes the situation of the Levinassian moral subject most succinctly: 'One recognizes morality by its gnawing sense of unfulfilledness, by its endemic dissatisfaction with itself. *The moral self is a self always haunted by the suspicion that it is not moral enough.*'[32]

## Textuality

So far I have tried to present the arguments of *Totality and Infinity* as clearly and cogently as I can. Obviously, to reduce more than three hundred pages of text to one short chapter involves a great deal of (perhaps over-hasty) paraphrase. At the same time, the difference between my chapter and *Totality and Infinity* is not simply one of length: the expository stance which I have adopted is at a far remove from Levinas's prose style. I have tried to make sense out of Levinas's text, but this inevitably entails a simplification (and perhaps a betrayal) of the extraordinary complexity of *Totality and Infinity*; the summary risks transforming the text into a smooth surface of propositions and arguments. In my account I have tried to stick to a pedagogic concern for clarity of exposition. But if I am justified in reducing Levinas's work to the terms that I have sketched out in the first part of this chapter, why does not Levinas avoid the need for such commentary by explaining his ideas more clearly? Why does he need to be so difficult? The answers to these questions relate to the kind of book *Totality and Infinity* is and to the nature of Levinas's project; and, having simplified his work in the first parts of this chapter, I should now muddy the waters a little.

Earlier I described *Totality and Infinity* as if it were exemplary in its construction, with a preface, four sections which develop the argument through a logical progression, and a concluding section. This already gives a false impression of the book. The latest French edition of the text in fact contains two prefaces, the original 1961 preface and one written in 1987 for the German edition of the book. Moreover the first section of *Totality and Infinity*, 'The Same and the Other', is in some respects also prefatory in its function since it summarizes arguments developed in the rest of the book (in his original preface Levinas refers to the 'preparatory character' of the first section of the book; *TI*, 16/30). Other aspects of the construction of the work seem to promise assistance to the reader, but may turn out to be less informative than we might have expected. Each subsection of *Totality and Infinity* has a heading, but those headings are sometimes remarkably unhelpful as indications of the ground covered in the subsection itself. Peperzak observes that 'Levinas's titles do not help very much to get an overview of the structure according to which his book has been composed'; rather than a systematic scheme we are apparently faced with 'a series of fragments that have been (re)arranged after their writing'.[33] The book is repetitive and fragmentary, constantly recapitulating past arguments or anticipating future ones. Or it may even seem circular: the discussion of desire with which the main text begins does not so much prepare the ground for what follows as make little sense without it. And, rather than a conclusion, *Totality and Infinity* ends with twelve sections grouped together as 'Conclusions', in the plural.

Peperzak suggests that the different parts of *Totality and Infinity* form 'a coherent text not broken by abrupt disruptions or startling turns'.[34] However, with too many prefaces and too many conclusions (which are anyway by no means entirely consistent with one another),[35] it may seem to some readers that the book is falling apart at the seams, apparently constructed as a unified whole but in fact disintegrating before our eyes. What is at stake here is whether the text has the character of a totality, in which even apparent contradictions or breaches can ultimately be shown to be part of the whole, or an infinity, in which the whole is revealed as inhabited by what it cannot contain. In the latter case, alterity turns out to be not only the *theme* of Levinas's text, but also the key to its complex textual performance. To *expound* alterity would also be to *expose* it, to bring it to light as an object of vision, reflection and knowledge; since this is the traditional move of the philosophy of the Same, alterity is also thereby annihilated as it is reconciled with that to which it had seemed external. It is therefore precisely what Levinas must avoid doing.

*Totality and Infinity*, then, cannot adopt a logical argumentative development leading to knowledge of the Other; instead, it offers a series of approaches pursued in proximity to the Other, aiming at exposure to alterity rather than exposition of it. In detail, this also entails a constant tussle with language in order to wrest it from its traditional contexts. Levinas's language twists and turns as if fitfully trying to throw off meanings that are never quite adequate. The Other is a 'reality without reality' (*TI*, 234/212; see also *TI*, 60/65) with which I may form a 'relation without relation' (*TI*, 79/80) or an 'unrelating relation [*rapport sans rapport*]' (*TI*, 329/295); the distance separating me from the Other is 'untraversable, and at the same time traversed' (*TI*, 56/62), and the Other opposes me with 'the resistance of what has no resistance' (*TI*, 217/199); violence is directed at a being which is 'both graspable and escaping every hold' (*TI*, 246/223). The text constantly evinces dissatisfaction and unease with its own language, as with its use of the word *experience*:

> The relation with infinity cannot, to be sure [*certes pas*], be stated in terms of experience, for infinity overflows the thought that thinks it. [. . .] But if experience precisely means [*si expérience signifie*] a relation with the absolutely other, that is, with what always overflows thought, the relation with infinity accomplishes experience in the fullest sense of the word [*l'expérience par excellence*]. (*TI*, 10/25)

The text emphatically rejects the word *experience* ('certes pas'), then redefines it ('si expérience signifie') and finds it, after all, to be perfectly apposite ('par excellence'). The passage turns back on the original proposition, examines it and reverses it. This does not simply negate what was first said; it involves a process of redefinition and recontextualization which tears the word away from its familiar sense and gives it a new, perhaps cleansed, meaning.

When discussing such paradoxes earlier in this chapter, I sought to explain why Levinas adopts such contorted verbal formulations. But such justification fails to account for the sheer strangeness of

Levinas's prose, as it tends to diminish the shock and disorientation experienced by even the best-qualified readers. Levinas's use of language is double-edged. Whilst words are rescued from their traditional contexts, their new definitions risk appearing arbitrary or senseless. The speculative restlessness of *Totality and Infinity* results in a constant remoulding of language. The reader is subjected to a conceptual bombardment by terms that are either invented or reallocated meaning by Levinas: totality, infinity, transcendence, exteriority, alterity, desire, the face, the face to face, epiphany, economy, separation, revelation, discourse, the feminine. Such terms constantly recur, being defined and redefined, their senses recalled and subtly modified on each new appearance. At the same time, this proliferation of terms sometimes seems to approach a collapse into senselessness as words merge into one another. Alterity, infinity, transcendence, exteriority and discourse are all figures of one another. The Other seems to be both nowhere and everywhere: 'The absolutely Other is the Other [*L'absolument Autre, c'est Autrui*]' (*TI*, 28/39); 'Signification is infinity, that is, the Other' (*TI*, 227/207); 'God is the Other' (*TI*, 232/211); 'The absolutely new is the Other' (*TI*, 242/219); 'The feminine is the Other' (*TI*, 297/265); 'The other that Desire desires is again Desire' (*TI*, 302/269). Words seem to be melting into an unhelpful synonymy. Terminological distinctions are implied and dissolved: *le moi* and *le soi* are used interchangeably to refer to the self; sometimes the text carefully distinguishes between *l'être* (Being) and *l'étant* (being), but sometimes uses the former to include the latter; Levinas opposes the philosophy of Being with the notion of exteriority, but also asserts that Being *is* exteriority (*TI*, 322/290); the scission between Same and Other is described as belonging to Being rather than making possible the transcendence of Being (*TI*, 302/269). The terminological bombardment effected within *Totality and Infinity* implies infinite nuances of meaning, and also threatens the reader with a dizzying breakdown of meaning as definitions constantly shift or merge into one another: 'To be I, atheist, at home with oneself, separated, happy, created – these are synonyms' (*TI*, 158/148).

The drama of *Totality and Infinity* lies in its struggle with the linguistic resources available to it. This is particularly the case in its use of the language of origins and the chronological narratives that are implied by it. Consistent with its phenomenological and ontological precursors, *Totality and Infinity* is concerned with original, fundamental, essential or ultimate realities. But in Levinas's text the language of origins is overlaid with competing implications. On the one hand *Totality and Infinity* suggests some sort of sequential narration whereby the anonymity of the *il y a* is replaced by the solitary subject in sole possession of the world; this subject then *encounters* the Other (words such as *rencontre* (encounter) or *accueil* (welcome) suggest an event that occurs in historical time); this imposes an ethical obligation which in turn can be taken as the foundation of society. On the other hand, the text implies that the subject only exists as a separate subject because of the presence of the Other. So on the one hand the self fully possesses the world *before* the encounter with the Other (language, for example, dispossesses me of 'a world *hitherto* mine' (TI, 189/174; my emphasis), whilst on the other hand the self only becomes itself *through* the encounter with the Other. Levinas denies that his account of the genesis of the subject should be understood in chronological terms, yet he continues to use language which suggests that it can and must be understood in precisely such a way. Different senses of *origin* compete and contradict one another, as the word seems to refer to both a fundamental state and an inaugural event.

For all its endeavours to define and maintain its own terminology, the text seems unable to control the implications of its language. The following passage, for example, both rejects and continues to draw upon a sequential narrative describing the relationship of self and Other:

> Being [*L'être*] is not *first* [*d'abord*], to give place afterwards [*ensuite*], by breaking up, to a diversity all of whose terms would maintain reciprocal relations among themselves, exhibiting thus the totality from which they proceed, and in which there would on occasion be produced a being [*un être*] existing for itself, an I, facing another I (incidents that could be accounted for by an impersonal discourse exterior to those incidents). [. . .] Separation is first [*d'abord*] the fact of a being [*un être*] that lives *somewhere*, from *something*, that is, that enjoys. The identity of the I comes to it from [*lui vient de*] its egoism whose insular sufficiency is accomplished by enjoyment, and to which the face teaches the infinity from which this insular sufficiency is separated. This egoism is indeed founded [*se fondę certes*] on the infinitude of the other [*l'infinitude de l'autre*], which can be accomplished only by being produced [*ne peut s'accomplir qu'en se produisant*] as the idea of Infinity in a separated being [*un être séparé*]. (TI, 237–8/215–16)

The twists and turns of Levinas's prose look like the effects of a losing battle against the temporal implications of his language. He begins by refusing a chronological narrative ('L'être n'est pas d'*abord*') in which Being gives way to a series of separate beings (the word *être* refers to both Being and beings here, whereas *étant* might have clarified the distinction). A little later, however, he substitutes his own chronological narrative. *First of all* ('d'abord' is repeated) separation concerns the individual self; identity derives from ('vient de') egoism. But this origin turns out to be non-originary, as Levinas traces the foundation of the self back to a more distant phase: egoism itself *is founded on* ('se fonde certes, sur') the other ('l'infinitude de l'autre' – why not 'l'Autre'?). And the final sentence quoted above complicates the issue still further: *l'infinitude de l'autre* is only realized when it is produced or produces itself (Levinas uses reflexive verbs to avoid implications of outside agency: 'ne peut s'accomplir qu'en se produisant'[36]) as the idea of the infinite in a separated being. So the Other is grounded in the self which is grounded in the Other.

The implied temporal sequence in the story of origins is evidently not the point, but the language of foundations, realization, production and so on continues to imply that it is. *Totality and Infinity* gets tangled up in the difficulties of giving a narrative form to a fundamental state. Moreover, the text constantly draws upon the authority of the language of origins and ultimate realities, even whilst denying the validity of such terms. The relationship with the Other, we are told, 'precedes all ontology; it is the ultimate relation in Being. Ontology presupposes metaphysics' (*TI*, 39/48); and, since this relation is also ethical, Levinas is also asserting that ethics has priority over ontology. The text invokes all the power of the rhetoric of origins: ethics is the bedrock, it precedes and has priority over everything else. But such rhetoric is also deemed to be singularly inappropriate: this foundation, when further scrutinized, requires a further underpinning, and it turns out to be founded precisely on that which it founds.

The difficulty derives from problems within Levinas's philosophical enterprise. He wants to show that there is something *outside, beyond* or *before* Being, a reality more fundamental than that of ontology; yet this search for grounds, foundations and origins itself belongs to the project of ontology. Levinas continues to rely upon a vocabulary and way of thinking which he also discredits. In an elegant account of the problems of time sequence, grounds and foundations in Levinas's thought, Bauman suggests that *before* has the sense of *better*, and that words such as *being* should be read as appearing under erasure ('sous rature').[37] Writing under erasure is a technique adapted from Heidegger by Derrida whereby a cross is superimposed over problematic words. The point of this is to show that the terms used are deficient, but that there is no preferable alternative to them; so words such as *being* may be retained, whilst their limitations are also implied.[38] To apply this notion of erasure to Levinas is fraught with problems. Where does erasure stop? If being, and the language of origins, essences, foundations, ultimate relations, are put under erasure, then why not the whole of Levinas's terminological network? In a heady paradox, words end up both retaining and losing their conventional meanings. Erasure cannot easily be arrested, and it opens up a dizzying possibility: all the speculative restlessness and conceptual energy of *Totality and Infinity* are deployed on the edge of a semantic abyss into which the whole text might collapse.

The text's unease with itself is largely explained by its simultaneous retention and problematization of its own key conceptual tools. Nowhere is this more evident than in the references to femininity. In *Le Deuxième Sexe* Simone de Beauvoir criticized Levinas's earlier work for reproducing the stereotypical view of woman as Other.[39] Later authors writing from a feminist perspective have seen a more positive side to Levinas's association of femininity and otherness.[40] Nevertheless, I would stress that, whatever the philosophical and ethical complexities of his conception of the feminine, it still acts as a focus for a set of remarkably deep-rooted, conventional and unproblematized views.

Levinas suggests that what he means by the feminine is neither an empirical nor a gendered presence (*TI*, 169/158, 286/256). At one point the empirical gender implied by the feminine is confused by the shift from the masculine *Aimé* to the feminine *Aimée*: the 'epiphany of the Loved [*Aimé*]' becomes the 'epiphany of the Beloved [*Aimée*]', and the text refers to 'the Loved, who is the Beloved [*l'Aimé qui est Aimée*]' (*TI*, 286/256). This confusion of genders could be seen as being in accordance with the process of erasure by which the feminine is wrested from its conventional context. But it does not explain why the term should be retained at all; and in the two passages on femininity in the second and fourth sections of *Totality and Infinity*, the feminine is linked with qualities belonging to the most conventional gender stereotypes: a gentle, self-

effacing, intimate, familiar presence in the home (*TI*, 165–6/155), weakness, tenderness, frailty, secrecy, voluptuousness, ambiguity, mystery, virginity which raises the desire for violation and profanation, beauty, eroticism, lasciviousness (*TI*, 286–95/256–61). In erotic love Same and Other come together, and together they engender a child (*TI*, 298/266). Peperzak argues that 'the whole metaphorics of fecundity seems to be detached from its biological connotations.'[41] But it is nearly impossible for either author or reader to achieve the detachment described by Peperzak; gendered vocabulary retains its connotations of gender even if we are told that it does not. Although Levinas gestures towards denying the strictly physiological implications of his discussion of fertility, paternity and filiality, his language never escapes its socially conditioned context. The femaleness of the feminine-Other is the physiological condition of the engendering of a child with the father-Same. Moreover, Levinas never questions the association of alterity with feminity; the self with whom the Other is contrasted is always implicitly male. Levinas discusses fertility in terms of fathers and sons as earlier he had talked about social relations in terms of *fraternity*. Fathers, sons and brothers occupy the foreground; maternity is mentioned only once, in reference to the son's relationship with his past. Underlying the fourth section of *Totality and Infinity* is a family scenario: the father's love for the woman results in the engendering of a son who assures the father's continuity into the future; and on the penultimate page of the book the relationship between self and Other is finally resolved through erotic and paternal love in what Levinas calls 'the marvel of the family' (*TI*, 342/306).

The point I am making here is that Levinas's language tells a different story from the one that *Totality and Infinity* seems intended to narrate. The primacy of ontology is reasserted when its language and concerns are retained; and the attitudes of patriarchy show through Levinas's analysis of the feminine despite implications that this should not be understood in empirical, gendered or physiological terms. The feminine-Other ends up being described as no more than a property of the masculine-Same. In fact, Levinas comes close to acknowledging as much. The explicit equation of the feminine with the Other ('The feminine is the Other'; *TI*, 297/265) contrasts with the admission that the feminine is treated in *Totality and Infinity* as part of the drama of the self, part of my own internal world: 'The feminine has been encountered in this analysis as one of the cardinal points of the horizon in which the inner life takes place' (*TI*, 169/158). Here, then, 'feminine alterity' (*TI*, 166/155), the exteriority of the feminine, is reconciled with interiority; and Levinas's text re-enacts precisely the move that it endeavoured to avoid, as it reproduces the reduction of the Other to the Same. The encounter with alterity is precisely what does not take place. Otherness, including the otherness of Levinas's own text, is constantly brought back to familiar structures. Unwittingly, Levinas's text demonstrates precisely the opposite of what it seemed intended to prove: it shows how the Other is inevitably suppressed and excluded from the text that had sought to preserve it.

In its language and the patterns of thought that go with it, *Totality and Infinity* constantly rehearses its own failure to make the step from Same to Other, ontology to ethics, self to transcendence. The text hovers on the brink of restoring the primacy of the Same that it was its aim to dislodge. However, perversely, in this potential failure lies the text's only possibility of success: to succeed as a philosophy of the Other, it must fail adequately to thematize its subject. The Other is that which *will not be said* in the language of ontology which *Totality and Infinity* continues to use. But perhaps the philosophical text can *stage* the encounter with the Other which it cannot describe. Rather than simply a sum of propositions and arguments, Levinas suggests that philosophy is 'a discourse always addressed to another. What we are now exposing is addressed to those who shall wish to read it' (*TI*, 302/269). Philosophy, then, is an address, an interpellation of the Other; as such, the encounter with the Other may be what happens in the act of reading rather than something captured within the text.

This suggests the possibility of a philosophical practice no longer restricted by the language of ontology. *Totality and Infinity* is a work in which the textual performance, for all its difficulty and strangeness, never quite matches the thematic call of the text to encounter the Other without the violent reduction of its alterity. But it anticipates the possibility of a *different* sort of practice which might participate in the strangeness that it thematizes. In the next chapter I shall discuss what is generally accepted as Levinas's second *magnum opus, Otherwise than Being or Beyond Essence*, a work which represents both a continuation of the ideas contained in of *Totality and Infinity* and an intense critical reflection on the language and practice of philosophy itself.

# Ethical Language: Otherwise than Being or Beyond Essence

## Derrida and Levinas

Three years after the publication of *Totality and Infinity*, the first and still the most influential detailed study of Levinas's thought appeared in the *Revue de métaphysique et de morale*, written by Jacques Derrida. Derrida's long article entitled 'Violence et métaphysique' adopts a stance which is respectful but uncompromising towards Levinas's work;[1] it analyses some of the 'silent axioms' (158, 162) which underlie Levinas's texts up to and including *Totality and Infinity*, and it casts a critical eye on his relationship with Husserl, Heidegger and the philosophical tradition in general. Derrida poses questions about the very foundations of Levinas's philosophical practice; and the radical rethinking which informs Levinas's later work, particularly *Otherwise than Being or Beyond Essence*, has been explained by some commentators as an attempt to take account of Derrida's questioning.[2] Derrida, then, can be regarded as playing a pivotal role in the development of Levinas's thought; and for this reason it is worth considering Derrida's account of Levinas, and Levinas's response, before discussing *Otherwise than Being* in detail.

Derrida's tone in 'Violence et métaphysique' is initially modest, as he insists that the questions that he will ask 'are certainly not objections: they are rather the questions which are posed to *us* by Levinas' (125). Derrida thus denies himself the magisterial command of one who claims to know better than his subject; and at the end of his essay he refers to the unprecedented boldness, depth and resolution of Levinas's endeavour (225). To those who have read the preceding pages of 'Violence et métaphysique', however, it may appear that Derrida's final compliments are a way of damning with exorbitant praise. Derrida draws attention to two kinds of problem in Levinas's work: apparent inconsistencies in his thinking, and blind spots in his readings of other philosophers. In relation to the first of these, he demonstrates for example how Levinas uses terms and categories in *Totality and Infinity* (Same and Other, exteriority) which had been rejected in his earlier work (161–2, 165); metaphors of light and the inside/outside dichotomy continue to govern Levinas's thinking despite his suspicions of them (165–7); and his identification of language and thought fits uneasily with his reservations on rhetoric, leading to the incoherent and self-defeating notion of a purified language which has nothing to say (218–20). Throughout his essay Derrida seeks to show that Levinas may have misunderstood the significance of his own thought.[3] On the question of speech and writing, for example, Levinas evinces a Platonic hostility towards the latter; but Derrida suggests that writing, which implies the absence of the speaker, may be more suitable for a philosophy of alterity than speech, which requires the potentially bullying or authoritarian presence of the speaker. So, Derrida can suggest, 'Can one not invert all of Levinas's propositions on this point?' (150).

Derrida's tactic of making his observations in the form of questions rather than assertions serves to insinuate shortcomings in Levinas's work in a polite but nevertheless insistent manner. This approach is most damning when Derrida compares Levinas with other philosophers. He regrets that Levinas has not patiently and systematically confronted the work of Kant (142); he suggests that Levinas may be closer to Kierkegaard than he acknowledges (143), that his interpretation of Buber may be inaccurate (156), that Hegel has already anticipated what he says (146), and indeed that he may be very close to Hegel at the very moments when he sets himself up in opposition to him (176). The most important and detailed comparisons in 'Violence et métaphysique' are with Husserl and Heidegger; and here Derrida suggests that on crucial points Levinas has misunderstood the two philosophers whom he studied for so long. He has got Husserl wrong on adequation (174–5) and intentionality (178), and he neglects Husserl's respect for the alterity of the Other (180). As for Heidegger, Levinas has misunderstood the nature of his ontology (201) and some of his key terms (202); the relation to Being does not have the dominance ascribed to it by Levinas (203), nor is it a relation of knowledge (205); and the Other is not subsumed under the category of Being (206–7).

Despite Derrida's cautious, respectful tone ('One will perhaps regret . . .' (142); 'Others will perhaps say . . .' (156)) he repeatedly implies that Levinas has crudely misread his most important forerunners. His views on Husserl cannot be held 'without abusing his [Husserl's] most consistent and most declared intentions' (184); Levinas's 'violent article' on Heidegger[4] is refuted by reference 'to Heidegger's most clear texts on this subject' (214), and Derrida offers to refer to 'a hundred passages of Heidegger' to correct another misreading (205). The discussion of Heidegger's *Mitsein* is typical of Derrida's approach. Levinas consistently distinguishes his own philosophy of alterity from *Mitsein* on the grounds that the latter maintains the priority of Being over otherness. Derrida counters that Levinas, like Sartre, has misinterpreted *Mitsein* as comradeship, solidarity or teamwork; a footnote refers to a scholarly work on Heidegger which supports Derrida's view, and which permits the rejection of Levinas's reading: 'The being which can address *Mitsein* is not, as Levinas often implies, a third term, a common truth, etc.' (217). Back in the main text, Derrida can now assert that Heidegger's 'thought of being' is in fact a version of the non-violent discourse desired by Levinas; it allows others their autonomy whilst liberating dialogue and facilitating what Levinas calls the face to face (217–18). So, the force of Derrida's argument is that Levinas sets himself up in opposition to Heidegger, but in fact misreads him so that the refutation actually relies upon and reproduces the thought of the philosopher being attacked. Levinas agrees with Heidegger at the very moment when he believes he is rejecting him.

The points Derrida makes are detailed and specific. Nevertheless, a consistent pattern does emerge; as Critchley puts it, in the 'dominant gesture' of 'Violence et métaphysique' Derrida shows how 'the transgression of phenomenology and ontology that is effected by Levinas's empirical metaphysics in fact presupposes the very things that it seeks to transgress.'[5] Despite Derrida's show of respect, Levinas might begin to appear as a very ragged thinker indeed. Levinas's break with his philosophical sources is presented as a misreading as he continues to rely upon concepts, metaphors and habits of thinking which he seeks to abandon. Thus he ends up confirming what he aimed to reject: 'Didn't Hegel already say this?' (146), 'Levinas is very close to Hegel, much closer than he would himself want, and this at the moment when he is opposing him in apparently the most radical manner' (147), 'as soon as *he speaks* against Hegel, Levinas can only confirm Hegel, he has *already* confirmed him' (176), 'Levinas and Husserl are very close on this point' (183), 'Levinas confirms Heidegger in his argument' (209).

The generosity of Derrida's article lies in its readiness to accept that Levinas's misreadings are not simply errors that undermine his project; they relate rather to the difficult nature of his philosophical endeavour as he struggles to wrest the language of philosophy from the tradition in which it is embedded. In Derrida's account, that tradition proves to be both more resilient and perhaps less invidious than Levinas realized: more resilient, because it cannot be so simply thrown off, yet less invidious because Levinas's precursors already share the respect for the Other which he apparently fails to find in them. Ultimately, Levinas's fundamental problem concerns the language of philosophy itself. Levinas's recourse to a language rooted in the primacy of the Same necessarily defeats his desire for a discourse fully exposed to the strangeness of the Other: 'So Levinas resigns himself to betraying his intention in his philosophical discourse' (224).

Bernasconi and Critchley have argued that to regard 'Violence et métaphysique' as a critique of Levinas is to misunderstand the essay;[6] instead, it should be regarded as a deconstructive or 'clôtural' reading which leaves Levinas's writing 'suspended and hesitant in the space between two metaphysics'.[7] Derrida's engagement with Levinas clearly does go far deeper than a simple critique. His intense and ongoing studies of Husserl and Heidegger put him in an almost unique position to assess Levinas's relationship to his most evident sources. Most importantly, Derrida's essay is also to some extent an act of philosophical self-recognition, as Levinas's ambiguous relationship to the language and values of the philosophical tradition is a reflection of Derrida's own position. Derrida perceives that Levinas's writing anticipates the difficulties faced by deconstruction. According to Feron, 'The essential point of Derrida's argument consists in recognizing that philosophical discourse can only say the Other in the language of the Same';[8] and this can be taken to summarize Derrida's dilemma as much as that of Levinas. In his essay on Levinas, Derrida is also describing the fundamental aporia of deconstruction, unable to be fully inside or outside its host discourse, determined in its habits of thought by that which it rejects.

Derrida's essay exposes basic tensions in *Totality and Infinity*, particularly in respect of the use of language and philosophical practice in general. Subsequent sections of this chapter will examine how Levinas responds to these tensions in his second major work, *Otherwise than Being*. To conclude this section I shall briefly indicate how Levinas implicitly acknowledges and parries Derrida's critique in his own article on the author of 'Violence et métaphysique'. Levinas's essay 'Tout autrement' was written for an edition of the journal *L'Arc* dedicated to Derrida's work and published in 1973; the essay, which was subsequently reprinted in Levinas's *Noms propres*, thus appeared in the year before the publication of *Otherwise than Being*.[9] In his essay Levinas makes no explicit reference to 'Violence et métaphysique', though there are clear indications that he is returning the compliments paid him by Derrida. Derrida had described Levinas as inaugurating something 'new, so new [*nouveau, si nouveau*]' (132); echoing this phrase, Levinas refers to Derrida's 'new style' and, adopting words used by Victor Hugo to describe the poetry of Baudelaire, he refers to the 'new thrill [*frisson nouveau*]' of Derrida's writing (*NP*, 66). Derrida and Levinas also describe each other as striving for a decisive break with the philosophical tradition. Derrida suggests that Levinas's thought 'calls on us to dislocate the Greek logos; to dislocate our identity, and perhaps identity in general' (122); and Levinas indicates that Derrida might effect a 'new break [*coupure*] in the history of philosophy' (*NP*, 65).

But if Levinas returns Derrida's compliments, he also reproduces the deeper and more critical structure of Derrida's argument. Levinas makes points about Derrida which are remarkably similar to those which Derrida had made about him. Derrida's thought represents both a breach and a continuity within the philosophical tradition, maintaining the history of philosophy even as it disrupts it (*NP*, 65). Moreover, having brought the authority of truth into question, Derrida continues to rely upon it in his own writing. Levinas suggests this with an unacknowledged but clear allusion to Derrida's essay on his own work. Derrida had thrown doubt on Levinas's assertions by asking, 'Is it certain [*Est-ce sûr*]?': 'Levinas says that "the primacy of ontology does not rest" on a "truism". Is it certain?' (198). Levinas picks up on this 'Is it certain?' and sees in it the re-emergence of the discredited criterion of truth:

Discourse in the course of which, as he is rocking the foundations of truth, [. . .] Derrida still has the strength to say, 'Is it certain?', as if anything could be secure at that moment and as if security or insecurity should still matter. (*NP*, 69)

Adopting a tone as polite but telling as that of Derrida in 'Violence et métaphysique', Levinas suggests that 'One might be tempted to use this recourse to logocentric language as an argument against that very language, in order to contest the de-construction that is produced' (*NP*, 69). And, in what I take to be a further allusion to Derrida's essay, Levinas observes that such an argument is a 'Path which perhaps Derrida himself has not always disdained in his polemic' (*NP*, 69).

Levinas finds in Derrida some of the inconsistencies that Derrida had found in Levinas. The tranquil tone of 'Autrement dit' is belied by an implicit agon. This becomes most evident when Levinas recounts a story which he says Derrida's texts evoke for him. During the French retreat in 1940, a half-drunk barber offers to shave the soldiers without charge:

> With his two companions he shaved them without charge [*il rasait gratis*] and it was today. The essential procrastination – the future *difference* – was absorbed into the present. Time was reaching its end with the end or the interim period of France. Unless the barber was as delirious as in the fourth form of delirium in the *Phaedrus* in which, since Plato, the discourse of Western metaphysics has been held. (*NP*, 67)

The anecdote plays upon the phrase *Demain on rase gratis* (roughly equivalent to 'Jam tomorrow'), which makes a promise which will never be fulfilled because tomorrow never comes. Critchley sees a complimentary side to the story: 'That Levinas should apply this image to Derrida shows that he considers that the *impossible* takes place in his work.'[10] But the compliment is at the very least double-edged. Levinas does not explicitly make the connection between Derrida and the barber, but the comparison is nevertheless implied. The barber is described as 'half drunk', or as 'delirious'; and the learned reference to Plato in this latter qualification[11] does little to distract from the more ordinary implications of the suggestion that Derrida may be delirious. The barber is a comic figure, unaware of the magnitude of the catastrophe that he is witnessing; his apparent realization of the impossible becomes a merely foolish gesture rather than a heroic enterprise.

The fact that Levinas's essay reproduces some of the respect, arguments and underlying agon of 'Violence et métaphysique' is too striking to be coincidental. The respective essays of Derrida and Levinas give the uncomfortable sense that each philosopher is vying for position with the other: Derrida uses his astonishing knowledge of the history of philosophy to find weak spots in Levinas's thought; Levinas plays his cards too close to his chest for us to see what he really thinks, yet oblique criticisms can be discerned. Behind the double-edged compliments in which both thinkers indulge, there is perhaps a deeper anxiety underlying their responses to one another's writing. Derrida and Levinas recognize something of their own projects and dilemmas in the work of the other. The ambivalence manifested in both essays can be read as a sign of the disturbance caused when a moment of self-recognition reveals problems that it would have been more comfortable not to acknowledge. Derrida would return to Levinas in his later essay 'En ce moment même dans cet ouvrage me voici';[12] Levinas, in the meantime, was already rethinking the bases of his philosophical practice; this would culminate the year after the publication of 'Autrement dit' with what some have seen as his sustained and considered response to Derrida, *Otherwise than Being or Beyond Essence.*

## Otherwise than Being or Beyond Essence

The importance of Derrida's 'Violence et métaphysique' is twofold. It has had a decisive influence on the reception of Levinas's work, particularly in the English-speaking world; the essay lies at the source of what Robert Bernasconi describes as one of the major objections to Levinas's work, namely that 'in the course of articulating his claim that ethics is beyond being and so unthematizable, he makes a theme of the unthematizable.'[13] Secondly, there is a consensus amongst commentators that Levinas's subsequent work, especially *Otherwise than Being or Beyond Essence*, can be read as his implicit response to Derrida. Both the language adopted and the themes addressed in *Otherwise than Being* have been found to bear unmistakable echoes of Derrida's discussion in 'Violence et métaphysique'.[14]

Levinas's second major work occupies much of the same territory as *Totality and Infinity*; at the same time it is a more intensely self-conscious text, attempting to confront and avoid the pitfalls of ontology to which, Levinas himself acknowledged, *Totality and Infinity* had succumbed.[15] A new vocabulary is adopted. Words such as the Same, metaphysics, transcendence, exteriority, totality and separation have either disappeared or occur relatively rarely. There is no further discussion of the feminine, and only a handful of obscure references to maternity (see for example *OB*, 121–3). On the other hand, the later text bristles with terms more or less absent from the earlier work: proximity, approach, obsession, hostage, persecution, expiation, substitution, illeity, enigma.[16] Even *l'Autre* and *Autrui* play a less important role, being largely replaced by *le prochain* (the neighbour). Peperzak explains this change of vocabulary in part by a shift in Levinas's perspective: whereas *Totality and Infinity* dealt with the Other, *Otherwise than Being* is concerned more with the position and meaning of the subject.[17] Yet such a distinction barely holds, since the subject already occupied a crucial place in *Totality and Infinity*. What is most important in the renewal of vocabulary, I would argue, is Levinas's reluctance to establish and maintain a rigid conceptual framework. Levinas's terminology is fluid and largely drawn from ordinary language. Both these factors contribute to the difficulty of *Otherwise than Being*. New terms are constantly being adopted and familiar words seem to be used in unfamiliar ways. The main aim of this chapter is to show that the problems of understanding posed by these and other features of the textual practice adopted in *Otherwise than Being* play a vital role in the work.

By any standards, *Otherwise than Being* is a bizarre and difficult text. Simon Critchley states that 'no attempt has yet been made to appreciate this book's strangeness, the disturbance it provokes within philosophical discourse.'[18] Étienne Feron observes how this strangeness can be found in the structure of the book as well as in its textual details; the apparently rigorous construction of *Otherwise than Being*, with 'The Argument' followed by 'The Exposition', is belied by the text which appears rather 'like a preliminary discourse, like a prelude or a preamble which might ceaselessly interrupt itself to start again in a way which is always new'.[19] Within *Otherwise than Being*, Levinas refers to aspects of his own text as severe (*OB*, 156/99), barbaric (*OB*, 273/178) or simply strange (*OB*, 281/183). Most readers, I suspect, would be inclined to agree.

*Otherwise than Being* is characterized by its heightened attention to language, as can be seen at both thematic and textual levels. The opening paragraph of the 'Preliminary Note' explains the use of the word *essence* in the full French title of the book, *Autrement qu'être ou au-delà de l'essence*: *essence* refers to *être* as opposed to *étant*, or the German *Sein* as opposed to *Seiendes*, or the Latin *esse*

rather than the scholastic *ens*. Levinas regrets that he did not dare
write *essance* (recalling Derrida's *différance*) even though this spelling could be justified by a long list of French nouns ending in the
suffix *-ance*;[20] and he ends the paragraph by informing us that,
instead of *essence, essentiel* and *essentiellement*, he will use the words
'eidos, eidetic, eidetically, or nature, quiddity, fundamental, etc.'
(*OB*, 9/xli). From the very beginning, then, questions of language
are foregrounded; yet the opening paragraph offers synonyms or
equivalences rather than definitions, and Levinas tends to repeat
his point rather than to elaborate or refine it. Later, he once again
regrets that he dare not write *essance* and tells us that essence is
equivalent to *esse* and *Sein* (*OB*, 13/3) or *être* (*OB*, 43/23). The
foregrounding of language does not point us beyond the text to the
being or essence named by *essence*; instead, attention is drawn to
the words as words, interconnected and interchangeable links in a
vast textual chain which never quite succeeds in capturing that
which lies beyond the text or beyond Being.

Many features of Levinas's textual practice seem calculated, at
the very least, to disorientate the reader, to delay rather than to
facilitate understanding. Hyphens are constantly used to break up
words into their constituent parts, as if Levinas wanted to fracture
them and peer inside them, preventing us from receiving their
meanings too readily: *ex-ception, an-archique, re-présentation, diachronie, épi-phénoménal, dés-inter-essement, dé-position, ex-pression*,
and so on. Italicization also serves to draw attention to the
constituent parts of words: '*souvenir*' (*OB*, 28/13), 'simul*tanéité*'
(*OB*, 258/166), 'trans*parence*' (*OB*, 275/179) and (most bizarrely)
'dés-intéres*sement*' (*OB*, 278/181).[21] Conversely, hyphens are also
used to join together separate words in new, unwieldy composites:
'The unlimited responsibility in which I find myself comes from
the hither side of my freedom, from a "prior to every memory"
[*antérieur-à-tout-souvenir*], an "ulterior to every accomplishment"
[*ultérieur-à-tout-accomplissement*]' (*OB*, 24/10); 'All my inwardness
is invested in the form of a despite-me, for-another [*contre-mon-gré-
pour-un-autre*]' (*OB*, 26/11). Levinas is both dismantling the lexis
and reconstructing it; the new words need to be both shorter,
displaying the linguistic building blocks from which they are
made, and longer, combining more and more elements in new
formulations.

Disturbances of smooth linguistic surfaces can also be observed
in larger syntactical units. Levinas's sentences can be dizzyingly
long or surprisingly abrupt, bluntly aphoristic or perversely

convoluted. Dashes and commas are used sometimes idiosyncrati-
cally to interrupt the flow, demanding the exercise of considerable
mental agility to maintain a clear sense of syntactical relations.
There is a marked preference for the redoubling of terms: subjectivity is 'as a passivity more passive than all passivity' (*OB*, 30/14);
Levinas seeks 'the infinity of the infinite' (*OB*, 27/12), 'the denuding of denuding' (*OB*, 83/49), 'enjoyment of enjoyment [*jouissance
de la jouissance*]' (*OB*, 118/73), 'the signifyingness [*signifiance*] of
signification' (*OB*, 158/101), and not the origin but 'the very origin
of the origin' (*OB*, 249/160).

Unsurprisingly, perhaps, paradox is one of the characteristic
tropes of *Otherwise than Being*. Subjectivity, for example, is both
'locus and null-site [*lieu et non-lieu*, place and no-place]' (*OB*, 30/
14); Levinas describes a debt which increases as it is paid off (*OB*,
27/12); and he refers to propositional language as both 'ancillary
and thus [*ainsi*] indispensable' (*OB*, 18/6), when the *thus* confuses
matters even further, suggesting not merely a paradoxical simul-
taneity but a causal relation determining the two elements of the
paradox: not just ancillary *and* indispensable, but indispensable
*because* ancillary. Most crucially for Levinassian ethics, the assumption of responsibility for the Other takes place in 'a past more
ancient than every origin, a pre-original and anarchical *passed*' (*OB*,
23/9); this is 'a past more ancient than any present, a past which
was never present' (*OB*, 45/24), the quest for which leads to a near-
dysfunctioning of language: 'The problem consists only [!] in
asking oneself if a beginning is at the beginning' (*OB*, 257/165).
Accepted oppositions (active/passive, original/derived) collapse
under the weight of such pressure, as sources and foundations are
pushed further out of reach in an intensely self-reflexive endeavour
to name receding goals. Whereas the vocabulary of *Totality and
Infinity* reflected the search for originary, fundamental states, the
practice adopted in *Otherwise than Being* brings into question the
validity of such a search. Levinas refers to an identity which is
'pre-original, anarchic, older than every beginning' (*OB*, 227/145);
given that he uses *anarchic* in the sense of 'having no origin', each
of the three qualifications of identity seems to say the same thing.
But a doubt arises: is this redundant repetition, or careful qualification of the noun with subtle nuances of meaning? If our response
to such questions is unsure, we are left unable to decide whether
Levinas's prose is cautiously precise or unnecessarily verbose. The
intelligibility of the text hinges or founders on the apparent
nonsense of the word *pre-original*: what precedes the origin which

nothing can (by definition) precede? Such paradoxes give and retract meaning in the same instant. I shall discuss the purpose of all this later; for the moment it should already be evident that the logical incoherence of Levinas's prose entails a rejection of logic as the privileged tool of intellectual analysis. Whatever Levinas is getting at cannot be reached within a conventionally coherent discourse.

Levinas's prose gives too much and too little. Sometimes paradoxical and sibylline, at other moments it can appear repetitive or tautological. Key notions are introduced with little warning and little real explanation.[22] Luce Irigaray has complained of Levinas's tendency to use words without defining or redefining them.[23] Most bizarrely, given Levinas's sensitivity to the dangers of falling into the language of ontology, the verb *être* (to be) is used liberally, almost with abandon. A shotgun wedding is arranged between ill-matched pairs of nouns: 'Being's essence is the temporalization of time' (*OB*, 53/29); '[Signification] is the glory of transcendence' (*OB*, 29/13); 'The Mind is a multiplicity of individuals' (*OB*, 200/ 126). Or whole lists of nouns may be indiscriminately linked: 'The work of being, essence, time, the lapse of time, is exposition, truth, philosophy' (*OB*, 53/30). This abundant, unqualified use of *to be* is so remarkable, so contrary to Levinas's vigilance towards the language of ontology, that its effect becomes parodic. The verb is deprived of its power of identification; the essences it locates are evanescent at the very moment that they are named: not so much Being as its mass-produced, cheaper and less functional version.

To put it plainly, the difficulty of Levinas's prose is not simply a product of the philosophical complexity of what he has to say. Meaning is endangered by a practice of writing that eludes ready comprehension. At moments, language is pushed to near-breaking point: 'Subjectivity is precisely [*précisément*] a node and a denouement – the node or the denouement of essence and essence's other [*le noeud et le dénouement – le noeud ou le dénouement de l'essence et de l'autre de l'essence*]' (*OB*, 23/10). The most ironic touch here is the word *precisely*, which asserts a rigorous exactitude in this vertiginous collision of incompatibles: and/or, node/denouement, essence/essence's other. It would be easy to dismiss all this as mere wordspinning. However, in *Otherwise than Being* the textual practice is an integral part of Levinas's philosophical endeavour. Every aspect of the text, including its ethical ambitions, is commanded by his account of the distinction between *le Dire* (Saying) and *le Dit* (the Said). In this account, which is discussed in the next section, Levinas makes explicit the stakes of his extraordinary – severe, barbaric, strange – textual performance.


## Saying and the Said

*Otherwise than Being* consistently shows an exceptional awareness of the problems which its textuality poses to its own intelligibility. It foregrounds the surface irregularities of language which impede easy comprehension, denying ready access to a firm set of philosophical propositions. From the earliest stages of the book, Levinas draws attention to the difficulties of expression with which his thought must contend: 'The *otherwise than being* is stated in a saying that must also be unsaid [*un dire qui doit aussi se dédire*] in order to thus extract the *otherwise than being* from the said in which the *otherwise than being* [*autrement qu'être*] already comes to signify only a *being otherwise* [*être autrement*]' (*OB*, 19/7). This sentence exemplifies some of the textual problems I have been describing. It presents a bewildering surface behind which there may be nothing. The italics, the threefold repetition of *otherwise than being*, the wordplay on *otherwise than being* and *being otherwise* are all too closely compacted to allow easy deciphering. Everything revolves around the key phrase 'a saying that must also be unsaid'. This becomes a crucial characterization of Levinas's philosophical prose. Later in *Otherwise than Being* he describes his procedure as 'an incessant unsaying of the Said [*un incessant dédit du Dit*] [. . .] a movement going from said to unsaid in which the meaning shows itself, eclipses and shows itself. In this navigation the element that bears the embarkation is also the element that submerges it and threatens to sink it' (*OB*, 278/181). So language, the element which conveys meaning, is also the element which endangers it, exposing it to the risk of collapsing into nonsense.[24]

And yet the text does make statements and propositions. The sentence quoted at the beginning of the previous paragraph makes perfect sense in the context of Levinas's endeavour in *Otherwise than Being*. The distinction between *autrement qu'être* (otherwise than being) and *être autrement* (being otherwise) is not simply a play on words. Levinas is attempting to approach something that does not belong to the order of Being, something that is other-than-Being; in order to do this he must avoid the danger of transforming this other-than-Being into simply another Being, albeit a different one. The danger lies within the very language which philosophers have adopted in order to pursue their enquiries. The rhetoric of presentation, demonstration, description and truth implies the existence of a stable, knowable reality which the philosopher can explicate; hence, such rhetoric relies upon the ontological assumptions which Levinas wishes to elude. In order to say the other-than-Being, language must be torn away from such ontological assumptions. To achieve this is no easy matter, since philosophical prose is both the site and the object of the struggle. So the textual disturbances which characterize the language of *Otherwise than Being* are the surface effects of deep tensions within the work. It is as if the text were trying to shake off its own propositional structure, whilst remaining aware that the success of such a project would be disastrous for the philosophical ambitions that the text continues to entertain. Despite the ambivalence which *Otherwise than Being* manifests towards the philosophical heritage, Levinas insists that his text does not abandon that heritage; he refers to his 'discourse that means to be philosophy [*discours qui se veut philosophie*]' (*OB*, 242/155), thus accepting that his project does not entail the rejection of philosophy as such. The extreme audacity of Levinas's text lies in its attempt to theorize the limitations of theory, to conceptualize and to exemplify a dimension of language which normally slips through the themes and propositions of philosophy.

The crucial distinction which informs all textual and thematic aspects of *Otherwise than Being* is that between *le Dire* (Saying) and *le Dit* (the Said).[25] Levinas suggests that philosophy has traditionally been concerned only with the Said. This comprises statements and propositions about, for example, the world, truth, Being, personal identity, which are susceptible to established protocols of dispute, verification or disproof. Giving priority to the Said entails a failure to recognize another distinctive dimension of language, which Levinas calls Saying: underlying, though not fully represented by, every utterance is a situation, structure or event in which I am exposed to the Other as a speaker or receiver of discourse. The Said presupposes Saying, which is thus, in Levinas's term, pre-original: it does not chronologically precede the Said, but it has priority over it because it constitutes its condition of possibility. When philosophers concentrate only on what is said, they overlook the essential exposure to the Other without which there would be neither utterance nor meaning.

The relationship between Saying and the Said should not be assimilated to that between the Saussurean terms *langue* and *parole*.

In Saussure's conception, *langue* is a semiotic system encompassing the potential for combination and difference in language; *parole* is no more than a contingent and limited actualization of *langue*. For Levinas, Saying and the Said are two aspects of language which bear their own distinct meanings; and, most importantly, their meanings may be in direct contradiction to one another. The Said is easiest to analyse because it comprises the themes, ideas or observations which we intentionally communicate to one another through discourse. Saying is more elusive because its meaning is precisely what cannot be encapsulated in the Said. Levinas is entirely aware that severe methodological problems derive from the attempt to make Saying into an object of philosophical enquiry. In thematizing Saying he is forcing it into the domain of the Said, and thereby (to adopt the dramatic language which he often uses) betraying it. His text twists and turns as it wrestles with this problem: Saying is never fully present in the Said, yet the Said also constitutes the only access we have to it; it leaves a trace on the Said but is never revealed in it; it is not a theme, but can only be discussed in terms of themes (*OB*, 64–7/37–8, 78–81/45–8).

The problems involved in talking about Saying are strongly reminiscent of those stemming from the encounter with the Other, which is transformed into an *alter ego* as soon as it becomes for me an object of scrutiny and knowledge. Saying, like the Other, can only be violated by discourses which implicitly or overtly seek authority over it. These similarities are not, of course, coincidental. The importance of Saying for Levinas stems from his designation of it as the site where my encounter with – or, in the vocabulary preferred in *Otherwise than Being,* my exposure to – the Other takes place. The Said is the domain which philosophy inevitably inhabits; it is also the birthplace of ontology because the themes and identifications on which ontology depends take place within it (*OB*, 74/42–3). Saying is the place (which is also a no-place, a utopia; *OB*, 77/45) for approach or proximity to the Other, where the infinite, or that which escapes Being, is to be sought.

Levinas's analysis of Saying and the Said occupies such an important place in his later thinking because it binds together the problem of language with his ethical concerns. In *Totality and Infinity* language was already conceived as playing a central role in ethical relations because the encounter with the Other always involves speech and response.[26] *Otherwise than Being* goes further: the exposure to the Other effected in Saying is at the very core of ethical relations. This explains why Levinas regards a proper understanding of Saying as urgent. Although he insists that Saying can never be viewed in isolation from the Said, he employs the notion of *le Dire sans Dit* (Saying without a Said) (*OB*, 78/45) as a potentially useful fiction which might provide a better understanding of the profound nature of language: 'What does Saying signify before signifying a Said?' (*OB*, 78/46). For Levinas, Saying has its own meaning, quite separate from anything that might be communicated by the Said. Levinas refers to 'the signifyingness proper to Saying [*la signifiance propre du Dire*]' (*OB*, 79/46), using the word *signifiance* rather than the more usual *signification*, which is reserved for the meanings conveyed in the Said. *Signifiance* refers to a more active process of meaning which lies behind the Said. *Signifiance* is what makes *signification* possible:

> To say [*Dire*] is to approach a neighbour, 'dealing him signifyingness' [*lui 'bailler signifiance'*]. This is not exhausted in 'ascriptions of meaning [*prestation de sens*]', which are inscribed, as tales in the Said. [...] Saying is communication, to be sure, but as a condition for all communication, as exposure. (*OB*, 81–2/48)

Levinas is attempting to effect what he calls a reduction from the Said to Saying. Despite his use of a phenomenological term, this reduction is at a far remove from the Husserlian *epoché*. It does not reveal fundamental structures of consciousness or the sovereignty of the transcendental Ego; on the contrary, the reduction to Saying leads back to something pre-original, pre-phenomenological, before the constitution of the Ego and the birth of consciousness. Attempting to disentangle what he calls the *intrigue* (plot) of Saying, Levinas also uncovers the prehistory of the subject. The subject, for Levinas, is not the humanist or existentialist originator of its own actions and meanings, but neither is it the structuralist or post-structuralist battleground of structures and ideologies. Prior to consciousness, hence also prior to choice, commitment, activity or passivity, the subject is exposed to the Other, capable of speaking and responding to the discourse of others. Most importantly, the ethical nature of this exposure is brought out by the verbal link between the ability to respond and responsibility: '*saying is to be responsible for others [dire, c'est répondre d'autrui]*' (*OB*, 80/47). This responsibility is without limits; it is not part of my private experience, not something contracted in the biography of an individual, neither freely chosen nor actively desired. Before I am even myself, I am responsible for the Other, absolutely and without appeal.

Levinas elegantly sidesteps the classic philosophical problems posed by the existence of other selves. From his point of view the problems are badly posed for two reasons: firstly, because they presuppose that the self *pre-exists* the encounter with others, whereas in Levinas's account the subject is constituted *by* and *as* its exposure to the Other; and, secondly, because they focus on questions of knowledge (How can I know that others exist, and what can I know about them?), whereas for Levinas it is ethics rather than knowledge which is at stake in the relationship with the Other.[27] Levinas's discussion of Saying leads to a conception of subjectivity which rejects both the humanist insistence on the subject's sovereignty and the anti-humanist dissolution of the subject and its responsibilities: 'One must show in Saying, qua approach, the very de-posing or de-situating of the subject, which nonetheless remains an irreplaceable uniqueness, and is thus the subjectivity of the subject' (*OB*, 81/47–8). The subject is deposed and desituated, consciousness and intentionality lose their status as the privileged sites of philosophical analysis; and yet the subject is unique and irreplaceable, its exposure being the essential precondition to ethics, speech, communication and (as we shall see later) social justice.

The subject is not described by Levinas in terms of consciousness, intentionality, interiority, self-possession, freedom, commitment or choice. It is neither 'in itself [*en soi*]' nor 'at home with itself [*chez soi*]' (*OB*, 83/49). It exists in proximity to the Other, it approaches the Other, achieving the conditions of communication in the 'risky uncovering of oneself, in sincerity, in the breaking up of inwardness and the abandon of all shelter, in exposure to traumas, in vulnerability' (*OB*, 82/48). The sincerity which Levinas mentions, like the *témoignage* (witnessing) to which he devotes an important part of *Otherwise than Being* (see *OB*, 223–38/142–52), does not consist in 'telling the truth'; rather it is a full – and truthful – exposure of the self to the Other, prior to the telling of truth and lies, not an event within the history of the subject, but the very nature of its existence:

> Not the communication of a Said, which would immediately cover over and extinguish or absorb the Said, but Saying holding open its openness, without excuses, evasion or alibis, delivering itself without saying anything Said. Saying saying itself, without thematizing it, but exposing it again. [. . .] No Said equals the sincerity of Saying, is adequate to the veracity that is prior to the true, the veracity of the approach, of proximity, beyond presence. Sincerity would then be Saying without the

Said [*Dire sans Dit*], apparently a 'speaking so as to say nothing', a sign I make to another of this giving of signs, 'as simple as hello', but ipso facto the pure transparency of an admission, the recognition of a debt. (*OB*, 223/142, 225/143)

In as far as Saying says anything that can be thematized, it is merely 'Me voici' ('Here I am').[28] However, the simplicity of this declaration is deceptive. It involves a conception of the subject (constituted by its exposure to the Other), the basis of ethical relations (founded on that exposure), and a reorientation for philosophy (now directed towards the *signifiance* of Saying rather than the *signification* of the Said). The stakes for Levinas are never higher than when his text appears most unassuming.

## Society and justice

The analysis of Saying uncovers the fundamental structure of subjectivity as exposure to the Other. However, the importance attributed to Saying does not entail a rejection of the meanings that can be communicated in the Said. Levinas's work has been criticized for privileging Saying over the Said to the extent that it does not matter what is said as long as there is exposure to the Other through Saying.[29] Such criticism rests upon a basic misunderstanding of Levinas's commitment to the importance of the Said, which is not weakened by the priority which he accords to Saying. Without the Said there is no philosophy (*OB*, 136/85) and, more importantly, no society, justice, judgement or ethics either. 'This is wrong' is a statement that belongs to the Said, however much it may depend upon a pre-original Saying; and it is not a matter of simple indifference whether I judge something to be right or wrong. There is in Levinas none of the neo-pragmatist relativism which insists that anything can be redescribed as good or bad if we alter the final vocabularies within which we operate.[30] Most importantly, and perhaps surprisingly, the intense reflexive self-questioning that takes place within *Otherwise than Being* does not condemn the book to an endless and fruitless contemplation of its own propositional capacities; in fact, the book is rather more helpful than *Totality and Infinity* for an understanding of ethical and social relations, and in particular for the possibility of establishing a theory of justice and an ethical society.[31]

Levinas's extension of his thought to social issues derives, like everything else, from the basic situation of the subject's exposure to the Other. This is not conceived as an event within the experience of the subject, since such a view would imply that the subject was already constituted before that experience took place. Levinas insists that the relationship with the Other is the (pre-)original event of subjectivity: 'the relationship with the non-ego precedes any relationship of the ego with itself' (*OB*, 189/118). Exposure to the Other is the bedrock of my selfhood; it is the condition of subjectivity, not an aspect of it.

At every stage of his discussion Levinas adopts ethical language, but he is not concerned with questions of moral choice. Choices are made by conscious subjects, whereas the responsibility that Levinas finds at the core of the relationship with the Other cannot be accepted or rejected in an act of conscious volition. For Levinas the whole drama of subjectivity is ethical from its very first moment. Responsibility is not an accident which befalls (and so might not befall) the subject (*OB*, 180/114); neither should it be understood as 'altruistic will, instinct of "natural benevolence" or love' (*OB*, 177/111–12). Such responsibility would be an attribute or property of the subject; Levinassian responsibility is less generous, more imperious and ineluctable, in that it belongs to the very nature of subjectivity. I am responsible for the Other because my existence as individuated subject is entirely bound up with my relation to him or her. Levinas describes this relationship as *obsession* because it entirely dominates me;[32] or, in terms repeated throughout *Otherwise than Being*, I am the *hostage* of the Other, I am *persecuted* because I cannot escape the dominance of the Other over me. To do so would be to relinquish my subjectivity.

The dramatic quality of Levinas's language (obsession, hostage, persecution) foreshadows an uncompromising twist in his thinking. The subject comes into existence through its exposure to the Other, hence subjectivity is characterized as '*the other in the same* [*l'autre dans le même*]' (*OB*, 176/111). In a pivotal play on words, Levinas suggests that *par l'autre* (from-the-other) is also *pour l'autre* (for-the-other) (*OB*, 175–6/111): because the encounter with the Other is constitutive of the subject, the subject is not – as Sartre argued in *L'Être et le néant* – *pour soi* (for-itself), but rather it is *pour l'autre* (for-the-other), bound to the Other and responsible for its deeds and misdeeds. And my responsibility extends even to acceptance of the violence which the Other may do to me: 'The subjectivity of a subject is responsibility or being in question in the form of the total exposure to offence in the cheek offered to the smiter' (*OB*, 176/111). From here it is only a small step to one of the most shocking and controversial formulations in *Otherwise than Being*: 'the persecuted one is liable to answer for the persecutor [*le persécuté est susceptible de répondre du persécuteur*]' (*OB*, 175/111). Hence the importance of substitution and expiation in *Otherwise than Being*: although I am unique and irreplaceable, I am constituted by the Other, I can be called upon to replace the Other, to expiate the crimes of the Other: 'The word *I* means *here I am* [*me voici*], answering for everything and for everyone' (*OB*, 180–1/114). Levinas does not seek to avoid the consequences of this:

> Every accusation and persecution, as all interpersonal praise, recompense, and punishment presuppose the subjectivity of the ego, substitution, the possibility of putting oneself in the place of the Other, which refers to the transference from the 'from the other' into a 'for the other', and in persecution from the outrage inflicted by the Other to the expiation for his fault by me. (*OB*, 186–7/117–18)

The responsibility that I take for the actions of the persecutor forms the basis of my goodness (*bonté*). Again, this goodness is not the result of a moral choice; it describes an obligation arising from the fact that, in my condition as subject, I am given over to the Other (*OB*, 187/118). All moral qualities derive from this fundamental ethical premise: 'It is through the condition of being hostage that there can be in this world pity, compassion, pardon and proximity – even the little there is, even the simple "After you, sir"' (*OB*, 186/117).

So Levinas describes a link between ethical relations and moral behaviour; yet the claim that this also requires that I expiate the crimes of my own persecutor takes the argument into murky waters. Should my goodness really extend so far, and does this mean that the victim of torture can be held to blame for the torturer's action? Some of Levinas's more extreme formulations would suggest that this is indeed the case. However, he does seek to avoid some of the consequences that might be drawn from this position. In the dialogues transcribed in *Ethics and Infinity* (*Éthique et infini*) Levinas insists that his 'extreme formulas' should not be taken out of context (*EI*, 96/99); glossing the phrase 'I am responsible for the persecutions that I undergo', he declares that this position cannot be universalized: 'But only me! My "close relations" or "my people" are already the others and, for them, I demand justice' (*EI*, 95/99). The point is already anticipated in *Otherwise than Being*:

The ego involved in responsibility [*Le Moi de la responsabilité*] is me [*moi*] and no one else, me with whom one would have liked to pair up a sister soul, from whom one would require substitution and sacrifice. But to say that the Other [*Autrui*] has to sacrifice himself to the others [*les autres*] would be to preach human sacrifice! (*OB*, 201/126; see also *OB*, 179/113)

Throughout *Otherwise than Being* Levinas prefers the term *le prochain* (the neighbour) to the more abstract *Autrui*; and, as in the above quotation, he tends to refer to *les autres* (others) rather than to *l'Autre* (the Other). The neighbour is not a philosophical abstraction: the word refers to a real person actually in my proximity. Likewise, the 'ego involved in responsibility' is not a philosophical fiction, such as the transcendental Ego of Husserl or the subject of the Cartesian Cogito; the ego ('le Moi') is me ('moi'), the actual historical self of the speaking subject, in this instance Emmanuel Levinas. And what Levinas demands of himself, he does not expect of others: 'to ask of the other more than he owes, is criminal' (*OB*, 179/113). Levinas's position, then, is uncompromising towards himself and generous towards others: his own responsibility is without limits, but he does not claim the authority to expect the same of you or me.

Levinas denies himself the move of universalist ethics which would impose the same duties and obligations on all rational subjects. The refusal to universalize would seem to block the general applicability of his thinking; yet Levinas does talk about society, justice and the state, as if the ethical questions he raises do nevertheless impinge on issues of public judgement and morality. This step beyond the responsibilities of the individual subject is made possible by *le tiers* (the third party), who makes clear to me that a world exists outside my relationship with the neighbour. In *Otherwise than Being* Levinas elaborates on the rather sketchy comments on the third party made in *Totality and Infinity*. The exposure to the Other brings the subject into existence as it also puts it in question; the presence of the third party in turn raises questions about my relationship with the Other:

The third party is other than the neighbour, but also another neighbour, and also a neighbour of the Other, and not simply his fellow. What then are the other and the third party for one another? What have they done to one another? Which passes before the other? The other stands in a relationship with the third party, for whom I cannot entirely answer, even if I alone answer, before any question, for my neighbour. The other and the third party, my neighbours, contemporaries of one another, put distance between me and the other and the third party. (*OB*, 245/157)

Levinas is careful to insist that, just as the encounter with the Other is not an event that takes place in historical time, the appearance of the third party is not an empirical event (*OB*, 246/158). The third party is always potentially present in the proximity of the Other, because the Other is never simply *my* Other; the Other implies the possibility of others, for whom I am myself an Other: 'I am another for the others' (*OB*, 247/158). The third party, then, prevents my relationship with the Other from becoming too cosily self-enclosed. I am made to realize that the Other does not exist merely for my sake, that my neighbour is also a neighbour to the third party, and indeed that to them it is I who am the third party.

The proximity of the third party reveals the potential existence of innumerable subjects any of whom, including myself, can play the role of Other to all others. So, the discovery of the third party disturbs the intimacy of my relationship with the Other, provoking a questioning which opens up broader perspectives and lays the foundations of society. The subject is led to question its place in the world, which brings about the birth of consciousness and instigates a concern for social justice. Society is not founded on a unity of species, such as humankind, but on a multiplicity of others, in which each subject is unique, recalcitrant to classification; and justice is not founded on universal principles or on some social contract designed to tame the 'natural instincts' of the human species. Rather than the application of pre-existing laws, justice entails a community of others in which each is responsible for all:

> This means concretely or empirically that justice is not a legality regulating human masses, from which a technique of social equilibrium is drawn, harmonizing antagonistic forces. That would be a justification of the State delivered over to its own necessities. Justice is impossible without the one that renders it finding himself in proximity. His function is not limited to the 'function of judgment', the subsuming of particular cases under a general rule. The judge is not outside the conflict, but the law is in the midst of proximity. Justice, society, the State and its institutions, exchanges and work are comprehensible on the basis of proximity. This means that nothing is outside of the control of the responsibility of the one for the other. (*OB*, 248/159)

Levinas rejects the view that conflict is essential to human relations; instead, he derives the outlines of a social theory from his notion of exposure to the Other as pacific. And despite the limitlessness of my responsibility, which extends even to expiation for the actions of the persecutor, I can also claim justice for myself because for others I am an Other:

But justice can be established only if I, always evaded from the concept of the ego, always desituated and divested of being, always in non-reciprocatable relationship with the Other, always for the Other, can become an other like the others. [...] My fate is important. (*OB*, 250/160–1)

The third party, then, acts as a corrective to the asymmetry of ethical relations. My responsibility for the Other is not matched by any reciprocal responsibility of the Other for me, I cannot in any way be compared to the Other. But the third party makes it possible to escape the moral chaos that Levinas's non-universalist ethics might entail. The Other does not become an *alter ego*, but I become another Other (*OB*, 247/159). So the asymmetry of my responsibility for the Other no longer means that I cannot expect respect and fair treatment.

Levinas concedes that his thought has a utopian aspect (*OB*, 282/184); yet his work certainly does not take place in ignorance of historical and political realities. *Otherwise than Being* is dedicated to the victims of the Holocaust (*OB*, 5/v); and, although the book has nothing to say about that specific atrocity, it refers insistently to the traumas experienced by the subject in history. Pity, compassion, forgiveness and proximity are, he suggests, in short supply (*OB*, 186/117); the just and egalitarian society is not yet instituted (*OB*, 248/159). The ethical relationship which Levinas finds at the core of subjectivity does not imply that humankind or society is inherently or necessarily moral. On the contrary, Levinas's writing is underlaid by a constant appeal to his readers to become more moral; and despite the abstractions of Levinas's prose his most powerful and moving lines are also the most concrete, as he repeatedly insists on the ethical call to give food to the hungry: 'not a gift of the heart, but of the bread from one's mouth, of one's own mouthful of bread' (*OB*, 120/74).

The combination of ethical utopianism and the awareness of historical violence which overshadows the text characterizes the distinctive humanism of Levinas's writing, a humanism which he describes in the title of one of his books as an *humanisme de l'autre homme* (humanism of the other man). Modern anti-humanism is right, Levinas suggests, though not entirely for the reasons it gives. It correctly abolishes the notion of the human person as the free, self-creating source of its own values; but it then fails to make Levinas's move of reinstating subjectivity in terms of substitution and responsibility. Humanism should be rejected on the basis of this understanding of humanity, which turns out to be more human and humane than what the humanists describe; as Levinas puts it, 'Humanism has to be denounced only because it is not sufficiently human' (*OB*, 203/128).

## The Enigma of philosophy

Levinas suggests that the fundamental task of philosophy may be 'indiscretion with regard to the unsayable [*l'indiscrétion à l'égard de l'indicible*]' (*OB*, 19/7). This engages his work in a project which it designates as bound to fail. Throughout *Otherwise than Being*, Saying is analysed from the standpoint of the Said, even though the reader is constantly reminded that the proper meaning of the former can never be formulated in the latter. So, *Otherwise than Being* shadows its own propositions, concepts and arguments (such as those discussed in the previous section) with a sense of their inadequacy. The work, Levinas insists in its final paragraph, 'does not seek to restore any ruined concept' (*OB*, 283–4/185); yet it does aim to remain philosophy (*OB*, 242/155), accepting the inevitable betrayals of Saying which characterize the Said. *Otherwise than Being* adopts a double movement of proposition and self-subversion ('a saying that must also be unsaid [*un dire qui doit aussi se dédire*]'; *OB*, 19/7); from this double movement emerges Levinas's view of the role, limits and capabilities of philosophy, which should be practised as a discipline aware of its own enigmatic nature.

The awareness within *Otherwise than Being* of problems arising from its own textuality is made clear from frequent references to, for example, 'the present study', 'the present analysis', 'this study', 'this work' or to the 'very moment' of writing.[33] Levinas is acutely conscious of the work of philosophy as a process or an act located in time rather than a definitive, timeless product. The concepts it proposes are unstable, often inadequately defined, and its conclusions are suggestively aphoristic rather than compelling. In reference to his methodological problems Levinas implies that the lack of clarity in *Otherwise than Being* derives from the tension between the structural requirements of philosophy and the less conveniently ordered nature of his material:

The different concepts that come up in the attempt to state transcendence echo one another [*se font écho*]. The necessities of thematization in which they are said ordain [*ordonnent*] a division into chapters, although it is

> not the case that the themes in which these concepts present themselves
> [*se présentent*] lend themselves [*se prêtent*] to linear exposition, and cannot
> really be isolated [*s'isoler*] from one another without projecting their
> shadows and their reflections [*leurs ombres et leurs reflets*] on one another.
> Perhaps the clarity [*clarté*] of the exposition does not suffer here only
> from the clumsiness of the expounder. (*OB*, 37/19)

Here, Levinas adopts the trope of light which, as his earlier work
had shown, plays such an important role in Western philosophy.
Yet the linear progression from darkness (ignorance, superstition,
philosophical naïvety) to light (knowledge, reason, wisdom) is
replaced by an unstable interplay of shadow (*ombres*) and reflections (*reflets*). *Clarté* (light, clarity) is not the ultimate goal of a
philosopher who aims finally to climb out of the Platonic cavern
and to behold the sun;[34] instead, light (or enlightenment) is an
occasional, perhaps even accidental, effect of philosophical
enquiry, no more to be trusted, no more definitive, than any of
Levinas's constantly evolving concepts. Sense is relayed back and
forth rather than established once and for all. Moreover, this is not
a process directed by the rational mind of the philosopher. The
language of the text implies the near-absence of the philosopher, at
least as individuated or rational subject, from the composition of
his text. The necessities of thematization prescribe or ordain
(*ordonnent*) the division into chapters; and reflexive verbs (*se font,
se présentent, se prêtent, s'isoler*) suggest that concepts are self-made,
self-propelling, excluding the author from responsibility for his
text and denying his status as its source.[35]

The difficulty of *Otherwise than Being* (and indeed of Levinas's
later texts in general, though with varying degrees of self-
consciousness) is of a different nature from that of, say, Kant's
*Critique of Pure Reason* or Spinoza's *Ethics*. In those cases the
problems of understanding derive, at least in the first instance, from
the intellectual effort required to follow the increasing complexity
of the argument. In the case of *Otherwise than Being*, fundamental
difficulties are caused by tensions within the text arising from a
deep unease with its own linguistic resources. This can be illustrated by the use of the verbs *être* (to be) and *consister* (to consist).
On the one hand, Levinas clearly signals that these verbs will be
used from the very beginning of *Otherwise than Being* to name 'the
hither side of being' (*OB*, 75/43); on the other hand, these are the
very verbs which transform the beyond-Being into Being, the other-
than-essence into essence. *Otherwise than Being* both rejects and
reinstates the language of ontology, and it portrays this paradoxical

stance as the very condition of a philosophy of transcendence. There can be no simple renunciation of the language and aims of ontology (other than silence or gibberish), since the power of the philosophical logos lies in its ability to absorb what interrupts it:

> Every contestation and interruption of this power of discourse is at once related and invested by discourse. It thus recommences as soon as one interrupts it. [. . .] If the philosophical discourse is broken [*se rompt*], withdraws [*se retire*] from speech and murmurs, is spoken [*se parle*, speaks itself], it nonetheless speaks of that, and speaks of the discourse which a moment ago it was speaking and to which it returns to say its provisional retreat. Are we not at this very moment in the process of barring the issue that our whole essay attempts, and of encircling our position from all sides? The exceptional words by which is said [*se dit*] the trace of the past and the extravagance of the approach – One, God – become [*se font*] terms, reenter into the vocabulary and are put [*se mettent*] at the disposition of philologists, instead of confounding [*désarçonner*] philosophical language. Their very explosions are recounted [*Leurs explosions mêmes se racontent*]. (*OB*, 262–3/169)

Again, the use of reflexive verbs ('se rompt', 'se retire', 'se parle', 'se dit', 'se font', 'se mettent', 'se racontent') attributes the restoration of philosophical discourse to a process beyond the will or choice of the philosopher. The metaphors for the disruption of philosophy escalate in violence: contestation becomes interruption, breakage, unhorsing (the etymological sense of *désarçonner*) and finally explosion. But the rejection of philosophy takes place within philosophy, and the escape from Being is obstructed by the very language in which it is planned.

*Otherwise than Being* openly confronts the observations made by Derrida in 'Violence et métaphysique' on problems within Levinas's project. The most sustained attempt to overcome, or at least to justify, the tensions within the text comes in the comments on scepticism, particularly in the section of the book entitled 'Scepticisme et raison' ('Scepticism and Reason') (*OB*, 256–66/165–71).[36] As Bernasconi observes, the references to scepticism in *Otherwise than Being* are not to any specific philosophical author or movement. Scepticism is one of the fundamental possibilities of philosophical thought; it appears 'at the dawn of philosophy', it is subject to 'innumerable "irrefutable" refutations', and yet 'it always returns as philosophy's legitimate child [*enfant légitime*]' (*OB*, 20/7); it is 'by turn refuted and returning [*revenant*, a ghost]' (*OB*, 38/19–20). Scepticism, in this account, is both the dead ancestor (*revenant*) and the living offspring (*enfant*) of philosophy.

It is refuted but persistent: 'Philosophy is not separable from scepticism, which follows it like a shadow it drives off by refuting it only to find it once again on its path' (*OB*, 260/168).

Levinas does not characterize his own position as a form of scepticism, though he does see an analogy between the sceptical argument and his own. Both are subject to refutation on grounds of logical incoherence. The classical refutation of scepticism draws attention to a basic contradiction within the sceptical stance: the sceptic claims that there is no truth, yet this claim is itself taken to be true; so the sceptic does believe that some propositions can be judged in terms of truth or falsehood, and scepticism thus reinstates what it aimed to abolish. Scepticism, then, produces the same internal tension as Levinas's text in its opposition between Saying and the Said: Saying is explicitly given priority, but the text implicitly reaffirms the primacy of the Said by its very status as a text. Even so, the refutation of scepticism does not destroy it; and similarly Levinas's text survives the potentially destructive tension between Saying and the Said. Indeed, the text as we have it is vitally informed by that tension, to the point of being unimaginable without it.

Just as the refutation of scepticism proceeded by disinterring hidden presumptions within the sceptical position, Levinas responds by disinterring presumptions underlying the refutation. The opponents of scepticism are arguing from the standpoint of a totality in which the sceptical claim 'There is no truth' must be part of the series of propositions to which it refers. To question this assumption Levinas draws a distinction between synchrony and diachrony. Synchrony unites all moments and all statements in a single unbroken time sphere where reason asserts its claim to universal validity; Saying and the Said are in contradiction with one another only if they are regarded as occurring in synchrony. Levinas proposes instead that the time of Saying and the time of the Said be viewed from the standpoint of diachrony (or *diachrony*, as the word is frequently printed). This diachrony owes little to the more common usage of the term in Saussurean linguistics to refer to the development of an object of study (for example language) through time; in Levinas's usage it refers to an inner fracture within the single moment, so that time is internally riven rather than unified in an all-encompassing totality.[37] When time is viewed as diachrony, Saying and the Said occur simultaneously (the two can never be isolated from one another), but without conflict. As John Llewelyn explains, this conception of diachrony resolves the contradiction within *Otherwise than Being* and within scepticism:

> [Statements that contradict each other logically] are contradictory only because they are posited together in the same time. The contradiction can sometimes be resolved by asserting them at different times. But the saying and the said are neither at the same time nor at different times. They are *in* different times. So the saying cannot be retrieved in the said.[38]

Levinas is not trying to persuade the reader that scepticism is right and its refutation misguided; he aims to show that both are valid, that neither can expect a definitive victory over the other. The power of scepticism is 'invincible and evanescent' (*OB*, 265/171), and its apparent contradictions are not fatal to either its opponents or its proponents. Saying and the Said can, indeed must, coexist despite the tensions between them. This has crucial consequences for Levinas's understanding of philosophy. Levinas acknowledges, as we have seen, that philosophy necessarily belongs to the domain of the Said, however much it may insist on the theoretical primacy of Saying. At the same time, it is central to Levinas's conception of the Said that it always contains the traces of Saying. In consequence, philosophy is also always a practice of Saying, characterized by exposure to and responsibility for the Other: 'The philosophical speaking that betrays in its said the proximity that it translates for us still remains, as a saying, proximity and responsibility' (*OB*, 261–2/168). As a practice of the Said, philosophy recuperates the disruptions of the logos and restores the smooth, totalized surface of the Same; but, as a practice of Saying, philosophy breaks up that smooth surface. Language is presented to a listener and the text exposed to its reader, hence made susceptible to interpretations which shatter the totalities of the Said:

> And I still interrupt the ultimate discourse in which all the discourses are stated, in saying it to one who listens to it, and who is situated outside the Said that the discourse says, outside all it includes. That is true of the discussion I am elaborating at this very moment. This reference to an interlocutor permanently breaks through the text that the discourse claims to weave in thematizing and enveloping all things. In totalizing being, discourse qua discourse thus belies the very claim to totalize. This reversion is like that which the refutation of scepticism brings out. In the written text, saying does indeed become a pure said, a simultaneousness of saying and of its conditions. A book is interrupted

discourse catching up with that which breaks it. But books have their fate; they belong to a world they do not include, but recognize by being written and printed, and by being prefaced and getting themselves preceded with forewords. They are interrupted, and call for other books and in the end are interpreted in a saying distinct from the said. (*OB*, 264–5/170–1)

Philosophy cannot totalize the world because it is part of it; and, in its openness to interpretation by the Other, the philosophical text recovers Saying submerged beneath its Said. *Otherwise than Being* appears to be a text which is self-absorbed to the point of excluding all contact with the outside world; yet Levinas insists that 'The reflection of discourse on itself does not imprison it within itself' (*OB*, 265/171). The text is always turned outwards, open in as far as it constitutes an address to the Other even if its ambitions to totalize appear to present an unbreachable closure.

So, at its most fundamental level philosophy is not for Levinas a collection of propositions; rather it is a risk (*OB*, 38/20) or a drama (*OB*, 39/20). And its most important message is the Enigma. Levinas introduced the term *Enigma* into his philosophy in the essay 'Énigme et phénomène', which is also where Saying and the Said are discussed for the first time. The Enigma, which in *Otherwise than Being* replaces the references to secrets in *Totality and Infinity*, is etymologically opposed to the phenomenon; whereas the phenomenon appears, the Enigma withdraws (*EDE*, 209). It is not a mystery to be explained, but an essential secret which cannot be fully revealed. It is part of all language: 'All speaking is enigma' (*EDE*, 212); and it is also 'transcendence itself, the proximity of the Other as Other' (*EDE*, 213). Hence it joins the long list of other terms in Levinas's writing which represent the disruption of totality: transcendence, alterity, infinity, Saying, responsibility, proximity, approach, substitution, expiation, ethics.

References to the Enigma abound in *Otherwise than Being*, characterizing both the unthematizable significance of Saying and the text's own performance. It is crucial that the Enigma serves to open up dialogue, interpretation and responsibility rather than to paralyse them. I respond because I do not know what the Other is saying to me. In the Enigma, then, two fundamental concerns of *Otherwise than Being* coincide: the text combines an intense reflection on its own status, limits and ambiguities with the ethical urgency of an address to the Other. In one of the most densely self-reflexive passages of the book, Levinas both interrogates his own text and picks up (implicitly) Derrida's comments on his earlier work:

The very discussion which we are at this moment elaborating about signification, dia-chrony and the transcendence of the approach beyond being, a discourse that means to be philosophy, is a thematizing, a synchronizing of terms, a recourse to systematic language, a constant use of the verb *to be*, a bringing back into the bosom of being all signification allegedly conceived beyond being. But are we being duped by this subreption? [. . .] By the very fact of formulating statements, is not the universality of the thematized, that is, of being, confirmed by the project of the present discussion, which ventures to question this universality? Does this discourse remain then coherent and philosophical? These are familiar objections! (*OB*, 242–3/155)

Much more explicitly than any of Levinas's preceding texts *Otherwise than Being* incorporates within itself its own self-critique, which also entails engaging in dialogue with Levinas's critics. There can be no doubt that Derrida's 'Violence et métaphysique' lies behind the passage just quoted. But Derrida is, for all his importance, just one figure in a dialogue ultimately addressed to the Other, and to the many others who may read the work. Despite and through the terminological proliferation which characterizes Levinas's writing in general and *Otherwise than Being* in particular, the role of philosophy is no longer to be understood as the refinement or elaboration of ever more numerous and ever more adequate concepts. The philosophical text communicates its own Enigma before it transmits pre-established knowledge or wisdom. It thus becomes, if it succeeds, a site where something happens, where my own responsibility for the Other – and for the Other's text which I am reading – comes into play.

*Otherwise than Being* is an astonishingly difficult text, and astonishment is, Levinas suggests, what the book is all about: 'It is this astonishment [*étonnement*] that has been the object of the book proposed here' (*OB*, 277/181). The boldest move made in *Otherwise than Being* is the attempt to find a textual practice appropriate to its central thesis about language. The difficulty of the work and the problems of understanding that it poses are not tangential to the point; they *are* the point. Interrogating Levinas's text becomes a process of self-interrogation, as local problems of understanding confront the reader with more fundamental questions: 'What does Levinas mean by responsibility?' slips into 'What is my responsibility, how am I responsible for my neighbour?' The reader makes the text, and in the process makes herself. This is at least the wager which *Otherwise than Being*, with its breathtaking philosophical prose, its rapid oscillations between proposition and subversion, is prepared to take. The refusal to elaborate a stable set of ideas and propositions produces a disorientation which is perhaps neither what we expect nor what we want from a philosophical text. The result may be irritating or fascinating, depending on the reader or her mood. Whatever response it elicits, Levinas's later work challenges fundamental assumptions about philosophy. What the text says should not suppress its status as an instance of Saying; whilst remaining philosophy, the text should also maintain its openness, its function as address, exposure and risk. The philosophical work becomes a site where the Enigma appears as such; and the principal function of the text is to instigate debate, in which responsibility and respect for the Other may be both thematized and exemplified.

# 4

# *Religion*

Whilst formulating the ideas discussed in the previous chapters and refining the philosophical practice associated with them, Levinas was also engaged in a long, persistent reflection on religious and biblical issues. Levinas is a thinker crucially informed by his Jewish roots, though he consistently maintains that he is a philosopher rather than a theologian. This chapter will discuss how his texts on religious themes feed off and feed into the philosophical work pursued in parallel to them.

Levinas's work may be crudely divided into two categories: philosophical studies; and essays on religious, specifically Jewish, subjects. Some of his essays on Judaism are collected in *Difficult Freedom* (*Difficile liberté*, first edition 1963, revised edition 1976); *De Dieu qui vient à l'idée* (1982) contains articles and interviews dealing with theological issues; and Levinas has also published a large number of talmudic commentaries, most of which were originally delivered orally at the annual meetings of the Colloque des Intellectuels Juifs de Langue Française. The earliest of these appeared in *Difficult Freedom*, and others are collected in *Quatre lectures talmudiques* (1968), *Du sacré au saint* (1977) (the latter two published together in English as *Nine Talmudic Readings*), *Beyond the Verse* (*L'Au-delà du verset*, 1982) and *A l'heure des nations* (1988).

The importance accorded to the religious aspect of Levinas's writing has varied depending on the interests of individual commentators. Those writing from a philosophical perspective have tended to pay little attention to religious themes or patterns of thought. Étienne Feron is typical in justifying the exclusion of

Judaism from his study of Levinas; he insists that '[Levinas's] major works are genuinely philosophical and do not in any way consist in the transposition, into a pseudo-philosophical discourse, of Jewish theology.'[1] Robert Gibbs alludes to approaches such as that of Feron when he comments drily that 'Levinas has been read as a philosopher, while the Jewish dimension of his thought has largely been ignored, or honoured by a mention and then ignored.'[2] For Gibbs, Levinas is one of the two most important Jewish thinkers of the century (the other being Rosenzweig).[3] From a religious point of view, authors have examined his work for its theological significance or used it to help define their own positions.[4] Jewish themes, and in particular Levinas's approach to the Talmud, have been discussed by authors with expert knowledge in the field.[5]

But there is little real disagreement among those who regard Levinas either as a religious thinker or as a philosopher. According to Gibbs, 'the most "Jewish" of his works are still philosophical';[6] or, as Susan Handelman argues, 'All of Levinas's key philosophical ideas are found in his Jewish writings.'[7] The Jewish writings, in these accounts, are different in style and approach, but they share the same interests and much of the same vocabulary: themes of alterity, responsibility, subjectivity, sociality and ethics dominate the talmudic commentaries as much as they do the philosophical texts. Conversely, those philosophical texts are replete with religious terms such as infinity and transcendence; biblical reference is used freely and lies behind crucial formulations ('Thou shalt not commit murder', 'Here I am [*Me voici*]')[8] and ideas.[9] The biblical Abraham, opposed to the Hellenic Ulysses, appears repeatedly as the privileged figure for Levinas's philosophical project as he leaves behind his home (ontology) to explore an unknown world (alterity) without expectation of return.[10] No attempt is made to disguise the religious aspect of Levinas's thought, even if its bases are not fully explained in the philosophical texts; in *Totality and Infinity* the relationship between self and Other is characterized as *religion* (*TI*, 30/40), and in *Otherwise than Being* the problems of transcendence and subjectivity are described as inseparable from the question of God (*OB*, 33/17). Religion, then, has been treated as unimportant for the philosophical reception of Levinas's thought and as the vital impulse which informs every aspect of his writing. But all commentators accept that there is a constant interchange of vocabulary and ideas between Levinas's philosophical and religious works.

The present chapter attempts to show that Levinas's texts on religious themes, whilst focusing on his Judaic roots and their importance for the modern world, are largely consistent with his philosophical texts in their vocabulary and concerns. The chapter is divided into three sections. The first, drawing mainly on *De Dieu qui vient à l'idée*, looks at the theological aspects of Levinas's philosophical positions; the second discusses his conception of Judaism; and the third examines his interest in the Talmud, in which his understanding of Judaism, ethics, language and philosophy all come together.

## Theology

In *Du sacré au saint* Levinas acknowledges that for him philosophy derives from religion (*SS*, 156/182). As he subsequently explains in an interview reprinted in *A l'heure des nations*, this does not mean that philosophy is servile to religion, nor that religion requires philosophy to give it intellectual dignity; rather, he suggests, religion and philosophy are 'two distinct moments, but both are part of the same spiritual process which is *the approach* of transcendence' (*AHN*, 204). Philosophy is part of a process in which religion is also involved, and the difficulties involved in talking rationally about God are the same as those raised by alterity in *Totality and Infinity* and *Otherwise than Being*; thematization serves to reduce its transcendence, to capture radical otherness in the webs of the familiar:

> One wonders if it is possible to speak legitimately of God without undermining the absoluteness which the word seems to signify. To have become conscious of God, is this not to have contained him within a knowledge which assimilates him, within an experience which remains – whatever its modalities – a learning and a seizing? And thus is not the infinity or the total alterity, or the newness of the absolute restored to immanence, to the totality which is maintained by the 'I think' of 'transcendental apperception', to the system at which knowledge arrives or aims to arrive throughout the whole of history? (*DVI*, 8)

In the essays collected in *De Dieu qui vient à l'idée* Levinas confronts the theological ramifications of his thought. He does not offer anything like an account of the nature of God, since this would entail a reversion to ontology. If philosophy takes knowledge of God as its object, it effectively makes God into a Supreme Being, an essence to be revealed. The endeavour to transgress ontological thinking undertaken in Levinas's philosophical texts would be inconsistent with any such conception. According to Levinas, ontological thinking, whatever the stated beliefs of its practitioners, is always fundamentally atheist. As a form of thought which gives all prestige to the Same, it denies transcendence; it acknowledges nothing outside itself and leaves no place for alterity. Repudiating the significance of anything which does not fall within its competence, philosophy claims for itself full authority over the domain of the meaningful; and rational theology, in so far as it accepts the need to justify its positions in intelligible discourse, accepts its subordination to philosophy (*DVI*, 94–5). This does not mean that Levinas is advocating mysticism, negative theology or naïve faith. Each of these, whether it characterizes the godhead as ineffable, defines it by reference to what it is not or insists that faith is not susceptible to rational testing, adopts an inherently ontological stance by treating God as a Being or presence. Even to talk of religious *experience* implicitly affirms the primacy of the ontological outlook: God is an object of knowledge revealed to the subject, experienced as a presence (*DVI*, 103). The alleged transcendence of God thereby turns out to be a kind of immanence: God is ultimately understood as part of our own world, a Being that we may experience or refuse to experience, of which we may have knowledge or be ignorant.

In the preface to *De Dieu qui vient à l'idée* Levinas describes the essays in the volume as constituting 'an investigation into the possibility – or even into the fact – of understanding the word God as a meaningful word' (*DVI*, 7). The issue raised in this preface is the one which dominates all Levinas's texts: is it possible to talk of something outside Being? All the problems of thematization and conceptualization posed by Levinas's philosophy crystallize around the question of God. The essays are not concerned with belief or non-belief, or with discussion of the existence or non-existence of God. Such questions are firmly rooted within ontology. Levinas endeavours to speak of God 'in a discourse which would be neither ontology nor faith' (*DVI*, 96). This excludes all knowledge of God, be it rational or intuitive, and all theology, be it positive or negative, which speculates on the nature of God. Instead, God becomes the privileged figure of that which strikes thought from the outside, utterly irreducible to Being and inconceivable in terms of the knowledge or experience of the subject.

Once again, Levinas draws on Descartes's Third Meditation to help explain his position. Descartes finds within the subject the idea of the infinite, an idea too exorbitant to be the product of the subject itself. It disrupts the self-confidence and self-containment of the Cogito since it reveals to the subject that it is not its own origin, nor is it the source of all its own thoughts and knowledge. The idea of the infinite cannot, according to Descartes, have been conceived by the subject because it is completely beyond its powers; neither does the idea befall the unsuspecting subject at any specific moment in its conscious life. Descartes is thus left to assume that the idea of the infinite is placed inside me at the very moment of my own creation: 'And in consequence, there is nothing else to say other than that, like the idea of myself, [the idea of the infinite] is born and produced with me at the moment when I was created.'[11]

So, the Cogito is fractured from the outset by the presence within it of something beyond its competence. Levinas has no interest in the next stage of Descartes's argument whereby the presence within the subject of the idea of the infinite turns out to be a proof of the existence of God. Descartes's conception of God as an 'eminent being' (*DVI*, 104) depends upon the language of ontology which Levinas rejects.[12] Levinas, then, is not concerned with the full context of Descartes's argument. Just as he has no qualms about using Plato's notion of the good beyond Being for his own ·purposes, suggesting that Plato may not have understood its full significance, Levinas appropriates the Cartesian idea of the infinite for his own ends: 'It is not the proofs of the existence of God which are important for us here, but the breaking of consciousness, which is not a repression into the unconscious but a sobering up or an awakening' (*DVI*, 104–5).

Centuries before Husserl, Descartes unwittingly destroys the universal validity of intentionality and its privileged role in the constitution of the subject (*DVI*, 105). From its first moments the subject is not characterized by consciousness and self-presence, but by the self-exceeding idea of the infinite:

> The placing within us of an idea which exceeds us overturns that self-presence which is consciousness, thus breaking through the defences and controls, thwarting the obligation to accept or adopt everything which enters from outside. (*DVI*, 107)

Consciousness is no longer the supreme arbiter of meaning which can assume authority over everything which enters from the outside. The subject is constituted by an original encounter with something which exceeds it. This is not, for Levinas, a proof of God conceived as a being in which one might believe or not believe. What it provides is rather a justification for using the word *God* as a name for that area of sense not commanded by consciousness. God is not an essence, substance or Being, since each of these terms belongs to the language of ontology; God is radical exteriority, transcendence encountered at the core of subjectivity. It 'explodes thought [*fait éclater la pensée*]' (*DVI*, 105), allowing it to go beyond itself, as Levinas suggests in one of his favourite formulations: 'Thus thinks a thought which thinks more than it thinks [*Ainsi pense une pensée qui pense plus qu'elle ne pense*]' (*DVI*, 13).

'The idea-of-the-Infinite-in-me' can, according to Levinas, be taken as synonymous with 'my relation to God' (*DVI*, 11). But this relation, like the relation with the Other, is not contracted between two beings who are fully present to one another. God is neither a presence nor an absence that could become present:

> An invisible God which no relation could attain because he is not a term in any relation, even one of intentionality, precisely because he is not a term, but Infinity. Infinity to which I am given over by a non-intentional thought of which no proposition in our language – not even the *to* [*à*] to which we have recourse – could translate the devotion. (*DVI*, 250)

Levinas frequently writes *à-Dieu* (to-God) rather than *Dieu* in order to avoid the implication that the noun refers to a substance with separate existence.[13] Instead, God is to be *approached* but never reached: the *à* of *à-Dieu* suggests movement towards God, whereas the more familiar word *adieu* to which Levinas's term alludes suggests a farewell to God as an ontological category. However, verbal devices such as referring to God as *à-Dieu* should not be taken as adequately resolving the problems of expression posed by divinity. Whenever Levinas characterizes God, he is obliged to exercise the most extreme caution with his language. He is not attempting to tie God down to a being or essence; rather he claims to be describing 'only the circumstances in which the very meaning of the word God comes to thought, more imperiously than any presence; circumstances in which this word signifies neither being, nor perseverance in being, nor any other world – nothing less than a world! – without, in these precisely precise circumstances, these negations turning into negative theology' (*DVI*, 252–3). Levinas's prose proceeds by negations (*neither, nor, nor, without, negations, negative*) and disruptions ('– nothing less than a world! –'), leading to the final twist: these negations should not be read as negative theology, since even negative theology turns out to be too positive. Saying what God is not permits the indirect characterization of what God is and thereby falls back into immanence and ontology.

God's alterity is not that of *Autrui*: 'God is not simply the "first other" [*premier autrui*] or the "other par excellence" [*autrui par excellence*] or the "absolutely other" [*absolument autrui*], but other than the other, other otherwise, other by an alterity prior to the alterity of the other [*autre qu'autrui, autre autrement, autre d'altérité préalable à l'altérité d'autrui*], prior to the ethical obligation to the neighbour, transcendent to the point of absence, to the point of its possible confusion with the bustle of the *il y a*' (*DVI*, 115). Levinas uses the term *illeity* to refer to this alterity (*DVI*, 113–14), accepting the possible confusion that might arise between the anonymous horror of the *il y a* and the unseizable nature of God. Illeity is first discussed in 'La Trace de l'Autre' (1963) (reprinted in later editions of *En découvrant l'existence avec Husserl et Heidegger*), and the term subsequently appears in *Otherwise than Being*. Derived from the pronoun *il*, illeity entails the refusal of any direct, personal or intimate relationship with God. Levinas rejects Buber's I–Thou relationship because it implies too much familiarity with the Other, who should be addressed with the more formal *vous*; but this *vous* is in turn too familiar, too direct an address for God. God is glimpsed only in the third person, neither a presence nor an absence, but a trace (*EDE*, 199–202), infinitely close and absolutely distant. Illeity is alterity at the furthest remove; and to be in the image of God is to stand in the trace of this illeity (*EDE*, 202). God is not the supreme Other, but rather the absent condition, or the incondition as Levinas frequently writes, of the encounter with the Other.

Perhaps unsurprisingly, the illeity of God is bound up with Levinas's ethics. The idea of the infinite, the (non-)relation to God or the *à-Dieu*, represents the fracture within the subject which makes possible the exceeding of ontology and the dislodging of the sovereignty of the Cogito or transcendental Ego. This is also what ensures that the subject is exposed to the Other, which in turn leads to Levinas's insistence on the ethics of substitution and responsibility. In fact, the essays in *De Dieu qui vient à l'idée* add little that could not already be found in Levinas's earlier texts, beyond a more sustained reflection on God than he undertakes elsewhere. All of Levinas's key terms turn up: Enigma, Saying, transcendence, ethics, responsibility, desire, infinity, substitution, hostage. Levinas repeatedly calls for a new kind of thought, one that escapes ontology and the endless return to the Same. At moments, however, his own thinking gives an uncomfortable impression of sameness, as familiar paths are retrodden yet again, with the dazzling combinations of his terminology sometimes suggesting that his texts are locked within their own perspective rather than open to new questions.[14] Levinas's writing is caught in a curious dilemma: refusing to make God the object of experience or knowledge, and rejecting even propositions to do with the existence or non-existence of God, the texts become increasingly verbose and repetitive in their disclosures of their own limitations.

Levinas does not offer a personal God, an interlocutor, a transcendent guarantor of justice or of the meaning of history. Instead, he depicts a trace or near-absence which shatters the unity of the subject, ties it by bonds of responsibility to the Other, and then leaves it its freedom to respect or neglect that responsibility. This is no comfortable religion providing divine succour in need, or answers to questions beyond our competence. In Levinas's version, the question is more important than the answer, the search more urgent than the solution (*DVI*, 172). His religion is what he calls a religion for adults (*DF*, 24–42/11–23), the model for which he finds in his interpretation of Judaism.

## Judaism

Levinas's philosophical texts give clear indications of their author's religious, and specifically Jewish, background. There are frequent references to the Hebrew Bible, and the conception of the subject as *chosen* (*élu*, suggesting *le peuple élu*, the chosen people) and *persecuted* has evident cultural and historical resonances. Notions such as alterity and the face have important Jewish sources.[15] More generally, central aspects of Levinas's philosophical project, in particular his assault on totality and systematic philosophy, have been attributed to the influence of the Jewish thinker Franz Rosenzweig, author of *The Star of Redemption* (1921).[16] In fact, although Levinas is best known for his philosophical essays and books, most of his teaching career and much of his published work have been devoted to Jewish matters.[17] In the final section of this chapter I shall discuss the talmudic commentaries and the particular combination of textual authority and interpretative freedom which they embody; this section examines the more general characterization of Judaism and Jewish thought given in the essays collected in *Difficult Freedom* (first published 1963; second edition published 1976, with some changes and additions).

In part, Levinas's essays on Judaism combat influential philosophical interpretations of Judaism, particularly those of Hegel and Sartre. Hegel described Judaism as a negative moment in history, a stage to be surpassed in the onward march of the Spirit (*DF*, 328–33/235–38).[18] Such a view adopts the standpoint of totality and sees Judaism as part of a pattern which surpasses it. Levinas, on the contrary, insists on the separate identity of Judaism which has not been made redundant by the Hegelian system, and which is not dialectically surpassed by Christianity. Judaism has its own living culture and traditions; and, most importantly, it presents the model of an ethical humanism with universal relevance. In his *Réflexions sur la question juive* (1946) Sartre also failed to recognize the independent existence of Jewish culture. He described Jewish identity as in a sense the creation of the anti-Semite. The latter projects on to the Jews his or her own negative attributes; the power of this projection is such that Jews are effectively obliged to accept the racist's identification of them, thus they become the anti-Semite's negative image. Sartre, it has been suggested, knew precious little about Jewish religion and culture at the time of writing *Réflexions sur la question juive*; for this reason he attempts to analyse Jewish identity without reference to Jewish beliefs and practices. But Levinas rejects the view that the Jew can be explained as a creation of the racists: 'Of course, we do not owe Judaism to anti-semitism, no matter what Sartre may have said' (*DF*, 315/225).[19] In his essays on Judaism, Levinas will endeavour to define what is specifically Jewish about Jewish thought and religion.

Some of Levinas's essays in *Difficult Freedom* are addressed specifically to a French Jewish audience and deal with issues of immediate concern to that audience: problems of assimilation, attitudes towards Israel, Jewish education, religious observance, prayer, the decline in study of Hebrew and the Jewish sacred texts. Particularly in the essays collected in the first section of the book, Levinas also deals with more general questions about the nature of Judaism and Jewish spirituality. Being Jewish, for Levinas, is not a matter of accepting various articles of faith, since the notion of a body of dogma constituting a credo comes very late in the history of Judaism (*BV*, 168/138–9); nor is it a matter of strict observance of Jewish law, even though he describes this as possibly the most characteristic aspect of Jewish existence (*DF*, 46/26). Levinas picks out three senses covered by the word *Judaism*: a religion, a culture and a sensibility (*DF*, 43/24). However separate these may seem, they are all part of the dynamic exchange which modern Judaism (by which Levinas means orthodox Judaism) maintains with its history and its sacred texts; and at the source of Jewish religion, thought and sensibility lies the triumph of monotheism over idolatry.

Jewish monotheism is not simply the replacement of a panoply of gods by a single supreme divinity. Levinas recounts a legend according to which Abraham, the founder of monotheism, was the son of a merchant of idols (*DF*, 29/14); in the absence of his father Abraham destroyed all the idols except one, hoping that the remaining idol would appear to be responsible for the destruction of the others. The father is not taken in, knowing that no idol is capable of such an act of destruction. Monotheism is not the victory of one god over all others; it entails a rejection of the principles underlying idol-worship:

> Monotheism marks a break with a certain conception of the sacred. It neither unifies nor hierarchizes the numerous and numinous gods; instead it denies them. As regards the divine which they incarnate, it is merely atheism. (*DF*, 29/14–15)

The proximity of Judaism to atheism is important, and I shall return to it shortly. Here, Levinas is suggesting that monotheism is atheist only in so far as it does not accept a certain interpretation of the divine. Monotheism refuses the notion that the world is inhabited by gods who possess and inspire mortals, carrying them beyond their powers and desires. Rather than sacred enthusiasm, Judaism provides a model of religious adulthood, valuing the fruits of education and mature deliberation over the unverifiable claims of mystical revelation:

> Judaism has decharmed the world, contesting the notion that religions apparently evolved out of enthusiasm and the sacred. Judaism remains foreign to any offensive return of these forms of human elevation. It denounces them as the essence of idolatry. (*DF*, 28/14)

The key role of Judaism in history has been, according to Levinas, to create 'a type of man who lives in a demystified, disenchanted world' (*DF*, 83/54). The Jews reject possession by the sacred because it negates their freedom, making them puppets of the godhead:

The numinous annuls the links between persons by making beings participate, albeit ecstatically, in a drama not brought about willingly by them, an order in which they founder. This somehow sacramental power of the divine seems to Judaism to offend human freedom and to be contrary to the education of man, which remains *action on a free being*. Not that liberty is an end in itself, but it does remain the condition for any value man may attain. (*DF*, 29/14)

Although Levinas talks in general terms about Judaism, his description offers only an incomplete account of Jewish religious and intellectual practice. Even in the European context, his interpretation of Judaism is partial and tends to neglect the importance of other branches of Jewish faith. From the eighteenth century the Jews of Eastern Europe were divided between the followers of Hasidism and their opponents. Hasidism, founded by the charismatic and enigmatic Israël Baal Shem-Tov, was a popular mystical movement with intellectual sources in Kabbalism and a predilection for legends and stories of miraculous happenings.[20] The word *Hasidism* comes from a word meaning fervour; and it is not uncommon in Hasidic stories for the prestigious Masters to address, praise or reprove God directly, as if God were a being with almost human attributes and failings. All this implies precisely the sort of relation to the godhead that Levinas dismisses as infantile. Brought up in a non-Hasidic community in Lithuania, Levinas interprets Judaism in a manner quite opposed to the popular mysticism of Hasidism.[21] For him, Judaism is essentially rabbinic Judaism ('The Judaism with a historic reality – Judaism, neither more nor less [*le judaïsme tout court*] – is rabbinic'; *DF*, 28/13), grounded in the Jewish sacred texts and an exacting, rigorous discipline of study and exegesis: 'The other path is steep but the only one to take: it brings us back to the source, the forgotten, ancient, difficult books, and plunges us into strict and laborious study' (*DF*, 81/52).

Levinas describes any experience which befalls us without our full collaboration as violent (*DF*, 18/6). On this account, the experience of the sacred through religious enthusiasm or fear and trembling entails a submission to violence which Jewish monotheism, in Levinas's interpretation of it, refuses. Judaism is characterized by its emphasis on the freedom and responsibility of the individual for his or her choices and actions. In this tradition, God still speaks, but, to echo a formula used repeatedly in the Talmud, God speaks in a human tongue,[22] addressing rational individuals and appealing to their intellect. Humans accede to the divine word by study, debate and deliberation rather than by sacred ecstasy which alienates them from their humanity (*DF*, 30/15). Here, there is no place for the sacred fool or the mad mystic; this is a religion for scholars and sages. In 'Le Pharisien est absent' (*DF*, 47–50/ 27–9) Levinas rehabilitates, and laments the absence of, the Pharisees, discredited in the Christian New Testament for the apparently nit-picking and provocative questions they ask of Christ. Such questioning, rather than a shortfall of spirituality, betokens its fullest realization in Levinas's religion of adults. An enquiring, rational mind seeks to explore the full significance of the sacred, to make every aspect of it available to scrutiny and debate, to leave nothing shrouded in the mystery and mystification òf the ineffable. Even if Levinas's own writing sometimes appears mystical in tone, implying that the most important subjects lie beyond the capabilities of human language, in principle at least he maintains that nothing should be exempt from thorough, rational enquiry.

Jewish monotheism, then, attains freedom from possession by the godhead and freedom of choice and action for the individual. Such freedom is not freely assumed. As a talmudic story discussed by Levinas at length in 'La Tentation de la tentation' (*QLT*, 65–109/ 30–50) implies, the Jews have little option but to accept their position as the chosen people.[23] Freedom, as always in Levinas's writing, is not (as it is in existentialist thought) the origin and first principle of subjectivity; it derives from the subject's original exposure to that which transcends it, in this case God. Once invested as free, however, the subject is responsible for its own freedom and denied recourse to an unambiguous and unfailing divine guide for its decisions and judgements. The intellectual freedom thus conferred necessarily brings with it the freedom to question and to doubt the godhead itself. For this reason Levinas suggests that Judaism lies close, by its very nature, to atheism:

> The rigorous affirmation of human independence, of its intelligent presence to an intelligible reality, the destruction of the numinous concept of the sacred, entail the risk of atheism. That risk must be run. (*DF*, 30/15)

Atheism is a possibility inherent in the monotheistic enterprise. Judaism finds God after, or whilst, contesting and denying the gods of myth and idolatry. Denial and belief go together; so, compared with idol-worship, atheism is only half a mistake:

To ignore the true God is in fact only half an evil; atheism is better than
the piety bestowed on mythical gods. [. . .] Monotheism surpasses and
incorporates atheism, but it is impossible unless you attain the age of
doubt, solitude and revolt. (*DF*, 31/16)

The risk of atheism must be taken but overcome; for humanity it is
the 'price of its adulthood [*rançon de sa majorité*]' (*DF*, 31/16).
The 'difficult freedom' named in the title of Levinas's collection
derives from the dilemma of Judaism as fiercely jealous of its
independence yet longing for God, demanding freedom yet desiring transcendence. The tense resolution of these conflicting im-
pulses is found in the ethical relationship with others, as Judaism
discovers 'the presence of God through one's relation to man' (*DF*,
31/16). God is not encountered directly, but approached in the
ethical relationship with the Other. Judaism thus turns out to be a
concrete, practical religion, concerned with immediately relevant
questions of individual behaviour and social justice. Such questions
do not replace contact with God, they are the site where such
contact occurs. Humankind remains free and God remains transcendent, encountered only in the respect that the subject shows
for the Other. Judaism, then, does not expect miracles of its God,
indeed it is forbidden to rely on them. When asked why God does
not feed the poor, Rabbi Akiba replied: 'So we can escape dam-
nation' (*DF*, 36/20). Social justice is the means by which humankind attains its own redemption, and working for a just society
thus becomes a pre-eminent religious act (*DF*, 38/21). The central
message of Jewish Scripture affirms that ethical relations are also
religious in nature: 'The fact that the relationship with the divine
crosses the relationship with men and coincides with social justice
is therefore what epitomizes the entire spirit of the Jewish Bible'
(*DF*, 36/19).

Levinas's discussion of Judaism moves seamlessly into areas that
he explores in his philosophical texts. His religious writings run
parallel to, and use much the same vocabulary as, the later essays
collected in *En découvrant l'existence avec Husserl et Heidegger* and
the longer works, *Totality and Infinity* and *Otherwise than Being*.
Numerous echoes and allusions can be found; for example, the
enigmatic aphorism 'ethics is an optic' which occurs at the beginning of *Totality and Infinity* (*TI*, 8/23) appears in similar or identical
form in a number of papers on Judaism and Jewish issues first
published in the fifties (*DF*, 33/17, 223/159, 382/202), during the
period when Levinas was working on *Totality and Infinity*. With

different emphasis (and on the whole a more accessible presentation), the language and positions adopted in Levinas's essays on Judaism are the same as those to be found in his philosophical works; indeed, his interpretation of the significance of Judaism makes of it the ideal (and idealized?) historical enactment of his ethics of respect for the Other. In an essay entitled 'La Pensée juive aujourd'hui' he makes clear how his own thought is Jewish; and at the same time his interpretation of Judaism emphasizes its relevance to his own work:

> But its [Jewish thought's] basic message consists in bringing the meaning of each and every experience back to the ethical relation between men, in appealing to man's personal responsibility – in which he feels chosen and irreplaceable – in order to bring about a human society in which men are treated as men. The realization of this just society *ipso facto* involves raising man up into the same society as God. (*DF*, 223/159)

There is, for Levinas, no conflict between being a Jewish thinker and a philosopher who writes for a non-Jewish audience. Judaism does not seek converts, but its central ethical message is not restricted to believers in the Jewish God. As Levinas frequently insists, Judaism is a universalism (*DF*, 38–40/21–2): not a Hegelian universal concrete, in which the drama of the whole is played out in the history of the part, but an experiment in humanity with significance extending beyond a particular group of people. Jewish monotheism is presented as a humanism (*DF*, 383/275); its message and central principles thus belong just as much in the language and context of philosophy as in essays on Judaism.

Ultimately, for Levinas, what ensures that the relevance of Judaism remains unsurpassed is its ability to retain contact with transcendence, with a source of meaning which remains open, available and untotalized. This is made possible by its sacred texts, particularly the Talmud, which require and sustain the constant renewal of sense through study and interpretation. The Talmud is at the heart of the rabbinic Judaism espoused by Levinas, and since the early sixties it has been the most consistent focus of his Jewish writings.

## The Talmud

The notion of the incarnation, of God made human, visible and palpable, is alien to the Jewish tradition. In Judaism God is not incarnated but *inscribed* in the Jewish sacred texts (*AHN*, 139); and Levinas characterizes Judaism by its intimate relationship with those texts: 'Judaism is definitely the Old Testament, but through the Talmud' (*BV*, 166/136). The Talmud, here, occupies a position just as important as the Hebrew Bible, and one which is pre-eminent in Levinas's understanding of Judaism. From 1960 onwards his talmudic commentaries became a regular feature at the annual Colloque des Intellectuels Juifs de Langue Française, which had been inaugurated in 1957. Levinas's Judaism is essentially talmudic, and talmudic commentary provides him with an opportunity to combine religious devotion with sustained intellectual enquiry.[24]

There are in fact two Talmuds, the Babylonian and the Jerusalem Talmud, containing texts deriving from separate rabbinic academies.[25] These texts are also known as the Oral Torah; they complement the so-called Written Torah, which refers in its restricted sense to the Pentateuch and more generally to the Hebrew Bible. The Oral Torah is so called because it consists of teachings (Talmud means teaching or study) which were part of an oral tradition until they were given a written form. The Talmud has two parts: the Mishnah, consisting of Hebrew texts, often containing prescriptions deriving from the Bible, and given written form during the second century of the common era; and the Guemara, containing commentaries and further discussion of the Mishnah, largely in Aramaic, and set down in writing during the fifth century of the common era. These discussions are further categorized as either Halakhah, comprising the normative aspect of the Talmud, or Aggadah, being more discursive or narrative in nature. Levinas's commentaries are principally based on the Aggadah on the grounds that it is more accessible to the novice, more available to interpretation (*QLT*, 12–13/4), and it does not require the intellectual musculature of Halakhah (*QLT*, 70/32).

Levinas suggests that the Talmud is no less authoritative than the Bible, though the texts are very different in nature.[26] The Talmud constantly refers to and elucidates the Bible, thus becoming the obligatory conduit through which the Bible is to be understood. Levinas shows the greatest possible respect for the Talmud and for the intellectual powers of the rabbis whose words it transcribes. In the Talmud, he suggests, the potential for thought has been fully and definitively realized. To use a phrase which Levinas repeats, 'everything has been thought [*tout a été pensé*]' (*DF*, 102/68; *QLT*, 16/6); everything (even the most unforeseeable aspects of the modern world; *DF,* 102/68) has been anticipated and theorized in advance; all wisdom and knowledge can be discovered by the student of the Talmud. However, the explanatory role of the Talmud in respect of the Bible and of modern life does not make of it a set of unquestionable rules, prescriptions and interpretations; on the contrary, the essence of the text lies in its restless questioning. Levinas constantly emphasizes the plurality of meanings to be found in the Talmud. Even opinions which are rejected are nevertheless recorded, as if nothing that has been or could be thought should be obliterated (*BV,* 141/114). And on issues of the utmost importance for religious Jews, divergent views are offered. The first two talmudic commentaries published by Levinas deal with Judaic conceptions of the Messiah, and here the reader is confronted with numerous competing options. According to different talmudic masters, in the messianic epoch social injustice will, or will not, be abolished (*DF,* 91–7/60–5); those who repent will be privileged over the morally pure, or vice versa (*DF,* 98/65); it will be a return to Eden, or to something better than Eden (*DF,* 99–101/ 66–8); the coming of the Messiah depends upon human action, or is independent of it (*DF,* 102–14/69–78); the Messiah's name will be Silo, or Yinon, or Hanina (*DF,* 124/85). Each of the rabbis who defend or reject these views can justify his opinion with biblical authority. The debate becomes what Levinas calls 'a combat that trades verses like blows [*une bataille à coups de versets*]' (*DF,* 108/ 72). More problematically still, the rabbis cite the same verses but interpret them differently (*DF,* 98/65–6). This is made possible both by the nature of Hebrew as a consonantal language, which makes possible diverse readings of the same word,[27] and by variant readings of context. According to Levinas, in such detailed disputes over meaning lies the essential strength of the Talmud, as it strives to examine every angle of the questions under discussion. Its authority derives not from its dogmatic prescriptions, but from its spirit of enquiry: 'This concern to relate the "opinions" and "options" back to the crossroads of the Problem, where they become dignified into *thoughts,* is the true spirit of the Talmud' (*DF,* 98/66).

In this account of the Talmud, then, contradictions, disagreements and ambiguities do not appear as unwanted disturbances to be overcome; they are precisely what gives the Talmud its vitality, permitting it to escape the specific historical circumstances of its compilation. Levinas's method of commentary endeavours to respect and exploit the plurality of meaning rather than to reduce it. In this, he is defending the Talmud and the practice of rabbinic commentary against the historical, philological and positivist approach which he traces back to Spinoza's *Tractatus Theologico-Politicus* (1670).[28] Denying the inspired origin of the Bible and rejecting the interpretations of what he calls the Pharisees, Spinoza outlines a number of principles for discovering the true meaning of Holy Scripture:[29] (a) the tongue in which it was written should be fully understood; (b) contents should be analysed and organized under thematic headings, so that all texts that deal with a given subject may be compared, and ambiguous, obscure or mutually contradictory passages can be isolated; (c) finally, a history of separate parts of Holy Scripture should be compiled, analysing the life of the original author, the transmission of the text, and how the various parts were united into a single work. Spinoza lays out a rational path for understanding Scripture, shorn of all superstition and based on the original context of text and author. He thereby makes himself one of the most important forerunners of the historical study of the Bible which acquired a central position in biblical studies from the nineteenth century onwards.

Although Levinas acknowledges that historical and philological criticism have a role to play (*DF*, 102/68), any attempt to uncover the single, original meaning of the sacred texts is in his view misguided. This does not entail rejecting Spinoza's rationalism in favour of recourse to irrationalism or intuition. On the contrary, the Talmud is a most rational text which addresses the intellect, even though the mode of address is different from what we might expect of a philosophical work (*QLT*, 33/14). What Levinas disputes, then, is not Spinoza's rationalism, but the model of textual meaning that underlies his view of Scripture. In Spinoza's account, ambiguities and obscurities should be resolved by better knowledge of the language spoken by the author, and inconsistencies explained by the fact that different parts of the text had different authors with contradictory intentions. Spinoza regards meaning as static and entirely located in the past; for Levinas, this approach neglects the importance of the reader, an indispensable participant in the process of meaning: 'But Spinoza will not have conferred a role in the production of meaning on the reader of the text' (*BV*, 206/173).

In a well-known talmudic story, Moses is transported into the future to hear a lesson given by Rabbi Akiba; disconcerted that he cannot understand the lesson, he is surprised to hear Akiba's wisdom attributed to the revelation made to Moses himself on Mount Sinai (*BV*, 163–4/134). The story illustrates how the author does not command, nor even necessarily understand, the full meaning of his text. The reader realizes meanings which may not have been consciously placed there. Levinas frequently describes the two-way process between text and reader as *solicitation*: the reader solicits the text with his or her current interests in mind, and is in turn solicited by the text to an exploration of meaning to which those current interests make an indispensable contribution.

Levinas adopts a mode of reading which concentrates on precisely those obscurities, ambiguities and contradictions which Spinoza had sought to eliminate, for it is in these that new possibilities of meaning may be developed. Several important principles guide the commentary:

1 The first of these concerns the coherence and unity of the text. However disparate its historical origins, the Bible and the Talmud are not to be regarded as random compilations. The text is treated as a coherent whole, with all its parts interrelated by necessary, if elusive, links (*SS*, 29/104, 167/189; *BV*, 166/136).[30]

2 Without denying the religious content of the Talmud, Levinas starts from the assumption that the text contains a rational discussion of problems with philosophical significance (*DF*, 101/68; *QLT*, 10/3). Although the language of the rabbis is different from that of an academic philosopher, it can readily be transposed into it; and the casuistry of the rabbis' thought (arguing from individual cases rather than abstract ideas) goes together with an abiding concern for general principles, though these cannot be separated from the individual examples which suggest and limit them (*QLT*, 48/21; *BV*, 21/202–3).

3 A quotation of a verse from the Bible does not represent a recourse to an unquestionable authority, but rather it invites the reader to explore the context of that quotation, to find the relationship between it and the context of the current discussion. Hence it opens up new possibilities of meaning within the text (*QLT*, 47–8/21).

4 The reader should always solicit the text in the light of his or her current concerns, despite the anachronisms that this may seem to entail (*DF*, 101/68; *SS*, 9/92). Levinas's standard move in his commentaries is to address the theme of the conference at which he is speaking through a text which has little apparent connection to it; so, a text on the damage caused by fire elucidates the theme of war (*SS*, 149–180/178–97), a text on haircutting is made relevant to the theme of the youth of Israel (*SS*, 54–81/120–35), the question of forgiveness prompts a reflection on Heidegger's attitude to Nazism (*QLT*, 56/25).

5 All opinions and interpretations should be respected; none should be overlooked or dismissed out of hand (*BV*, 141/114). Contrary views may all have validity because their proponents all have access to an aspect of the truth, as a talmudic formula implies: 'These and those alike [*Les unes comme les autres*] are the words of the living God' (*BV*, 167/137).

6 Finally, nothing in the Talmud is arbitrary or fortuitous, so anything may be taken as a legitimate subject for interpretation. In his commentaries Levinas draws upon similarities between words, unusual spellings, the numerical values of words,[31] etymologies (even dubious ones) or ambiguities deriving from Hebrew syntax. This represents an intense attention to the letter of the text, with all its associations and peculiarities, based on the conviction that everything is, or may be, significant.

These guiding principles evidently leave a great deal of space for interpretative freedom. They exemplify the hermeneutic stance deplored by Spinoza, and certainly do not provide a route to the single correct reading advocated in recent years in literary theory by E. D. Hirsch.[32] Levinas acknowledges that Jewish interpretation resembles in some of its aspects the hermeneutic waywardness of deconstruction (*BV*, 66/47–8). However, this is not dissemination conceived as the destruction or dispersal of meaning. Talmudic commentary rests upon the presumption that the text has something to say, but that its message cannot be restricted to its obvious or surface meaning.[33] Further levels of meaning will only be discovered by exerting pressure on the text. Levinas suggests the degree of violence that this may entail by his development of a talmudic reference to Raba, who was so immersed in study that he rubbed his fingers until the blood spurted out:

As if by chance, to rub in such a way that blood spurts out is perhaps the way one must 'rub' the text to arrive at the life it conceals. Many of you are undoubtedly thinking, with good reason, that at this very moment, I am in the process of rubbing the text to make it spurt blood – I rise to the challenge! Has anyone ever seen a reading that was something besides this effort carried out on a text? To the degree that it rests on the trust granted the author, it can only consist in this violence done to words to tear from them the secret that time and conventions have covered over with their sedimentations, a process begun as soon as these words appear in the open air of history. One must, by rubbing, remove this layer which corrodes them. (*QLT*, 102/46–7)[34]

Here, Levinas generalizes his own practice of talmudic commentary to describe all reading and criticism. The extreme pressure which is exerted through critical attention is an act of violence, but one which nevertheless aims to restore meaning lost or obscured through the passage of time. So Levinas implies that the meanings he uncovers are genuinely present in the texts he analyses. At the same time they are also the commentator's meanings, the specific answers to his or her questions, and potentially unique to each reader. Each commentary adds to the meaning of the text or realizes something that without the unique character of the commentator would have remained undiscovered. Commentary is thus necessary to the text (*BV*, 108/87); indeed the Talmud is already constructed as a series of commentaries, discussions and commentaries on commentaries to which Levinas's own commentary adds yet further layers. Commentary itself demands interpretation (*BV*, 126/102), making the process potentially endless (though curtailed in practice by the need to make binding decisions and judgements). The number of possible readings is equal to (or perhaps even greater than) the number of actual readers:

> It is as if the multiplicity of persons [. . .] were the condition for the plenitude of 'absolute truth'; as if every person, through his uniqueness, were the guarantee of the revelation of a unique aspect of the truth, and some of its points would never have been revealed if some people had been absent from mankind. (*BV*, 163/133)

There is for Levinas no contradiction between the absolute respect for the authority of the text and the uniqueness of each interpretation. The meaning of the Talmud is inexhaustible, so each reading may be both new and entirely faithful to the letter and spirit of the text. Revelation, in this account, is not something that occurred once and for all on Mount Sinai; it is repeated, continued and modified with every act of reading: 'the voice of Revelation, as inflected, precisely, by each person's ear, would be necessary to the 'Whole' of the truth. [. . .] the multiplicity of irreducible people is necessary to the dimensions of meaning' (*BV*, 163/133–4). Revelation and exegesis go hand in hand, which explains the extraordinary status of the Talmud in Levinas's rabbinic Judaism. God does not speak directly to the commentator; the divine word is available in the Talmud, requiring interpretation, and offering different nuances to every reader. Exegesis is an act of piety and adoration every bit as important as prayer, and the sacred texts require a practice of interpretation that entails both an 'audacious hermeneutic' and 'listening piously to sovereign orders':[35] combining freedom and restraint, entirely respectful of the text but fully open to new possibilities of meaning.[36] Commentary thus emerges as a never completed project, a restless activity with conclusions which can only ever be provisional. Everything has been thought in the Talmud, but its full significance will never be definitively elucidated.

The bold commentator sees in the text what no one else had, or could have, seen. Levinas's commentaries combine modesty (he usually begins with a statement of his inadequacy to the task before him), scholarship, reliance upon the work of other commentators, and a speculative daring which develops possibilities of meaning further and further removed from the obvious sense of the text. A good example of this is provided by the parable of a man with two wives, one young and one old; the young wife pulls out his white hairs and the old wife pulls out his dark hairs, to the point that he is left bald on both sides (SS, 176/194). Levinas acknowledges the faintly humorous aspect of the anecdote and then extends its significance to make of it a parable of the conflict between tradition and modernity. For the young, the past (which Levinas compares to the prescriptions of Halakhah) is like grey hair: pure form that has lost its colour. The young wife plucks out the grey hairs, as the young uproot traditions by interpreting texts to the point that they no longer mean what they seem to say. The old woman respects the traditional view, takes the sacred texts literally and does not regard them as requiring rejuvenation. She plucks out the dark hairs, representing the innovations to be brought from youthful vitality, impatience and interpretation. The text, then, describes the conflict within the community of Israel between the young and the old, revolutionaries and traditionalists. More generally, it condemns the bigamy of the spirit which loses its sovereignty when it becomes the site of dispute between opposing cults: 'maturity as conservatism and youth as a search for novelty at any price' (SS, 177/195). The commentary itself attempts to maintain a balance between innovation and tradition which eluded the hairless husband. It develops implications permitted by the text and by traditional protocols of reading, whilst attempting to find the unique resonance of the text for the commentator's current concerns. Neither tradition nor innovation, freedom nor constraint, rigid forms nor bold interpretations, are allowed to dominate as Levinas maintains an exchange between the text and his own situation, between the search for new meanings and well-established exegetic frameworks.

Levinas claims to have learned his method of commentary from an enigmatic and prestigious master, Rav Chouchani, with whom he studied the Talmud in the years following the war (see *QLT*, 22/8). The mysterious Chouchani serves to link Levinas with Élie Wiesel, the novelist and winner of the Nobel Peace Prize. After the liberation of Buchenwald, Wiesel lived and studied in Paris, where he also came under the influence of Chouchani;[37] and, like Levinas, Wiesel has dedicated a significant part of his work to the study of Jewish sacred texts. In the introduction to *Célébration talmudique*, a collection of some of his lectures on the Talmud, Wiesel echoes many of the principles which inform Levinas's commentaries: the inexhaustible richness of the text, the constant invitation to participation that it offers, the respect for the Other which it embodies, its enigmatic nature and the resulting impulse to investigate further, its essential unity and logic despite apparent incoherence and inconsistency.[38] Some of the differences between Wiesel's Judaism and Levinas's also emerge, however. Wiesel's Hasidic background shows through his talmudic scholarship. He informs his reader that he is not writing 'a scholarly or scientific work',[39] although his knowledge of the Talmud seems to be as broad and detailed as Levinas's. As his title suggests, his aim is to celebrate rather than to analyse:

> My principal aim was simply to recount my love [*raconter mon amour*] for the Talmud, and my passion for its teaching, through its fabulous characters. [. . .] My ambition? To listen and to make others listen to a Jewish child, lost in his memories, recounting nostalgic love stories [*racontant de nostalgiques histoires d'amour*] in which Jerusalem remains the centre and the life force.[40]

Here it is possible to see clearly the differences between Wiesel's approach to the Talmud and Levinas's. Wiesel's vocabulary implies the enthusiasm and longing, and the love for stories, which characterize Hasidism ('to recount', 'love', 'passion', 'memories', 'recounting nostalgic love stories'). Each of his chapters is organized around one or more of the talmudic rabbis. Whereas Levinas takes particular passages and studies them in detail, Wiesel recreates a character. For Wiesel, the Talmud is populated by fascinating and prestigious figures, whereas for Levinas it is primarily a text, philosophical in significance if not in expression; a text which poses a myriad of detailed and general problems of interpretation to be analysed by the commentator. Levinas is no less passionate than Wiesel, but the channel through which his passion passes is the thorough, patient and rigorous line-by-line examination of the text.

Levinas's reflection on talmudic commentary has important parallels in contemporary hermeneutic thought. He compares his approach to the interpretative stance implied in Ricœur's aphorism 'The symbol gives cause to think [*Le symbole donne à penser*]' (see *BV*, 107/86).[41] What Ricœur calls a symbol plays the same role as the text in Levinas's commentaries, acting as an incitement to thought which can never be exhausted, and for which no single interpretative protocol (philological, historical, formalist, structuralist, psychoanalytic and so on) is adequate on its own (see *QLT*, 18–20/7). The emphasis on the constant exchange between text and reader, and on the uniqueness of every reading, also links Levinas's practice to the hermeneutic philosophy of Hans-Georg Gadamer. Like Levinas, Gadamer argues that every act of understanding is different from all others: 'It is enough to say that one understands *differently, if one understands at all*.'[42] This does not mean that the interpreter is the sole and entire source of the interpretation. The text is not, as it appears for example in the work of Stanley Fish,[43] an empty vessel with no content of its own. The hermeneutic positions of Levinas and Gadamer preserve the possibility of a real encounter with the text. In Gadamer's terminology, the act of reading brings about a fusion of horizons, whereby the horizon of the text, although never fully comprehended, comes into contact with and extends the reader's horizon.[44] Interpretation is saved from arbitrariness, subjectivism, or what Gadamer calls 'hermeneutic nihilism',[45] by the fact that it is rooted in a tradition that is to some extent shared by most interpreters at any given time or in any given country. Although each reading is new and different, it is not simply wilful and utterly unrelated to all previous readings because it is guided by assumptions which are common to other contemporary readers. In Gadamer's hermeneutics meaning is dynamic but not arbitrary; the same can be said of Levinas's talmudic readings, which are rule-bound, but bound by rules which leave significant space for innovation. As in Gadamer's hermeneutics, the openness of the text poses the problem of how to discriminate between different interpretations;[46] and, like Gadamer, Levinas resolves the difficulty by his insistence that all valid reading and all genuine innovation are firmly grounded in the continuity of tradition:

But, what is more, a distinction is allowed to be made between the
personal originality brought to the reading of the Book and the pure play
of the fantasies of amateurs (or even of charlatans); this is made both by
a necessary reference of the subjective to the historical continuity of
reading, and by the tradition of commentaries that cannot be ignored
under the pretext that inspirations come to you directly from the text. A
'renewal' worthy of the name cannot avoid these references, any more
than it can avoid reference to what is known as the oral Law. (*BV*, 164/
135)

Like much contemporary literary theory, then, Levinas insists
that the reader plays an active role, but not an exclusive role, in
the production of meaning. This leads to the conclusion that
readers may legitimately offer interpretations which cannot possibly have been consciously intended by the original authors.
Those who locate meaning in the intentions of the author, and aim
to uncover it through historical, biographical and philological
criteria, inevitably find such a possibility intolerable; from Spinoz-
a's repudiation of the Pharisees to Hirsch's attack on Gadamer, the
implication that the text can mean what its author cannot have
meant has been virulently rejected. On the other side of the debate,
Levinas's belief that in the Talmud 'everything has been thought'
depends upon the implication that the text inevitably and always
exceeds the intentions of any given author. He does not shirk from
the anachronisms that this entails: 'We begin with the idea that
inspired thinking [*la pensée géniale*] is a thought in which everything
has been thought, even industrial society and modern technocracy'
(*DF*, 102/68).

   *Beyond the Verse*, particularly the essay 'De la lecture juive des
Écritures', represents a distinct development and philosophical
reflection on the view of language implied in Levinas's earlier
talmudic commentaries. Levinas adapts the formula 'Thought
thinks more than it thinks' to make it '[The text] contains more
than it contains' (*BV*, 135/109, 204/171). The theological explanation for this is that the word of God cannot simply be transposed
into human language: Holy Scripture is polysemic because it
preserves the intractability of divine language to simple propositions (*BV*, 7/x–xi). Levinas goes beyond this to suggest that interpretation responds to an excess of meaning inherent in language
itself:

   The reading processes that we have just seen at work suggest, first, that
   the statement commented upon exceeds what it originally wants to say;
   that what it is capable of saying goes beyond what it wants to say [*son*

*pouvoir-dire dépasse son vouloir-dire*]; that it contains more than it contains; that perhaps an inexhaustible surplus of meaning remains locked in the syntactic structures of the sentence, in its word-groups, its actual words, phonemes and letters, in all this materiality of the saying which is potentially signifying all the time. Exegesis would come to free, in these signs, a bewitched significance that smoulders beneath the characters or coils up in all this literature of letters. (*BV*, 135/109)

Every aspect of language is potentially interpretable, which implies a virtual surplus of meaning which no speaker or author could possibly command. Levinas uses the word *inspiration* to describe this aspect of language: 'Inspiration: another meaning [*sens autre*] which breaks through from beneath the immediate meaning of what is meant to be said, another meaning which beckons to a way of hearing that listens beyond what is heard, beckons to extreme consciousness, a consciousness that has been woken' (*BV*, 137/ 111). Language is inspired because an 'other voice [*voix autre*]' (*BV*, 137/111) can be heard behind the voice of the speaker, saying things that the speaker could not have intended.

On an immediate level, Levinas is justifying the special status accorded within the orthodox tradition to the Jewish sacred texts, explaining their inexhaustible semantic plenitude, the continuing revelation which they effect and the permanent call for exegesis which they make on their readers. But Levinas is also making a more general point about language, and one which might poten- tially dislodge the Bible and the Talmud from their privileged position. All language is actually or potentially *inspired* in the sense given to that term by Levinas, for this inspiration is not attributed principally to some divine figure whispering messages into unsus- pecting ears. Inspiration is (in terms discussed in the previous chapter) the excess of Saying over the Said; the inevitable failure of the latter to contain the former means that there is always some- thing else in language to be interpreted, although the excess of meaning is never fully grasped in any particular interpretation. In this sense, then, inspiration is the fundamental attribute of language itself: 'One may wonder whether man, an animal endowed with speech, is not, above all, an animal capable of inspiration, a prophetic animal. One may wonder whether the book, as a book, before becoming a document, is not the modality by which what is said lays itself open to exegesis, calls for it; and where meaning, immobilized in the characters, already tears the texture in which it is held' (*BV*, 136–7/110). And this conception of language leads directly back to Levinas's philosophical writings:

the 'other voice' which speaks in all language disrupts the primacy of consciousness (since consciousness is not in full command of the meanings the speaker produces), participates in the encounter with alterity and infinity, hence also plays a crucial role in the ethical relations described by Levinas. By different routes (and with a sense of humour lacking in his other texts)[47] Levinas's talmudic commentaries and essays on Judaism constantly return to the issues which dominate his philosophical writings.

But if inspiration and the surplus of meaning are inherent in all language, how are the Bible and the Talmud different from any other text? Levinas's answer to this question is decidedly weak: Holy Scripture contains, he suggests, 'another secret [*un autre secret*], an additional essence that purely literary texts have perhaps lost' (*BV*, 204/171), but he gives little clue as to what this secret might be. Levinas leaves open the possibility that the real difference between sacred and secular texts lies in the kind of attention they receive rather than any inherent quality. Levinas's commentaries on the Talmud and his discussion of the nature of sacred texts develop into a theory of textuality and interpretation applicable to all texts and all speech. Levinas accepts that inspiration, and hence plurality of meaning and the call to interpretation, are characteristic of all writing:

> The act of saying causes a vibration of something that precedes whatever is thought within it. Interpretation draws it out and is not just perception, but the formation of meaning. From this point of view, every text is inspired: it contains more than it contains. (*BV*, 204/171)

Levinas distinguishes between the Greek and Hebrew traditions, between the elliptic, elusive nature of the Hebrew sacred texts and the Greek search for clarity, conceptualization and explanation;[48] he accepts that in this sense his own language is Greek, as he translates the obscurities of the Jewish texts into a language accessible to his Western academic audiences (*AHN*, 203). However, he acknowledges that the 'Greek' text may not be as different from the 'Hebrew' as this distinction suggests:

> But one day you discover that even philosophy is something plural and that its truth is hidden and contains various dimensions, and is endlessly deepening, and that its texts contradict one another, and that internal difficulties are at work within its systems. (*AHN*, 199)

This theory of textuality has now expanded to the point where it also encompasses the text in which it is enunciated and Levinas's own practice as commentator and philosopher. One of the principal implied targets of Levinas's remarks on the nature of commentary is Spinoza, whose guidelines for the interpretation of Scripture are at a far remove from the principles adopted by Levinas. Moreover, Levinas suggests that Spinoza's writings are themselves susceptible to the kind of reading and multiple rereading which can be applied to the Talmud. The meaning of Spinoza's texts is not limited to what their author may have intended: 'while there may be numerous interpretations of Spinozism itself, they do not exclude its truth but testify to it' (*BV*, 206/173). The truth of the text lies not in any single meaning, but in its openness to new revelations and successive reinterpretations. In Levinas's account this is as true of the philosophical text as it is of the literary or sacred text, and it is as true of Levinas's philosophy as it is of Spinoza's. Levinas effectively concedes that his own writing may be obscure and enigmatic, awaiting explanation in the partial light of his reader's interests. This is certainly borne out by Levinas's ambiguous position on the contemporary philosophical scene, and by the wide variety of responses to which his work has given rise. The next chapter examines Levinas's place in modern French thought and looks at some of the different ways in which his texts have been understood by his readers.

# 5

# Levinas and his Readers

It is not unusual for introductions to ethics written in English to contain no reference to Levinas;[1] in France, on the other hand, he is widely regarded as the most important ethical thinker of the twentieth century. It would be easy to explain the discrepancy in terms of the frequently invoked distinction between Continental and Anglo-American philosophy. According to this distinction, French philosophers are separated from their English-speaking counterparts by incompatible interests, styles and assumptions. However, despite widespread respect for his work, Levinas also remained outside the philosophical mainstream in France for much of his career. French accounts of post-war French philosophy seem unsure how to locate him in relation to his contemporaries. Vincent Descombes's *Le Même et l'autre*, written specifically with an English-speaking audience in mind,[2] takes as its title two terms judged to be central to French thought since 1933, and with a relevance to Levinas which should by now be evident; yet Descombes makes no reference to Levinas in the book, concentrating instead on Jean-Paul Sartre, Maurice Merleau-Ponty, Michel Foucault, Louis Althusser, Jacques Derrida, Gilles Deleuze and Jean-François Lyotard. In the first paragraph of *La Pensée 68*, an account of aspects of French thought in the sixties and seventies, Luc Ferry and Alain Renaut specifically exclude Levinas (along with Paul Ricœur) from their discussion,[3] choosing to direct their fire on the sexier figures of the French intellectual scene: Foucault, Derrida, Pierre Bourdieu and Jacques Lacan. And in a series of lectures on contemporary French philosophy given in London by a number of French- and

English-speaking philosophers and published in 1987, Levinas is mentioned only once, and then in reference to Derrida's article on him in *L'Écriture et la différence*.[4]

Levinas is difficult to place in either the general field of ethics or the more local scene of modern French philosophy. The difficulty arises from the impossibility of assimilating his work to any easily identifiable school or system of thought. In the series of lectures mentioned in the previous paragraph, Pascal Engel, who is himself in the difficult position of an analytic philosopher working in France, has contrasted characteristic attitudes of analytic philosophers with what he calls 'widely held beliefs' amongst French philosophers:[5] for the former, philosophy is a common enterprise subject to discussion and argument, whereas for the latter it is solitary; for analytic philosophers there can be progress in philosophy, whereas for French thinkers truth and objectivity are suspect values, argument has more to do with rhetoric and eloquence than logic and truth, so no ultimate agreement can be expected; for analytic philosophers good philosophy may be dull, specialized and technical, whereas French philosophy celebrates geniuses, giants of thoughts, who are more like artists than specialists. Despite its caricatural aspect (which Engel denies),[6] this account does give an insight into attitudes embedded within French philosophical practice. Yet Levinas, who by no stretch of the imagination could be described as an analytic philosopher, cannot easily be identified with the French position either: he distrusts rhetoric and maintains a notion of philosophical truth;[7] he readily acknowledges intellectual debts and seeks to correct errors or shortcomings in the work of important philosophical precursors, as if progress in philosophy were indeed possible; and, most importantly after Derrida's first article on his work, he does respond to criticism and attempt to rethink his positions in the light of it.

In France, Levinas's major texts are all available in relatively inexpensive paperback editions, yet I suspect they are more bought than read. The importance of his work is readily acknowledged, though its significance remains unclear. His thought is, in the words of one commentator, 'too well and too little known, too often schematized and too rarely understood adequately'.[8] If reading Levinas poses difficulties at very basic levels, as previous chapters have attempted to illustrate, explaining his curious position within his philosophical context is no less hazardous. In this chapter I shall attempt to show how that curious position is maintained by a complexity bordering on elusiveness within his writing and his central notions, and by the consequential latitude for reading and misreading that this gives his readers. These factors combine to form what I call the Levinas effect: the difficulty of Levinas's texts permits his commentators to find in them a reflection of their own interests and attitudes.

## Levinas and contemporary philosophy

Descombes's *Le Même et l'autre* analyses developments in French philosophy between 1933 and 1978. The period begins with Alexandre Kojève's influential lectures on Hegel's *Phenomenology of Mind* which were reputedly attended by an astonishing array of French intellectuals: Sartre, Merleau-Ponty, Lacan, Georges Bataille, Raymond Aron, Pierre Klossowski and André Breton. Kojève's interpretation of Hegel marked a shift in the sense of the word *dialectics*: from its pejorative sense as a philosophy based on appearance or wordplay, it becomes the prestigious tool by which the opposition between Same and Other is constantly surpassed in the movement towards totalization.[9] The relationship between Same and Other was thus put, and was to remain, at the centre of philosophical debate, even though dialectical totalization was to swing in and out of fashion. Kojève's audience formed what has been dubbed 'the generation of the three Hs', so called because their principal philosophical authorities were Hegel, Husserl and Heidegger. In Descombes's narrative, the generation of the three Hs was to be replaced in the late fifties and sixties by the generation of the three 'maîtres du soupçon' (masters of suspicion), Marx, Nietzsche and Freud.[10] For the younger thinkers of the period, the project of totalization, the description of Being or of the transcendental structure of consciousness, gave way to a distrust of totalities and a subversion of subjectivity.

One reason for the omission of Levinas from *Le Même et l'autre* may be that he fits so uncomfortably within the narrative which Descombes elaborates. Born in 1906, the year after Sartre and two years before Merleau-Ponty, and unquestionably one of the earliest French expositors of Husserl and Heidegger, Levinas belongs resolutely to the generation of the three Hs. Despite his disagreements with them, Husserl, Heidegger and to a lesser extent Hegel remain constant points of reference in his writing throughout his career. According to Descombes, 'those who persist in calling on

the three Hs or on one of them after [1960] will be the first to admit
that their position is not the dominant one. Moreover, this fact
requires of them, in discussion, to take account of the common
doxa by anticipating the objections that might be made to them in
the name of the new trinity.'[11] This is simply not true of Levinas.
In the sixties and later, he makes no concessions to the outmoded-
ness of his allegiances. In the preface to *Totality and Infinity*,
published in 1961, Levinas acknowledges his debt to Husserl (*TI*,
14/28–9) whilst not even mentioning Marx, Nietzsche or Freud.
For Descombes the adherents of the three Hs are the unreconstructed champions of totality, carrying away Same and Other in a
dialectical movement towards Absolute Knowledge;[12] but in *Totality and Infinity* Levinas explicitly rejects such totalization. Belonging
to the generation of the three Hs, he fails to exhibit some of its
defining characteristics.

Levinas never renounces his debt to the three Hs, rarely alludes
to the 'masters of suspicion', yet adopts positions regarding totalization and consciousness closer to those espoused by the younger
generation of philosophers coming to the fore in the sixties.
However, Levinas remains philosophically marginal, and his
ambiguous relation to the generation of the three Hs is reproduced
in relation to their structuralist and post-structuralist successors. In
*La Pensée 68* Ferry and Renaut outline the four essential characteristics that came to dominate French thought in the late sixties and
subsequently: (a) the theme of the end of philosophy; (b) the
paradigm of genealogy; (c) the dissolution of the idea of truth; and
(d) the historicization of categories and the end of reference to the
universal. Levinas does avoid reference to universal values; but at
the same time he gives short shrift to the idea that philosophy is at
its end, he continues to talk of truth, and he shows no interest in
genealogy and little in history. Two further strands in the thought
of the period put Levinas out of sympathy with the younger
generation of thinkers: anti-humanism and the assault on subjectivity, the two linchpins of *La Pensée 68*. Sartre had been mocked for
describing existentialism as a humanism in the title of an infamous
lecture delivered in 1945;[13] in 1972 Levinas revived the discredited
term in the title of his own *Humanisme de l'autre homme*, claiming
with a touch of provocation that his essays should not be taken as
representing 'a lack of attention with regard to the dominant
opinions of our time, which have been defended with such brill-
iance and mastery' (*HAH*, 7). Levinas is no more converted to the
assault on subjectivity than he is to contemporary anti-humanism.

He described *Totality and Infinity* as 'a defence of subjectivity' (*TI*, 11/26); even if Levinassian subjectivity does not have the self-founding prestige of the Cartesian Cogito or the Husserlian transcendental Ego, the subject plays an irreplaceable role in the dramas of responsibility and substitution which are at the centre of Levinas's ethics.

Levinas himself has poked fun at the battle cries of Parisian intellectual fashion:

> The end of humanism, of metaphysics – the death of man, the death of God (or put God to death!) – apocalyptic ideas or slogans of the intellectual high society. Like all the manifestations of Parisian taste – or distaste – these phrases are imposed with the tyranny of the latest fashion, but they are priced within the range of every pocket and become degraded. (*HAH*, 95)

However, what makes a thinker unfashionable in 1960 or 1970 might put him or her in fashion in 1980 or 1990. From being a highly respected but marginal figure, in recent years Levinas has found himself right at the centre of mainstream French philosophical concerns. This is in large measure due to the ethical turn of post-structuralist thought from the late 1970s onwards. Ferry and Renaut write *La Pensée 68* with the explicit aim of reopening the questions of subjectivity and humanism, questions which Levinas had never abandoned and which seemed prematurely resolved by the fashionable allegation that man is dead. In her contribution to a series of lectures published in 1987 Michèle Le Dœuff suggested that the idea of an ethical end was not valued in contemporary French philosophy.[14] However, in the same series of lectures signs of change can be seen. The British philosopher David Wood defended Derrida against the common accusation that his work leaves no basis for ethics; and Wood argued that 'Derrida's own most serious confrontation with the question of ethics can be found in his long and brilliant discussion of the French Jewish philosopher Emmanuel Levinas, in his essay "Violence and Metaphysics".'[15] Derrida's ethics were beginning to be presented as distinctly Levinassian,[16] and the work of extremely able commentators such as Robert Bernasconi and Simon Critchley contributed to a greater understanding of the ethical aspects of modern French philosophy. In his book of 1992, *The Ethics of Deconstruction*, Critchley argued powerfully that 'Derridian deconstruction can, and indeed should, be understood as an ethical demand',[17] and he undertook a full-scale confrontation between the work of Derrida and that of Levinas.

It is unclear – indeed, opinions differ – whether the ethical turn of post-structuralism represented a new departure, or rather a heightened awareness of something that had been there all along.[18] Certainly Derrida's essay on Levinas had been available for reading since the early sixties; but not until much later did its ethical aspects receive the sustained scrutiny of commentators. Whatever the case, Le Dœuff's comments on the lack of value accorded to ethical ends in French philosophy now look outdated. A long series of books by the most prominent thinkers directly confront ethical issues: Michel Foucault's histories of sexuality (1976–84), Julia Kristeva's *Pouvoirs de l'horreur* (1980), Jean-Luc Nancy's *L'Impératif catégorique* (1983), Luce Irigaray's *Éthique de la différence sexuelle* (1984), Philippe Lacoue-Labarthe's *La Fiction du politique* (1987), Jean-François Lyotard's *Moralités postmodernes* (1993) and Derrida's *Force de loi* (1994). Implicitly or explicitly, Levinas's account of alterity is an almost obligatory point of reference in such works, with ethics understood as the questioning of the self as it encounters the irreducible Other. As if by a quirk of philosophical fashion, in the eighties and nineties Levinas's work has come to occupy a pivotal position in French philosophical debate.

Levinas's ambiguous attitude towards the French mainstream is reproduced in his rare explicit discussions of contemporary thought. He has little time for notions such as the end of philosophy and the death of man; but he also concedes that the proponents of such views have a serious point:

> The crisis of humanism in our age doubtless has its source in the experience of human failure which is made evident by the very abundance of our means of action and the extent of our ambitions. [...] The dead without burial in wars and the extermination camps give credence to the idea of a definitive death and make care for oneself tragi-comical, and make illusory the claim of the rational animal to a privileged place in the cosmos, and illusory also his capacity to dominate and integrate the totality of being in a consciousness of self. (*HAH*, 73–4)

If anti-humanism is misguided, then so is humanism in so far as it maintains belief in an essence of humankind (*OB*, 203/127–8); Levinas's 'humanism of the other man' is a humanism shorn of essences, of self-possessing, self-grounding consciousness, or even of firm moral certainties.

In his response to humanism, once again we see Levinas neither fully inside nor entirely outside the options which seem to be available to him; and this ambiguity is reproduced in his often elusive references to the intellectual currents of his time. He rarely refers to the 'masters of suspicion', and it would seem likely that he has a relatively poor knowledge of their work. On one of the few occasion when he does refer to them, in the essay 'Idéologie et idéalisme',[19] he accords them an important role in the demystification of rationality (*DVI*, 18). But characteristically Levinas equivocates in his assessment of the consequences of this demystification. The Marxian revolt is ethical in origin, but destroys that origin by portraying ethics as no more than a ruse of ideology (*DVI*, 19); structuralism puts into question the status of the subject, but the privilege it gives to theoretical reason leaves no place for human value (*DVI*, 22). Contemporary philosophy in general simply replicates pre-established schemes, evacuating all possibility of genuine discovery or true alterity (*DVI*, 23–5). Levinas is typically either ambivalent or reticent in his comments on modern thought and modern thinkers. He refers to Althusser (*DVI*, 20), to Deleuze and Guattari's 'machines désirantes' (*DVI*, 22) and to dissemination (*DVI*, 32), but remains elusive in his attitude towards them. Elsewhere, he supports psychoanalysis for its contribution to the critique of consciousness, but criticizes it for its fixation on a handful of endlessly repeated fundamental and elementary fables (*EN*, 44–5); and he admits to a lack of interest in and understanding of structuralism whilst also describing Claude Lévi-Strauss as the most eminent thinker of the century.[20]

The difficulty of pinning down Levinas's attitudes to contemporary philosophy is compounded by the extraordinary complexity of his prose. The final sentence of chapter 2 of *Otherwise than Being* refers to 'the death of God', 'the end of man' and 'dissemination', all buzzwords of French philosophy during the late sixties and seventies (*OB*, 99/59); but any hope that the passage will help us understand Levinas's position is likely to be disappointed: the sentence is (in the Livre de Poche edition) thirteen lines long, contains two passages in parentheses, one between dashes, six relative clauses and no main verb. The linguistic complexity is such that it risks looking as much like a defensive gesture as a necessary counterpart to the profundity of thought. Consistently, Levinas gives with one hand and takes away with the other, appearing reluctant to commit himself unambiguously to conventional terminology or any of the fashionable schools of thought; as I shall discuss later in this chapter, this is precisely what allows him to be (nearly) all things to all people, overtly hostile to few and readily assimilable to a startling variety of different positions.

Levinas has characteristics of both an insider and an outsider. He has remained outside the fashions and factional disputes of recent French thought;[21] at the same time there is something classically French about his manner of doing philosophy. Ferry and Renaut describe the cult of paradox and the search for marginality as defining features of *La Pensée 68*;[22] and, whatever separates him from contemporary thinkers, marginality and paradox play as great a role in his writing as in the most fashionable works of the period. Moreover, the founding philosophical insight of Levinas's mature work, namely the belief that Western philosophy has been based on a systematic privileging of the Same over the Other, is typically French in its sweeping generalization. Bruno Latour describes as characteristic of French philosophy its tendency to announce 'the complete subversion of everything that has been thought in the past by everybody'.[23] Indeed, one of the things which may excite or repel English readers as they first encounter French thought is the sheer immodesty of French philosophers' projects. In the case of Levinas, his view of Western philosophy as ontology (systematically suppressing alterity) has the status of an enabling simplification; it throws a flattering, dramatic light on his own work. In that respect ontology functions in much the same way as metaphysics in the early work of Derrida.[24] The history of thought is presented as a flawless monolith which is at worst the product of some forgotten conspiracy or at best misguided since its origins.

The curious position of Levinas both within and outside mainstream French intellectual life has been stressed by Louis Pinto in his sociological account of modern French philosophy.[25] In 1982 the newspaper *Le Monde* published a series of articles by twelve philosophers, including Levinas, Derrida, Descombes, Michel Serres, Jean-Toussaint Desanti, Clément Rosset, Manuel de Dieguez and Élisabeth de Fontenay. Pinto arranges the authors in an ordered list stretching between what he calls the two poles of academic discourse, prophetism and orthodoxy (170–1). Ferdinand Alquié, former Sorbonne professor and author of a series of scholarly books published by the most distinguished academic presses, appears as the extreme representative of academic orthodoxy. His article takes a classic philosophical subject (the extent and limits of scientific knowledge) and adopts generally accepted

conventions of argumentation and demonstration; Derrida represents the extreme case of the prophetic avant-garde, announcing
cataclysmic shifts in thought and exploring new philosophical
forms. His article is structured around a telephone conversation
and deals with problems of language relating to the nature and
status of philosophical practice.

On Pinto's scale, Levinas comes slightly closer to the pole of
orthodoxy than to the pole of prophetism. But Pinto argues that, of
the twelve authors, Descombes and Levinas stand apart from the
rest, the first because he seems to belong to neither of the two
poles, and Levinas because on the contrary 'he seems precisely to
achieve a particularly subtle combination of characteristics from
each of [the two poles]' (175). Levinas produces 'a discourse which
conforms to scholarly rules' (198), with references, a tripartite plan,
an explicit thesis and a sober style; at the same time, 'he gives
himself the philosophically sovereign task of thinking beyond "the
history of the West"' (198). Levinas thus follows 'a trajectory which
combines contradictory attributes' (199). Pinto relates Levinas's
non-confrontational manner to his cultural, racial and institutional
marginality: as a Jewish émigré who for much of his career did not
have a French university post, Levinas underplays his prophetism,
seeking acceptance as an insider within the philosophical establishment rather than to break out of it. Levinas avoids polemical
confrontation and respects the stylistic and rhetorical norms of the
scholarly institution; and he prefers to adopt and ennoble ordinary
words ('face', 'substitution', 'hostage') rather than to create bold
neologisms. So there is enough in Levinas to placate the traditionalists; but there is also enough to excite the philosophical avant-
garde. Like the most daring of contemporary thinkers but in less
transgressive forms, Levinas is engaged in a radical revision of
Western philosophy and the search for new ways of thinking. Pinto
finds features in Levinas's philosophical practice which make it
possible for him to appear as both a defender of tradition and a
champion of the avant-garde; and Pinto refers to the 'objective
irony' which has achieved what might have seemed impossible,
'the conversion into a strange, disturbing and abyssal work of the
philosophical product of a way of thinking characterized by
restraint, horror of being conspicuous and explicit fidelity to
tradition' (204).

## Problems of reading

Levinas begins to look strangely assimilable to different (perhaps even incompatible) philosophical positions. His reluctance to take sides in academic polemics, his respect for scholarly norms and the ambitiousness of his philosophical project combine to make him appear the potential ally of all or the real ally of none. In the previous section I showed how some of the ways in which the recent history of French thought has been narrated either omit Levinas or consign him to an ambiguous position. This is not simply because we have not yet found the 'right' way of telling the story in which Levinas would be restored to his 'proper' role. The elusiveness of Levinas is essential to the texture of his writing and thought, and I suspect that all schematic histories will leave him somehow on the sidelines. The Levinas effect to which I referred earlier arises from a lack of explicitness, a tendency to say not quite enough, which sometimes permits the reader the illusion of having grasped Levinas's point but which retains the potential to put any such act of understanding into doubt. In this section I shall illustrate how this works in detail by looking at two of Levinas's key terms, the *il y a* and the face, to show the possibilities of misprision that they bring with them.

In the preface to the second (1978) edition of *Existence and Existents*, written thirty years after the original work, Levinas refers to the discussion of the *il y a* as the most important part of his book (*EE*, 10; not translated in the English edition). It is, he says, a notion which he still uses, and he insists on its significance for his later philosophical development. The term itself is potentially misleading. On the one hand Levinas adopts an ordinary French expression which most French speakers would frequently use and think they understand. On the other hand the phrase brings with it a philosophical baggage which serves to complicate matters. It is the normal French equivalent of the Heideggerian *es gibt*, referring to the donation by Being to beings of light, freedom and truth;[26] it had been used by Sartre in *L'Être et le néant* (1943) only a few years before the publication of *Existence and Existents*.[27] But Levinas claims ignorance of philosophy published during the war in France,[28] and he sternly warns against the Heideggerian association of the term *il y a*: 'It was never either the translation or the copy of the German expression and its connotations of abundance and generosity' (*EE*, 10; not translated in the English edition). So both the ordinary and the philosophical senses of *il y a* turn out to be unhelpful.

In the first reference to the *il y a* in the text of *Existence and Existents* the difficulty of the notion is already apparent. The *il y a* is, Levinas says, a fact of existence which is more general than the division between Being and Nothingness; it is a state in which the subjective existence of existential philosophy and the objective existence of philosophical realism are confused (*EE*, 20–1/20). It invalidates the available tools of philosophical analysis. Later it is described as impersonal and anonymous, transcending the distinction between interior and exterior, engulfing all subject, person or object; it is a presence when all things have disappeared, a *rien* which is not a *néant*, a universal absence which is also an absolutely inevitable presence; it is what is immediately there without language, a silence which can be heard (*EE*, 93–5/57–8). The immense difficulties posed by the notion should be clear. Since there is no subject to experience it (the subject is a hypostasis which breaks from the *il y a*) and no language in which to speak of it, it must remain incommunicable to subjects whose knowledge is bound to speech and experience. Levinas's prose is at its most tense and desperate at such moments, and once again the figure of giving with one hand and taking with the other comes to mind: 'If the term experience were not inapplicable to a situation which involves the total exclusion of light, we could [*pourrions*] say that the night is the very experience [*l'expérience même*] of the *there is* [*il y a*]' (*EE*, 94/58). The cautious conditional of *could* is made derisory by the categorical rejection of adequacy which precedes it ('inapplicable', 'total exclusion'); yet the experience then becomes the 'very experience', the apparent epitome of what we have been told it cannot be.

When Levinas returns to the *il y a* in *Time and the Other*, he writes in terms similar to those adopted in *Existence and Existents*:

> Let us imagine all things, beings and persons, returning to nothingness.
> Are we going to encounter pure nothingness [*le pur néant*; this sentence omitted from the translation]? What remains after this imaginary destruction of everything is not something, but the fact that there is [*il y a*]. The absence of everything returns as [*comme*] a presence, as the place where the bottom has dropped out of everything, as an atmospheric density, as a plenitude of the void, or as the murmur of silence. There is [*Il y a*], after this destruction of things and beings, the impersonal 'field of forces' of existing. Something that is neither subject nor substantive. The fact of existing imposes itself when there is no longer anything. And

it is anonymous: there is neither anyone nor anything that takes this existence upon itself. (*TO*, 25–6/47–7)

The only available ways of describing the *il y a* seem to be negation ('not something [. . .] neither subject nor substantive [. . .] there is no longer anything') or simile (the word *comme* occurs five times in one sentence). However, the procedure of negation disqualifies the use of simile by implying that the *il y a* cannot be compared to anything without falsifying it. The text hovers on the edge of nonsense: 'The absence of everything returns as a presence, [. . .] as a plenitude of the void, or as the murmur of silence.' Similes are adopted but simultaneously undercut by the implication that tenor and vehicle have nothing in common; and Levinas's text strains to describe something that it characterizes as lying beyond any experiential or cognitive measure.

In *Totality and Infinity* and *Otherwise than Being* Levinas occasionally refers to the *il y a*, but does little to develop the notion beyond its expression in the forties. He tends to allude to his own former work rather than to offer anything new ('an always deeper abyss which we elsewhere have called *there is* [*il y a*]', *TI*, 94/93). When called upon to explain the notion in the interviews with Philippe Nemo collected in *Ethics and Infinity*, Levinas recalls childhood memories: 'One sleeps alone, the adults continue life; the child feels the silence of his bedroom as "rumbling [*bruissant*]". [. . .] It is something resembling what one hears when one puts an empty shell close to the ear, as if the emptiness were full, as if the silence were a noise' (*EI*, 37–8/48). Levinas repeats familiar paradoxes, and it is tempting to act as if (and to believe) one understands. When discussing the *il y a*, critics have an unnerving tendency to write as if the notion were relatively unproblematic: a flat paraphrase, a rapid comparison with Heidegger and an allusion to Blanchot will apparently do the job nicely.[29] But things are not so simple. Levinas produces a flurry of similes and comparisons in an attempt to convey the *il y a*, yet he also makes it clear that none of those figures should be accorded unmitigated explanatory power. The desire for elucidation founders on the enigmatic nature of the *il y a*. For readers the sense that we have grasped the point is perhaps more misleading than the recognition that we have not; and the reader's self-conscious bemusement is perhaps what Levinas aims to achieve in order to avoid allowing us over-hastily to assimilate the *il y a* to familiar experiences.

The difficulties of the *il y a* are replicated in the notion of the face. Again, the term has a long history in Levinas's thought. Already in *Time and the Other* he referred to 'the encounter with a face which at once gives and conceals [*donne et dérobe*] the other' (*TO*, 67/78–9). The word *face* is an ordinary word with which all speakers will be familiar; yet, having chosen such an ordinary word, Levinas then divests it of its common meanings. Part of the difficulty of the notion lies in the resulting tension between what we think we understand and the repeated insistence that we have still not yet got the point. The face, in Levinas's account, should not be confused with the part of the head where the eyes, nose and mouth are to be found. In the face, the Other is presented to me directly and as utterly external to me (*EDE*, 173). But the manner of that presentation is not at all clear, since the face cannot be seen or experienced in any way that would make it the object of my intentional acts:

> The face [*Le visage*] does not resemble the plastic form [*la forme plastique*], which is always already deserted, betrayed by the being which it reveals, like the marble from which, already, the gods which it reveals take their leave. It [*Elle*] is different from the animal face in the brutish stupidity of which being is not to be found. In the face what is expressed [*l'exprimé*] *is present* in the expression, it expresses its expression itself, it always remains master of the meaning which it delivers. 'Pure act' in its way, it [*il*] refuses to be assigned an identity, cannot be reduced to what is already known, brings help to itself, as Plato says, speaks. The epiphany of the face is entirely language. (*EDE*, 173)

Levinas's lapidary, aphoristic prose makes few gestures towards patient exposition, and even grammatical links between sentences are less than clear.[30] The allusion to Plato is misleading, since Plato's reference to speech (as opposed to writing) being able to bring aid to itself has nothing to do with the discussion of the face;[31] but the allusion does serve to facilitate – if only at a rhetorical level – the connection between the face and language which comes to occupy a central place in Levinas's account. The Other is established as interlocutor rather than as an object of perception or experience, and the face is divested of any literal reference the word might imply by the description of it as language.

The face receives its most extended treatment in *Totality and Infinity*, after which it occupies a less central position in Levinas's writing. The most persistent misunderstanding to which the face gives rise is the assumption that it is something which can be seen. This misunderstanding is hardly surprising, since faces are generally thought of as being at least potentially visible, and the French word *visage* is anyway etymologically related to vision. Since this error is always likely to be made, Levinas repeatedly corrects it:

> The way in which the Other presents himself, exceeding *the idea of the Other in me*, we here name face. This mode does not consist in figuring as a theme under my gaze, in spreading itself forth as a set of qualities forming an image. The face of the Other at each moment destroys and overflows the plastic image it leaves me, the idea existing to my own measure and to the measure of its *ideatum* – the adequate idea. (*TI*, 43/50–1)

So we are constantly warned not to confuse the Levinassian face with anything we might see, thematize and appropriate. Yet the temptation – I would say the inevitable temptation – never quite goes away. Even such a sensitive and intelligent interviewer as Philippe Nemo gets rapped on the knuckles for persistently failing to get the point. In *Ethics and Infinity* Nemo asks Levinas about his phenomenology of the face, 'that is, the analysis of what happens when I look at the Other face to face' (*EI*, 79/85). Levinas suggests in response that phenomenology may be the wrong word, since phenomenology describes what appears. The look is associated with perception and knowledge, therefore it annihilates the face in Levinas's sense by bringing it within the sphere of the Same. Levinas insists that 'The best way of encountering the Other is not even to notice the colour of his eyes! When one observes the colour of the eyes one is not in social relationship with the Other' (*EI*, 79–80/85). Levinas explains that 'what is specifically the face' is that which cannot be reduced to perception. But Nemo, persevering in his endeavour to make Levinas's thought accessible to a popular audience, still seems to have missed the point, since he continues to talk about faces as if they were real objects of perception: 'War stories tell us in fact that it is difficult to kill someone who looks straight at you' (*EI*, 80/86). Levinas does not even respond to this. He refuses the popularizing simplification and continues his own line of thought: 'The face is signification, and signification without context' (*EI*, 80/86).

Not surprisingly, given the centrality and difficulty of the notion of the face in Levinas's writing, a great deal of critical energy has been directed towards it. Étienne Feron, one of Levinas's best commentators, observes of the face that 'the best known notion in Levinas's thought, and the one which is sometimes held to be characteristic of it, is perhaps also the most vague at the time of

*Totality and Infinity.'*[32] Feron explains that the face is distinguished
from the phenomenon, yet conceived in almost identical terms; it
is described as both noumenal, because in the face the Other is
presented in its essence as Other, and concrete, because the Other
is presented to me in person. Levinas insists that the face cannot
become the object of an intuition, but writes about it as if it can; he
describes the face as if it were the foundation of sense, and also as
if it represented a surplus of meaning which breaches all foundations; taken from the vocabulary of vision and light, the face
manifests that which transcends the light.

In *Fragments of Redemption* Susan Handelman also concedes that
'[Levinas's] notion of the face is often quite ambiguous and subject
to varying definitions which are more like networks of associations
than any precise stipulations.'[33] Drawing on articles by James Ponet
and Richard Cohen,[34] she gives an excellent overview of some of
the sources and meanings of the term. The Hebrew word *ponim*
and Rosenzweig's *The Star of Redemption* are suggested as important
influences; the face is the 'distinctive mark of the individual human
personality' as opposed to 'impersonal, anonymous Being'; it
replaces and displaces the term *phenomenon*; it is the part of the
body with most openings to the exterior, 'the locus of sensitivity
and vulnerable exposure to the world'; and the face of the Other is
not just the object of my gaze, it looks back at me as both witness
and judge.

All these points are useful, well made and well supported. But
two suspicions are aroused: firstly, that through such explanations
the notion of face becomes more coherent and more persuasively
justified than in Levinas's own texts; and, secondly, that all such
attempts at analysis almost inevitably fall into Nemo's error of
talking about the face as if it were a physical, observable part of a
human body. Despite being fully aware that the encounter with
the face is not primarily or essentially a matter of visual perception,
Handelman continues to talk as if it were: the 'distinctive mark of
the individual human personality', the 'locus of sensitivity and
vulnerable exposure to the world' and the 'defeated, wounded
look in the face of the other' only make sense on the assumption of
specific, empirical acts of vision.

Handelman is far from alone in adopting strategies of explanation which rely upon assumptions which she knows to be erro-
neous. In fact, it is hard to see how it can be avoided. In 'Violence
et métaphysique' Derrida states that 'the face is not in the world
because it breaches and exceeds totality';[35] but elsewhere in the

article he talks of the face as something that sees and is seen, and which is located in the upper part of the human body.[36] In even the most rigorous analysis, a moment comes when the face appears as something to be accounted for at least in part in phenomenal terms. When this happens, the commentator risks missing the point of Levinas's own descriptions. The face may be a real part of the human body available to be encountered, seen and experienced; but for Levinas it is before all else the channel through which alterity presents itself to me, and as such it lies outside and beyond what can be seen or experienced. Both the reality of the encounter and the elusiveness of the face are crucial to Levinas's argument. Without the possibility of real encounters, the Other would be a senseless abstraction; but if the encounter were only phenomenal and thus could easily become an object of perception or knowledge, then it would be reduced to just another non-event in the subject's sovereign possession of the world. Levinas plays on the possible confusion of the faces of other people with the face of the Other, yet at the same time he imposes on his readers and commentators the almost impossible task of maintaining the distinction between them; any failure to do so risks being qualified as a misreading.

Given the extraordinary difficulty of Levinas's key terms, it is hardly surprising that errors or lapses of vigilance may occur. Levinas, it should be said, does not always go out of his way to avoid misunderstandings. The combination of ordinary language and his extremely complex prose style produces a heady mixture of familiarity and strangeness. Critics tend to respond by smoothing out the kinks, offering explanations of philosophical complexities and acknowledging few loose ends or rough surfaces which might present insurmountable problems of interpretation. And commentary on Levinas consists in filling in the gaps and ellipses, supplying the missing links and producing a more coherent and persuasive text than the original. Typically, I believe (and this certainly corresponds to my own experience), reading Levinas entails in constantly recognizing and rediscovering those parts of his writing which make sense to us, whilst passing over those parts which remain rebarbative. Understanding as much as we do may be at the cost of a necessary blindness towards what continues to elude us. Commentary becomes an art of paraphrase in which fundamental questions are more or less skilfully evaded.

The problems involved in understanding the *il y a* and the face are characteristic of difficulties posed throughout Levinas's writing. Other key notions employ the same fraught combination of ordinary language with paradox which places them right at the edge, or perhaps just beyond the edge, of intelligibility. In a sense Levinas's texts are sources of signification in the same way that the face is in his account of it: they signify, but what they signify is not a message or signified that precedes them; they signify themselves, accessible as enigma and challenge rather than as a stable body of meaning. Like the Talmud, Levinas's manner of writing displaces any fixed message, so that the text becomes the site where an event of meaning takes place rather than where established meanings are communicated. The complexities, repetitions, ellipses and paradoxes ensure that any such event may be infinitely renewable, and always different. In the previous chapter we saw how Gadamer's dictum, 'one understands *differently, if one understands at all'*, could be applied to Levinas's understanding of the Talmud. In the next section of this chapter we shall see that it could equally be applied to Levinas's own work, which has been subjected to a number of very different interpretations and appropriations.

## Readers

In 1980 a collection of essays published under the title *Textes pour Emmanuel Levinas* brought together articles by an impressive collection of intellectuals: Maurice Blanchot, Jeanne Delhomme, Jacques Derrida, Mikel Dufrenne, Jean Halperin, Edmond Jabès, François Laruelle, Jean-François Lyotard, André Neher, Adriaan Peperzak, Paul Ricœur and Edith Wyschogrod.[37] Most of the articles in the volume directly address Levinas's work. In the introductory essay François Laruelle suggests that there may be a unifying thread behind the diverse responses to Levinas: 'I am not the keeper of world History, but my brother's keeper; I am not the keeper of Being, but the keeper of the Jews' (12–13). However, Laruelle is aware that this risks restricting the essays in the volume to an extremely bland message; in fact, *Textes pour Emmanuel Levinas* offers a remarkably wide range of very different responses to Levinas's work. Laruelle gives an explanation for this when he states that 'it is the characteristic of Levinas to go and seek us in our uniqueness' (12). Laruelle implies that what is distinctive about Levinas is his ability to elicit something from his readers. This is borne out in the collection of essays; all of the authors who address Levinas's work directly find that it provides them with a congenial occasion to talk of their own concerns in their own manner.

The same variety of academic postures, ranging between the opposing poles of prophetism and orthodoxy, can be seen here as in the pieces from *Le Monde* studied by Louis Pinto. Once again, Derrida could be placed at the extreme pole of prophetism: he is represented in the volume by his second article on Levinas, 'En ce moment même dans cet ouvrage me voici', which adopts the form of a dialogue.[38] Derrida's article would be joined by Jabès's poem-meditation 'Il n'y a de trace que dans le désert'. Occupying the opposite pole of academic orthodoxy would be Ricœur's detailed reading of Husserl and Edith Wyschogrod's heavily footnoted essay on the primacy of touch in Levinas's thought. The different academic styles adopted by contributors to the volume support Pinto's comments on his article for *Le Monde*: the contradictory characteristics which Levinas manages to combine in his work help to make him compatible with authors of very different intellectual orientations.

The articles collected in *Textes pour Emmanuel Levinas* are as different in substance as they are in style. The principal interpretative grid through which different images of Levinas emerge is the opposition between continuity and discontinuity. For some of the authors, Levinas's thought continues the philosophical tradition to which it belongs. Ricœur places his own essay on Husserl within the field of study inaugurated in France by Levinas, whom he describes as 'the founder of Husserlian studies in France' (169).[39] Wyschogrod compares Levinas to philosophical forebears such as Aristotle and Berkeley, and Lyotard discusses him alongside Kant. Differences between thinkers are sanctioned in such portrayals as a legitimate aspect of ongoing philosophical debates; continuity is fully reconcilable with specific disagreements between philosophers. In Levinas's case, the argument for continuity has a particularly important Jewish variant, represented in this volume by Jean Halperin's article 'Liberté et responsabilité: Sagesse juive'. For Halperin, the differences between Levinas's religious and philosophical works are only superficial; the 'profound sources' (61) of his thought are to be found in the Jewish tradition and especially in Levinas's deep knowledge and rigorous respect for the Talmud.

It is no coincidence that the authors who emphasize the continuity of Levinas's thought with tradition are themselves the most orthodox of the contributors to the volume.[40] Others, in both manner and argument, emphasize discontinuity. Maurice Blanchot, whose career was spent outside the academic establishment, gives no references to Levinas's work and concedes that some of his quotations may be inaccurate because he is quoting from memory (80).[41] The title of his article, 'Notre compagne clandestine' ('Our clandestine companion'), implies a community of spirit between himself and Levinas; and he portrays Levinas's independence of mind in a way which makes it an image of his own position outside the institutions of philosophy. At one point the close connection between the two thinkers is clearly signalled when Blanchot quotes Levinas referring to the *il y a* as reinterpreted through Levinas's reading of Blanchot.[42] Rather than a thinker deeply rooted in tradition, Levinas appears as someone who philosophizes 'against the current', 'according to his own paths' (82); if his concerns are shared with others, he nevertheless broaches them in his own manner, following paths that have been neglected by 'philosophical tradition' (82). *Otherwise than Being* may be a work of philosophy, though this is what Blanchot calls a 'philosophy of rupture' (86). He emphasizes the uncanny, disturbing nature of a thinker who 'cuts and breaks with a tradition with which he is entirely familiar' (85). Blanchot offers a very different conception of Levinas's relation to tradition from the commentators mentioned in the previous paragraph: whereas for them dissent from established views permits the dialogue which ensures the continuity of tradition, for Blanchot Levinas's differences are absolute, making it impossible to assimilate him to a tradition with which he is familiar but to which he does not belong.

Like Blanchot, Derrida stresses the strangeness of Levinas's writing when compared with orthodox, institutionalized philosophical practices.[43] Levinas provokes a 'strange event [. . .] something unprecedented but so ancient [*quelque chose d'inouï mais de si ancien*]' (21). The use of the word *ancient* here does not imply that Levinas is tied to familiar or traditional themes; on the contrary, what is ancient is also unprecedented (*inouï*, unheard of), radical and – because radical – suppressed in mainstream philosophy. Referring to Levinas's use of quotation from the Bible, Derrida highlights the eerie effects of Levinas's writing:

> Almost always, with him, this is how he sets his text to work, interrupting the weaving of our language and then weaving together the interruptions themselves, another language [*une autre langue*] comes to disturb our own. It does not inhabit it, it haunts it. Another text, the text of the other [*Un autre texte, le texte de l'autre*], without ever appearing in its

original language, comes in silence, following a more or less regular cadence, to dislocate the language in which it is translated, to convert the translation, to turn it over, to fold it into the very thing that it was supposed to import. It disassimilates it. (29–30)

In Derrida's essay Levinas appears as an elusive thinker, his language haunted by alterity, with contexts melting away to permit an unprecedented philosophical event: 'The edges of the phrase are shrouded in mist. [. . .] The sentence is not evasive but its borders slip away. [. . .] The shore is lacking, the edges of a phrase belong to the night' (22).

In Derrida's earlier essay, 'Violence et métaphysique', Levinas appeared to be locked in a heroic struggle with the philosophical tradition, which he could neither accept nor evade. The shift from metaphors of combat to the mercurial image offered in the later essay might say as much about the development of Derrida between 1963 and 1980 as it does about that of Levinas. In fact, one of the most uncanny and valuable insights offered by the articles in *Textes pour Emmanuel Levinas* comes from the revelation of how readily Levinas's writing seems to lend itself to the very different purposes of the various contributors. Lyotard's endeavour to separate prescriptive and descriptive utterances finds as much support in Levinas as Derrida's disruptions of philosophical language, Ricœur's interest in phenomenology (and elsewhere his concern for the problem of subjectivity)[44] and Halperin's Judaic traditionalism. The ambiguity and lack of explicitness of Levinas's writing act as an invitation to others to supplement his thought, to fill the lacunae and speak on his behalf. Blanchot makes explicit what is implicit in the practice of other commentators; at the end of his essay, he describes his own formulation of the problems of post-Holocaust philosophy as the thought which 'traverses, bears the whole of Levinas's philosophy', and which 'he proposes to us *without saying it*' (87; my emphasis).

In the work of his admirers Levinas can adopt a variety of guises to suit nearly all occasions: as pseudo-deconstructionist, theologian or proto-feminist, for example.[45] In Zygmunt Bauman's search for a postmodern ethics, Levinas offers the best available support;[46] and Marc-Alain Ouaknin goes one step further, finding in Levinas the seamless reconciliation of postmodern ethics and rabbinic Judaism.[47] I am not suggesting that these readings are wrong; each is admirably supported and persuasively argued. Nevertheless, I am struck by the broad, almost universal assent to Levinas's thought, and the relative ease with which his astonishingly difficult writing can apparently be cited in support of the most diverse intellectual projects. What I am calling the Levinas effect is the ability of the Levinassian text to appear differently to each of its readers. Levinas seems to deliver whatever it is the reader wants, to the point that commentary on his writing rapidly becomes a reflection of the commentator's own desire.

There are dissenting voices amongst Levinas's commentators, though even here a variant of the Levinas effect can be witnessed. Levinas's account of femininity has been criticized by authors such as de Beauvoir and Derrida.[48] Most importantly, Luce Irigaray has argued that Woman in Levinas's writing is viewed as a negative image of Man.[49] Femininity merely represents 'that which sustains desire, that which rekindles pleasure'.[50] So the feminine is not genuinely Other; Woman is simply a projection of male desire. Levinas's description of pleasure is unacceptable to Irigaray because female desire is obliterated, and Levinas abandons the feminine Other 'in order to return to his responsibilities in the world of men-amongst-themselves'.[51] Levinas thus remains a patriarchal thinker: 'After having been so far – or so close – in the approach to the other sex, in my view to the other, to the mystery of the other, Levinas clings on once more to this rock of patriarchy in the very place of carnal love.'[52] Irigaray's position is powerfully argued and, I think, compelling; yet it is striking that her criticism comes entirely from within the set of problems (alterity, respect, appropriation) which she shares with Levinas; her criticisms of him adopt criteria which his texts would fully support. Likewise, when Derrida implies that Levinas adopts a posture of mastery in respect of femininity,[53] the argument is damaging only because Levinas is alleged to be doing precisely what he aims to avoid. Michèle Le Dœuff has argued that, when male philosophers speak of women, they characteristically deviate from their own best standards.[54] This is certainly what Irigaray and Derrida suggest in relation to Levinas on femininity: he aims to approach alterity without appropriating it to the Same, but fails. The failure gives rise to criticism only because the initial aim is accepted unquestioningly.

Criticisms of Levinas are almost invariably made on the basis of Levinas's own criteria.[55] So even those who take position against him are endeavouring to correct him in the light of what (they think) he should be, to make Levinas more Levinassian. For Levinas's readers it is treacherously difficult either to stand *inside* his writing and to claim with any confidence to have heard its genuine message, or to stand *outside* it and to examine it according to criteria which are not dictated by the texts themselves. The Levinas effect colours acts of both appropriation and criticism; in the first case Levinas appears to be more or less what we want him to be, and in the second he falls short of what we expect of him only because he fails to match his own principles. Either way, Levinas is protean in the variety of forms he can adopt and in the difficulty confronting anyone who wishes to pin him down. This could be seen as either a strength or a weakness, as a cause of irritation or a sign that Levinas is in tune with the demands made by avant-garde theories of textuality. His texts may be regarded as an ambiguous space in which readers encounter the Other and define themselves, or as frustratingly elusive, refusing to elaborate a clear set of ideas in sober philosophical prose. Whatever the response, it tells us as much about our own expectations and desires as it does about Levinas. And ultimately the Levinas effect mirrors the frailty and strength of the Other: the text is always available for appropriation by its reader, just as, in Levinas's account of the history of philosophy, the Other is ultimately restored to the Same; but the residual sense that, despite such appropriation, the Other or the text has not yet been fully grasped, ensures the survival of alterity and its continuing resistance to the authority of the Same.

# Conclusion

Levinas's ethics revolve around the possibility that I might encounter something which is radically other than myself. Western philosophy, Levinas suggests, has missed the encounter because it has always sought to appropriate the Other, to neutralize the threat it poses to the autonomy and sovereignty of the Same. The ethical encounter has a hermeneutic counterpart in the question of how far we actually receive anything from the objects of our interpretation: in reading, do we genuinely learn anything from the text, or does the text merely provide an occasion for the replication of what we already know? Some modern theorists have argued that a text can give us nothing which is genuinely new or unexpected; reading entails the repeated and inevitable reproduction of the norms, values and conventions of the interpretative communities to which we belong and which effectively make us what we are.[1] The encounter with the textual Other does not take place.

The possibility of an encounter with the Other, in both ethical and hermeneutic senses, is the cornerstone of Levinas's thought. But this encounter, if it happens, does not disclose univocal meanings or rigid moral obligations. The Talmud, as analysed in his readings of it, is too polysemic to permit of any practical restriction to the diversity of possible interpretations; but, provided that it follows established protocols of commentary, each interpretation elicits something which is authentically to be found in the text. Meaning, in this conception, is not conceived as something that can be reduced to a message, objectively present in the text and identical for all readers. Rather, it is an event, unique but not arbitrary, produced in the moment of encounter between text and commentator.

For Levinas, commentary is a form of encounter with the Other; and, just as texts do not offer simple, unambiguous messages, neither do ethical encounters provide a stable set of rules to govern moral behaviour. Ethics, in Levinas's sense, does not provide a path to knowledge of right or wrong, Good or Evil; it is a point of contact with that which challenges me most radically, and through that challenge my identity and relation with the world are thrown into question. My response to the encounter defines my own ethical nature. The results of hermeneutic and ethical encounters are not, then, strictly predetermined; they are produced in the encounter itself. Levinas illustrates this in his commentaries on the Talmud, and chapter 5 indicated how readings of Levinas's own texts *produce* meanings as much as they *reproduce* Levinas's presumed intentions. The openness to alterity, fundamental if the encounter is to take place, is mimicked in the textual openness to the production of new readings. And this in turn can give rise to radically different evaluations: Levinas might be portrayed as lacking rigour, with central notions inadequately defined, to the point that even the most careful and sophisticated readers are frequently left mystified; or alternatively he might appear as someone who creates a new role for philosophy, destabilizing its fictions of mastery, making a space receptive to the as yet unheard language of the Other. I am attracted by the latter reading but cannot quite bring myself to dismiss the former.

What is most powerful about Levinas's writing is his insistence on ethics as a challenge to the subject rather than as a solution to its problems. The restlessness and rawness of Levinas's enquiry derive from the urgency of his topic. He has described his life as 'dominated by the presentiment and the memory of the Nazi horror' (*DF*, 406/291); and *Otherwise than Being* is dedicated to the victims of Nazism (*OB*, 5/v). Moreover, the Holocaust is only one in the list of barbarisms which characterize the century:

> A century which in thirty years has known two world wars, totalitarian-isms of the left and right, Hiroshima, the gulags, the genocides of Auschwitz and Cambodia. A century which is drawing to an end with the spectre of the return of all that these barbaric names evoke. Suffering and evil imposed deliberately, but which no reason could limit in the exasperation of reason which has become political and detached from all ethics. (*EN*, 114)

This passage makes it clear that a strong moral impulse lies behind Levinas's ethics. The role assigned to philosophy is not to provide solutions, but to prevent the cynicism of political reason from silencing other dimensions of thought.

In his descriptions of the encounter with the Other, Levinas acknowledges that the subject may respond with violence on finding that its mastery of the world is endangered. Murder is always possible, even banal (*TI*, 217/198–9). But Levinas does not dwell on this possibility. Having dedicated *Otherwise than Being* to the victims of the Holocaust, he has little to say about the unethical realities which brought about their murder. Instead, his work is commanded by a simple but far-reaching question: what would it mean if, rather than responding to the threat of the Other with violence, we endeavoured to accept our dispossession of the world, to listen to the voice of the Other rather than to suppress it? Thematically, this leads to Levinas's accounts of subjectivity, responsibility, substitution and justice. It also entails a reorienta-tion of the whole philosophical project: rather than just talking *about* the Other, the philosophical text becomes engaged in the project of giving the Other a voice, of trying to find an idiom in which the Other may be heard through the chatter which serves to silence it.

In this respect, Levinas is the philosophical counterpart of those seeking in numerous theoretical and practical ways to empower traditionally muted or disenfranchised groups. The silenced, sup-pressed or victimized Other might be defined, for example, by race, gender, religion, class or position within an institutional hierarchy. Levinas offers an ethics without rules, imperatives, maxims or clear objectives other than a passionate moral conviction that the Other should be heard. His texts provide a philosophical framework which readily offers itself for incorporation within the most diverse ethical projects. From a critical perspective, he may appear to be too much of a chameleon. He leaves too many questions unanswered and the status of his own discourse remains unclear; he suits too many by giving too little. More positively, his work is perhaps one of the boldest modern attempts to derail philosophy so that it can explore new territories. His work remains poised between the urgent ethical demand to reveal the far side of thought and the knowledge that the voice of the Other remains still unheard.

# Notes

## Chapter 1   Phenomenology

1 See Hammond, Howarth and Keat, *Understanding Phenomenology*, 1.

2 See respectively Levinas, *Théorie de l'intuition dans la phénoménologie de Husserl* (1930) and 'Martin Heidegger et l'ontologie' (first published in 1932, emended version in *En découvrant l'existence avec Husserl et Heidegger*). On Levinas's role in the dissemination and reception of Heidegger's thought in France, see Rockmore, *Heidegger and French Philosophy*, especially 72–3, 128–9.

3 See Ricœur, *A l'école de la phénoménologie*; Lyotard, *La Phénoménologie*; Derrida, *La Voix et le phénomène*; and Husserl, *L'Origine de la géométrie*, translation and introduction by Derrida.

4 Ricœur, *A l'école de la phénoménologie*, 285, 287; Sartre, 'Merleau-Ponty vivant', 192.

5 Rockmore refers to Levinas as presenting 'a somewhat violent reading of Husserl's thought, with important Heideggerian components'; see Rockmore, *Heidegger and French Philosophy*, 129.

6 See Adorno, *The Jargon of Authenticity*.

7 Levinas quotes Husserl's *Logical Investigations* (1900–1) in *PH*, 178; see also Heidegger, *Sein und Zeit*, 27. Subsequent references to *Sein und Zeit* are given in the text; the English quotations are from *Being and Time*, translated by Macquarrie and Robinson.

8 See Descartes, 'Première Méditation', in *Œuvres et lettres*, 267–73.

9 Husserl, *Cartesian Meditations*, 82; see also *Méditations cartésiennes*, translated by Peiffer and Levinas, 69. Subsequent references to this work are given in the text; the first reference is to Peiffer and Levinas's French translation, and the second is to the English translation by Dorion Cairns. No German edition of the *Cartesian Meditations* was authorized or published during Husserl's lifetime.

10 See Rockmore, *Heidegger and French Philosophy*, 73.

11 Derrida, *Marges de la philosophie*, 151: 'So we can see that *Dasein*, if it is *not* man, is nevertheless *not anything other* than man.'

12 Macquarrie and Robinson explain their decision not to translate *Dasein* in a footnote to *Being and Time*, 27: 'The word "Dasein" plays so important a role in this work and is already so familiar to the English-speaking reader who has read about Heidegger, that it seems simpler to leave it untranslated. [...] Though in traditional German philosophy it may be used quite generally to stand for almost any kind of Being or "existence" which we can say that something *has* (the "existence" of God, for example), in everyday usage it tends to be used more narrowly to stand for the kind of Being that belongs to *persons*. Heidegger follows the everyday usage in this respect, but goes somewhat further in that he often uses it to stand for any *person* who has such Being, and who is thus an "entity" himself.'

13 Rolland, 'Sortir de l'être par une nouvelle voie', Introduction to Levinas, *De l'évasion*, 14.

14 Bell, *Husserl*, 12.

15 See Bell, *Husserl*, 235, n. 23.

16 This privileging of presence accounts in part for the discredit into which phenomenology fell during the structuralist and post-structuralist periods, when presence was one of the chief targets of suspicion and theoretical attack; see the following note.

17 With exemplary rigour and attention to detail, in *La Voix et le phénomène* Derrida shows how Husserl posits the self-presence of consciousness, whilst his analyses of the sign, interior monologue and time imply that such self-presence is always contaminated by absence. Given Derrida's knowledge of Levinas's writings (as indicated by his long essay 'Violence et métaphysique: Essai sur la pensée d'Emmanuel Levinas' (1964), which is discussed in chapter 3), and given the convergence of their respective readings of Husserl, it is perhaps surprising and noteworthy that Derrida's study contains no reference to Levinas's work.

18 The passage to which I refer here is from the preface to the second edition of *Existence and Existents*, which does not appear in the English translation of the work.

19 Heidegger, *Lettre sur l'humanisme*, 86. The English translation of the quotation is that given by Macquarrie and Robinson in a footnote to *Being and Time*, 255.

20 On phenomenology as a philosophy of light, see Ouaknin, *Méditations érotiques*, 39–41.

21 Husserl's Fifth Meditation has given rise to widely divergent assessments. Derrida, in 'Violence et métaphysique', defends Husserl against the charge that he suppresses the alterity of the Other (180–4) and describes the 'power of resistance to Levinas's criticisms' of the Fifth Meditation (194). Ricœur's reading, on the other hand, broadly converges with that of Levinas in the suggestion that the Fifth Meditation fails to solve the tension between the absolute primacy of the transcendental Ego and the existence of the other consciousnesses; see Ricœur, *A l'école de la phénoménologie*, for example 267–73, and on the Fifth Meditation in general, 197–225. More bluntly, David Bell describes how the reduction to the sphere of ownness is 'vacuous at best, and at worst it is incoherent' (*Husserl*, 217).

22 Leibniz, *The Monadology*, 248: 'each simple substance has relations which

express all the others, and, consequently, [. . .] it is a perpetual living mirror of the universe.'
23 Levinas discusses this passage in *MT*, 43–6.

### Chapter 2   Same and Other: *Totality and Infinity*

1 See for example 'L'Ontologie est-elle fondamentale?' (1951), 'Le Moi et la totalité' (1954) (both reprinted in *Entre nous*), 'La Philosophie et l'idée de l'Infini' (1957) and 'La Ruine de la représentation' (1959) (both reprinted in *En découvrant l'existence avec Husserl et Heidegger*).
2 See Peperzak, *To the Other*, 131.
3 Plato, *Republic* 7.509b.
4 These two definitions of ethics are given in Singer, 'Introduction', *Ethics*, 4.
5 Jacques Derrida, 'Violence et métaphysique', 124. Using a more dramatic image, Susan Handelman compares the effect of Levinas's prose to a 'battering'; see Handelman, *Fragments of Redemption*, 180.
6 Plato, *Phaedrus* 275e; Plato's *Phaedrus* is one of the most frequently cited texts in *Totality and Infinity*; for Levinas's use of Plato's views on rhetoric, see in particular *TI*, 66–75/70–7. However, as I discuss in chapter 4, in the context of Jewish hermeneutics Levinas accords to some texts an authority which is not consistent with the Platonic distrust of the written word.
7 This 'truism' is by no means universally accepted, and particularly in recent years a number of authors have contested it in the most vigorous terms; see, for example, Ferry and Renaut, *La Pensée 68*, 311–38.
8 See Althusser, *Lenin and Philosophy and Other Essays*, 116–19.
9 Descartes, 'Méditation troisième', in *Œuvres et lettres*, 294.
10 See, for example, Plato, *Sophist* 254–5.
11 Plato, *Timaeus* 35b.
12 Descartes, 'Méditation troisième', 295.
13 On Levinas's use of *tu* and *vous*, with particular reference to his engagement with the work of Martin Buber, see Robert Bernasconi, ' "Failure of Communication" as a Surplus: Dialogue and Lack of Dialogue between Buber and Levinas', in Bernasconi and Wood (eds), *The Provocation of Levinas*, 100–35.
14 Important parallels might be observed between Levinas's thought and contemporary reflections on desire, such as Lacan's account of its unfulfillable nature, or Deleuze and Guattari's notion of *machines désirantes* (desiring machines) in *Capitalisme et schizophrénie: L'Anti-Œdipe*; for a cogent account of Lacan's views on desire, see Bowie, *Lacan*, 130–41.
15 Problems in the notion of the face are further discussed in chapter 5.
16 For the contrast between teleological and deontological theories, see Williams, *Ethics and the Limits of Philosophy*, 16; the former are characterized as 'theories that take as primary the idea of producing the best possible state of affairs', whereas the latter 'take as basic a notion of obligation or duty'. See also Nancy (Ann) Davis, 'Contemporary Deontology', in Singer (ed.), *A Companion to Ethics*, 205–6.
17 See Plato, *Republic* 352d.
18 For a forthright expression of the non-cognitivist position, see Wittgenstein, 'A Lecture on Ethics', in Singer (ed.), *Ethics*, 146–7: 'My whole tendency

and I believe the tendency of all men who ever tried to write or talk Ethics or religion was to run against the boundaries of language. This running against the walls of our cage is perfectly, absolutely hopeless. Ethics so far as it springs from the desire to say something about the ultimate meaning of life, the absolute good, the absolutely valuable, can be no science. What it says does not add to our knowledge in any sense.'

19 On the mistake of presenting *Totality and Infinity* as an ethics, see Peperzak, *To the Other*, 123–4.

20 See Sartre, *L'Être et le néant*, 502: 'The essence of the relations between consciousnesses is not *Mitsein*, it is conflict.' For comparison of Levinas and Sartre on the nature of the encounter with Other, see Finkielkraut, *La Sagesse de l'amour*, 25–34; see also Christina Howells, 'Sartre and Levinas', in Bernasconi and Wood (eds), *The Provocation of Levinas*, 91–9.

21 On the absence of foundations in postmodern ethics, with particular reference to Levinas, see Bauman, *Postmodern Ethics*, for example 73–81.

22 For discussion of Levinas's thought in the context of the Holocaust, see Finkielkraut, *La Sagesse de l'amour*, 162–9. Finkielkraut argues that there is no contradiction between Levinas's philosophy of responsibility and the knowledge of Nazi crimes; the latter represent a methodical refusal of the proximity of the Other and the threat to the sovereignty of the self that it represents.

23 The Bible repeatedly instructs its readers to show particular solicitude and generosity towards strangers, widows and orphans; see, for example, Deuteronomy 24: 17–22.

24 See Bauman, *Postmodern Ethics*, 220.

25 Bauman, *Postmodern Ethics*, 51.

26 See Critchley, *The Ethics of Deconstruction*, 225–37.

27 Critchley, *The Ethics of Deconstruction*, 227.

28 Bauman, *Postmodern Ethics*, 84. Ouaknin concurs in describing Levinas's thought as 'the establishment of a postmodern ethics' (Ouaknin, *Méditations érotiques*, 129).

29 Bauman, *Postmodern Ethics*, 15

30 Bauman, *Postmodern Ethics*, 245.

31 For a rejection of the notion that postmodern ethics are relativistic, see also Bauman, *Postmodern Ethics*, 14–15. Bauman argues that modern societies are parochial when they promote their own ethical codes as universally valid; postmodern ethics, on the other hand, reveal a moral self without alibis or excuses, unable to take refuge behind the particular codes imposed by any given society.

32 Bauman, *Postmodern Ethics*, 80.

33 Peperzak, *To the Other*, 142.

34 Peperzak, *To the Other*, 142.

35 See Peperzak, *To the Other*, 202–5.

36 On the use of *se produire*, see also *TI*, 11/26.

37 Bauman, *Postmodern Ethics*, 71–3.

38 For Derrida's use of erasure, see *De la grammatologie*, 31. Norris, in *Deconstruction: Theory and Practice*, describes erasure in the following terms: 'The marks of erasure acknowledge both the *inadequacy* of the terms employed – their highly provisional status – and the fact that thought simply cannot manage without them in the work of deconstruction. By

this graphic means [. . .] concepts are perpetually shaken and dislodged' (69).

39 De Beauvoir, *Le Deuxième Sexe I: Les Faits et les mythes*, 15. For Levinas's somewhat unreconstructed view of femininity (which he is nevertheless cautious to present as only an account of Jewish sources), see also 'Le Judaïsme et le féminin' (*DF*, 51–62/30–8), and 'Et Dieu créa la femme', (*SS*, 122–48/161–77).

40 See, for example, Tina Chanter, 'Feminism and the Other', and Alison Ainley, 'Amorous Discourses: "The Phenomenology of Eros" and Love Stories', both in Bernasconi and Wood (eds), *The Provocation of Levinas*, 32–56 and 70–82. A sympathetic account of some problems in Levinas's treatment of femininity is given in Ziarek, 'Kristeva and Levinas: Mourning, Ethics, and the Feminine'.

41 Peperzak, *To the Other*, 195. See also Chanter, 'Feminism and the Other', 46–7.

**Chapter 3  Ethical Language:** *Otherwise than Being or Beyond Essence*

1 Derrida, 'Violence et métaphysique: Essai sur la pensée d'Emmanuel Levinas'; references, given in the text, are to the version published in Derrida's *L'Écriture et la différence*.

2 This point is made by several of the contributors to Bernasconi and Critchley (eds), *Re-Reading Levinas*; see in particular the essays of Robert Bernasconi and John Llewelyn. On Derrida's relationship with Levinas in general, see Critchley, *The Ethics of Deconstruction*.

3 It appears on this point that Derrida is adopting an implicit distinction between the letter and the spirit of Levinas's thought; yet Derrida suggests that Levinas is wrong to apply such a distinction in his studies of Husserl. See 'Violence et métaphysique', 128–9.

4 Derrida is referring to 'Heidegger, Gagarine et nous', in *Difficult Freedom*, 323–7. Derrida's description of the article as violent is in response to the alleged errors it contains, rather than to the tone of Levinas's comments on Heidegger.

5 Critchley, *The Ethics of Deconstruction*, 93.

6 See Bernasconi and Critchley, 'Editors' Introduction', in *Re-Reading Levinas*, xii.

7 Critchley, *The Ethics of Deconstruction*, 93.

8 Feron, *De l'idée de transcendance à la question du langage*, 260.

9 For detailed discussion of this essay and its ramifications, see Critchley, *The Ethics of Deconstruction*, 145–87. A translation of the essay appears as 'Wholly Otherwise', translated by Critchley, in Bernasconi and Critchley (eds), *Re-Reading Levinas*, 3–10.

10 Critchley, *The Ethics of Deconstruction*, 153.

11 Levinas is referring to Plato, *Phaedrus* 244–5. The passage describes the madness of the lover who, in beholding the beauty of the world, is reminded of true beauty and of true being.

12 Derrida, 'En ce moment même dans cet ouvrage me voici', in Laruelle (ed.), *Textes pour Emmanuel Levinas*, 21–60, and in *Psyché: Inventions de*

*l'autre*; this article, and the collection in which it first appeared, are discussed in chapter 5.

13 Bernasconi, 'Skepticism in the Face of Philosophy', in Bernasconi and Critchley (eds), *Re-Reading Levinas*, 149.

14 Bernasconi, for example, describes Derrida as Levinas's 'main interlocutor' in *Otherwise than Being*; see 'Skepticism in the Face of Philosophy', 154. See also Feron, *De l'idée de transcendance à la question du langage*, 258–68. Levinas never refers explicitly to 'Violence et métaphysique' in *Otherwise than Being*, though Derrida's *La Voix et le phénomène* is mentioned in one footnote (*OB*, 63/36).

15 See Levinas's preface to the German edition of *Totality and Infinity* (*TI*, I–II; not reproduced in the English translation).

16 It is in the nature of Levinas's writing that terms such as these cannot easily be defined since their meaning emerges only gradually and is anyway susceptible to important modifications. Schematically, proximity and approach refer to the subject's relationship with the Other in words which seek to avoid implications of comprehension or appropriation. Other terms in the list attempt to describe the subject's responsibility for the Other: I am besieged and held captive by the Other (obsession, hostage, persecution), and can be called to account for the Other's actions (substitution, expiation). The term *enigma* will be discussed in the final section of this chapter, and *illeity* will be discussed in chapter 4.

17 See Peperzak, *To the Other*, 212.

18 Critchley, *The Ethics of Deconstruction*, 8.

19 Feron, *De l'idée de transcendance à la question du langage*, 118.

20 But Levinas is less reticent about using *essance* elsewhere; see, for example, *DVI*, 78, and *EN*, 82. On *différance* see Derrida, 'La Différance', in *Marges de la philosophie*, 1–29.

21 In none of these cases are the italics in the French text reproduced in the English translation.

22 See, for example, the comments on *obsession*, *OB*, 133/83.

23 Irigaray, 'Questions to Emmanuel Levinas: On the Divinity of Love', in Bernasconi and Critchley (eds), *Re-Reading Levinas*, 113.

24 See *EI*, 103–4/107, where Levinas describes the oscillation between *dire* (saying) and *dédire* (unsaying) as 'a proper mode of philosophizing [*un mode propre de philosopher*]'. See also *NP*, 69: '[The truth of truths] is in the Said and in the Unsaid and in the Otherwise-said [*dans le Dit et dans le Dédit et dans l'Autrement dit*].'

25 Levinas first discusses this distinction at length in 'Énigme et phénomène', originally published in 1965 and reprinted in *En découvrant l'existence avec Husserl et Heidegger*, 203–16.

26 See Feron, *De l'idée de transcendance à la question du langage*, 76.

27 See *OB*, 82/48: 'The plot of proximity and communication is not a modality of cognition. The unblocking of communication, irreducible to the circulation of information which presupposes it, is accomplished in Saying. It is not due to the contents that are inscribed in the Said and transmitted to the interpretation and decoding done by the Other.'

28 See, for example, *OB*, 228/146. The phrase is based on the Hebrew *hineni*, which occurs frequently in the Bible; Levinas quotes Isaiah 6: 8. See Handelman, *Fragments of Redemption*, 265–6, which refers to Genesis 22: 1.

29 See Feron, *De l'idée de transcendance à la question du langage*, 327, for a version of this criticism.
30 See Rorty, *Contingency, Irony, Solidarity*, 73; Rorty refers to what he calls ironists who realize that 'anything can be made to look good or bad by being redescribed.'
31 An important part of the work done on Levinas has been from the standpoint of the social sciences; see, for example, Burggraeve, *From Self-Development to Solidarity*.
32 On obsession, see also 'Langage et proximité', in *En découvrant l'existence avec Husserl et Heidegger*, especially 228–31, 233–4.
33 On the use of the phrase 'En ce moment même', see Derrida's second article on Levinas, 'En ce moment même dans cet ouvrage me voici'.
34 See Plato, *Republic* 7.514–16.
35 Similar implications can be found in near-contemporary French discussions of authorship; see, for example, Roland Barthes, 'The Death of the Author' (1968), and Michel Foucault, 'What is an Author?', both in Lodge (ed.), *Modern Criticism and Theory: A Reader*, 167–72 and 197–210 respectively.
36 On scepticism in Levinas, with particular reference to 'Scepticism and Reason' and its relevance to Derrida's comments, see Jan de Greef, 'Skepticism and Reason', in Cohen (ed.), *Face to Face with Levinas*, 159–79; Robert Bernasconi, 'Skepticism in the Face of Philosophy', in Bernasconi and Critchley (eds), *Re-Reading Levinas*, 149–61; and Critchley, *The Ethics of Deconstruction*, 156–69.
37 On synchrony and diachrony in Levinas, see Jeanne Delhomme, 'Savoir lire? Synchronie et diachronie', in Laruelle (ed.), *Textes pour Emmanuel Levinas*, 151–65.
· 38 John Llewelyn, 'Levinas, Derrida and Others *vis-à-vis*', in Bernasconi and Wood (eds), *The Provocation of Levinas*, 153.

## Chapter 4 Religion

1 Feron, *De l'idée de transcendance à la question du langage*, 10.
2 Gibbs, *Correlations in Rosenzweig and Levinas*, 10.
3 Gibbs, *Correlations in Rosenzweig and Levinas*, 4.
4 See, for example, Guibal, ... *Et combien de dieux nouveaux II: Levinas*; Vandevelde, *Expression de la cohérence du mystère de Dieu et du salut*; de Vries, *Theologie im Pianissimo und zwischen Rationalität und Dekonstruktion*; Smith, *The Argument to the Other*. A particularly interesting example of an attempt to use Levinas's work as part of a theological project is provided by Marion; see, for example, *L'Idole et la distance*.
5 See Ouaknin, *Méditations érotiques*; Chalier, *Judaïsme et altérité*; Banon, *La Lecture infinie*; Handelman, *Fragments of Redemption*.
6 Gibbs, *Correlations in Rosenzweig and Levinas*, 154.
7 Handelman, *Fragments of Redemption*, 270.
8 For discussion of these expressions see chapters 2 and 3 respectively.
9 On possible biblical sources of the notion of the face, see, for example, Handelman, *Fragments of Redemption*, 208–17; on alterity, see Chalier, *Judaïsme et altérité*.

10 See Robbins, *Prodigal Son/Elder Brother*, 106, for discussion of the role of Abraham as a figure of Jewish alterity within the philosophical text.

11 Descartes, 'Méditation troisième', in *Œuvres et lettres*, 299; quoted in *DVI*, 107.

12 Descartes refers to God as 'a substance which is infinite, eternal, unchanging, independent, all-knowing, all-powerful, and by which myself, and all the other things which are (if it is true that there are things which exist), have been created and produced' ('Méditation troisième', 294).

13 On the problems of naming God, see also 'Le Nom de Dieu d'après quelques textes talmudiques' (*BV*, 143–57/116–28).

14 See, for example, *DVI*, 116, which begins to look like a parody of Levinas's style: 'This traumatism – which cannot be assumed – inflicted by the Infinite on presence or that affection of presence by the Infinite – that affectivity – becomes apparent as submission to the neighbour: thought thinking more than it thinks – Desire – reference to the neighbour – responsibility for the other.' For a different view, see Chalier, *Levinas: L'Utopie de l'humain*, 161; Chalier claims that in *De Dieu qui vient à l'idée* Levinas brings together 'various fundamental articles which open new perspectives in his thought'.

15 See note 9 above.

16 The relationship between Levinas and Rosenzweig has been discussed in, for example, Gibbs, *Correlations in Rosenzweig and Levinas*; Handelman, *Fragments of Redemption*, 182–7; and Cohen, 'The Face of Truth in Rosenzweig, Levinas, and Jewish Mysticism'. Levinas acknowledges the influence of Rosenzweig in the preface to *Totality and Infinity*; Rosenzweig is described as 'too often present in this book to be cited' (*TI*, 14/28), and the text itself contains no references to his work. Levinas has discussed Rosenzweig in a number of essays; see, for example, 'Franz Rosenzweig: Une Pensée juive moderne' (*OS*, 71–96/49–66), and 'La Philosophie de Franz Rosenzweig' (*AHN*, 175–85).

17 In 1946 Levinas was made Director of the École Normale Israélite Orientale, an organization established to train teachers for Jewish schools in the Mediterranean Basin; in 1967 he was appointed as Professor of Philosophy at the University of Nanterre and in 1973 at the Sorbonne. He retired in 1976.

18 Levinas's discussion of Hegel is based on Bourgeois, *Hegel à Francfort ou Judaïsme, Christianisme, Hégélianisme*.

19 See also *DF*, 79/50: 'You are born a Jew; you don't become one'; Levinas is alluding to de Beauvoir, *Le Deuxième Sexe II: L'Expérience vécue*, 13: 'You are not born a woman, you become one [*On ne naît pas femme: on le devient*].' Levinas acknowledges that his parody of de Beauvoir is only a 'half truth' (*DF*, 79/50).

20 For a controversial account of the history of Hasidism which stresses its intellectual sources, see Scholem, *Major Trends in Jewish Mysticism*. Hasidic stories have been collected and adapted by, for example, Martin Buber in *Tales of the Hasidim*, and discussed by Élie Wiesel in his *Célébration hassidique*.

21 Levinas alludes ironically to Hasidism in *DF*, 17/6; and later he deplores the modern world 'in which Jews understand only Hasidic tales' (*DF*, 50/29).

22 Levinas suggests that the formula 'The Torah speaks the language of men' is repeated eighteen times in the Talmud; see *BV*, 7/x.

23 Whilst referring to the Jews as the chosen people, Levinas warns against the feelings of superiority which might derive from the sense of occupying a privileged position in the order of the world; in his account, being chosen entails obligations rather than privileges; see, for example, *DF*, 39/21.

24 An excellent introduction to Levinas's talmudic commentaries is given in Annette Aronowicz's 'Translator's Introduction', in Levinas, *Nine Talmudic Readings*, ix–xxxix.

25 Levinas presents the Talmud in the Introduction to *QLT*, 9–25/3–11. His commentaries are taken from the Babylonian Talmud, which has authority over the Jerusalem Talmud. My discussion draws both on Levinas's texts and on a number of invaluable works: see in particular Banon, *La Lecture infinie*; Handelman, *The Slayers of Moses*; Hartman and Budick (eds), *Midrash and Literature*.

26 See Levinas's 'De l'écrit à l'oral', preface to Banon, *La Lecture infinie*, 8; see also *BV*, 165/135–6.

27 On the consonantal nature of Hebrew and the possibilities of interpretation which it allows, see Banon, *La Lecture infinie*, 188–203.

28 Levinas discusses Spinoza in 'Le Cas Spinoza' (*DF*, 152–7/106–10), 'Avez-vous relu Baruch?' (*DF*, 158–69/111–18) and 'L'Arrière-plan de Spinoza' (*BV*, 201–6/168–73).

29 See Spinoza, *Tractatus Theologico-Politicus*, chapter 7, 'Of the Interpretation of Scripture'.

30 On the presumption in Jewish hermeneutics that the sacred texts constitute a coherent whole, see Banon, *La Lecture infinie*, 89–90.

31 Hebrew letters have a numerical value, so words can also be read as numbers. See, for example, *BV*, 132/209: the numerical value of the word *Torah* is 611; when this is added to the two commandments heard directly from the voice of God, this makes 613, taken by one rabbi to be the number of commandments given by God to Moses.

32 Hirsch defends the notion of a single correct interpretation, in, for example, *Validity in Interpretation*.

33 On the different levels of interpretation in Jewish hermeneutics, see Banon, *La Lecture infinie*, 205.

34 For discussion of this passage, see Aronowitz, 'Translator's Introduction', xvii.

35 Levinas, 'De l'écrit à l'oral', in Banon, *La Lecture infinie*, 10. See also *SS*, 15/96: 'Obedience or boldness? Safety in proceeding or a taking of risks? In any case neither paraphrase nor paradox; neither philology nor arbitrariness.'

36 On this issue in Jewish hermeneutics, see Judah Goldin, 'The Freedom and Restraint of Haggadah', in Hartman and Budick (eds), *Midrash and Literature*, 57–76.

37 See Wiesel, 'Le Juif errant', in *Le Chant des morts*, 119–44, and 'La Mort d'un juif errant', in *Paroles d'étranger*, 108–13.

38 Wiesel, *Célébration talmudique*, 10–13.

39 Wiesel, *Célébration talmudique*, 14.

40 Wiesel, *Célébration talmudique*, 14.

41 On this phrase, see Ricœur, *Le Conflit des interprétations*, 284: '"The symbol

gives cause to think": this sentence which enchants me says two things; the symbol gives; I do not put meaning in it, it is the symbol which gives meaning; but what it gives is "to think" [*à penser*], something to think about, [...] so the sentence suggests both that everything is already said as an enigma, and yet that everything must be begun and begun again in the dimension of thinking.' See also Ricœur, *Finitude et culpabilité II: La Symbolique du mal*, especially 324–5.

42  Gadamer, *Hermeneutik 1: Wahrheit und Methode*, 302.

43  See Fish, *Is there a Text in this Class?*, 327: 'Interpretation is not the art of construing but the art of constructing. Interpreters do not decode poems; they make them.'

44  Gadamer, *Hermeneutik 1: Wahrheit und Methode*, 311–12.

45  Gadamer, *Hermeneutik 1: Wahrheit und Methode*, 100.

46  Hirsch, for example, claims that Gadamer's hermeneutics provides no reliable means of distinguishing between competing interpretations; see Hirsch, *Validity in Interpretation*, 245–64.

47  This point is also made by Aronowicz, 'Translator's Introduction', xv–xvi, xxi; see also Handelman, *Fragments of Redemption*, 314.

48  The distinction between Greek and Hebrew has been discussed at length by Levinas's commentators; see, for example, Aronowicz, 'Translator's Introduction', ix–xv.

## Chapter 5  Levinas and his Readers

1  Bernard Williams, for example, does not even mention the name of Levinas in his *Ethics and the Limits of Philosophy*, neither do any of the contributors to Singer (ed.), *A Companion to Ethics*.

2  Descombes, *Le Même et l'autre*. The book was commissioned by Cambridge University Press, and published in English as *Modern French Philosophy*.

3  Ferry and Renaut, *La Pensée 68*, 21.

4  David Wood, 'Beyond Deconstruction?', in Griffiths (ed.), *Contemporary French Philosophy*, 180.

5  Pascal Engel, 'Continental Insularity: Contemporary French Analytical Philosophy', in Griffiths (ed.), *Contemporary French Philosophy*, 2–4.

6  See Engel, 'Continental Insularity', 4.

7  This can be seen, for example, in his retention of a Platonic distinction between rhetoric and genuine discourse; see *Totality and Infinity*, 66–75.

8  Feron, *De l'idée de transcendance à la question du langage*, 5.

9  See Descombes, *Le Même et l'autre*, 22.

10  Descombes, *Le Même et l'autre*, 13.

11  Descombes, *Le Même et l'autre*, 13–14.

12  Descombes, *Le Même et l'autre*, 61.

13  Sartre, *L'Existentialisme est un humanisme*, first published 1946.

14  Michèle Le Dœuff, 'Ants and Women, or Philosophy without Borders', in Griffiths (ed.), *Contemporary French Philosophy*, 48.

15  Wood, 'Beyond Deconstruction?', 180.

16  Bennington, for example, makes Derrida sound distinctly like Levinas in *Legislations*, 192: 'The relation with the other as such (the 'as such' is important, marking that what is at stake here is respect for the *alterity* of

the other, not an attempt to reduce that alterity to familiarity) [. . .] marks
[Derrida's] thinking as profoundly ethical.' More generally, the concern for
the Other has been described as one of the hallmarks of post-structuralism;
see Haber, *Beyond Postmodern Politics*, 6.

17 Critchley, *The Ethics of Deconstruction*, xi.

18 Supporting his point with an allusion to 'Violence et métaphysique',
Derrida himself argues that deconstruction had been concerned with
ethical issues from its earliest stages; see *Force de loi*, 21.

19 The article, first published in 1973 and reprinted in *De Dieu qui vient à l'idée*
(17–33), is based on lectures given in 1972.

20 See Levinas's comments in Poirié, *Emmanuel Levinas: Qui êtes-vous?*, 131.

21 This is indicated, for example, by the publicity wrapper which appeared
around the original edition of *Existence and Existents*; it mocked the
existentialist vogue of the forties with the declaration 'Où il n'est pas
question d'angoisse' ('In which anxiety is not discussed').

22 Ferry and Renaut, *La Pensée 68*, 51–5.

23 Bruno Latour, 'The Enlightenment Without the Critique: A Word on
Michel Serres's Philosophy', in Griffiths (ed.), *Contemporary French Philosophy*, 83.

24 In the opening pages of *De la grammatologie*, for example, Derrida lumps
together large parts of the history of philosophy, referring to it as 'the
*history of metaphysics*' which despite all differences stretches 'from Plato to
Hegel (even passing through Leibniz), but also, outside its apparent limits,
from the presocratics to Heidegger' (11).

25 Pinto, *Les Philosophes entre le lycée et l'avant-garde*; page references are given
in the text.

26 For discussion, see chapter 1, pp. 22–3.

27 Heidegger warns against the possible confusion of his *es gibt* and Sartre's
*il y a* in *Lettre sur l'humanisme*, 86.

28 Although it was not published until 1947, *Existence and Existents* was
written during the war in a German prisoner-of-war camp; this explains,
according to Levinas, 'the absence of any consideration of those philosophical works published, with so much impact, between 1940 and 1945' (*EE*,
10/15).

29 All three elements are found, for example, in Poirié, *Emmanuel Levinas: Qui
êtes-vous?*, 16, and Peperzak, *To the Other*, 18. (The allusion to Blanchot is
implicit in the phrase 'rumbling and rustling', referring to Blanchot's
'remue-ménage'; see note 42.)

30 The subject of the second sentence ('Elle') must be 'la forme plastique';
from the point of view of sense, it would be easier (though grammatically
impossible) to take 'Le visage' as the subject. The 'il' of the penultimate
sentence presumably refers to 'l'exprimé', but again it is tempting to read
it as referring to 'le visage'.

31 Plato, *Phaedrus* 275e.

32 Feron, *De l'idée de transcendance à la question du langage*, 51; the rest of this
paragraph is based on 51–5.

33 Handelman, *Fragments of Redemption*, 209; the rest of this paragraph is
based on 209–11.

34 See Ponet, 'Faces: A Meditation', and Cohen, 'The Face of Truth in
Rosenzweig, Levinas, and Jewish Mysticism'.

35 Derrida, 'Violence et métaphysique', 154.

36 Derrida, 'Violence et métaphysique', 146, 149.

37 Laruelle (ed.), *Textes pour Emmanuel Levinas*; page references will be given in the text.

38 The article is also published in Derrida's *Psyché*, 159–202, and translated by Ruben Berezdivin as 'At this very moment in this work here I am', in Bernasconi and Critchley (eds), *Re-reading Levinas*, 11–48.

39 Ricœur's essay is reprinted in *A l'école de la phénoménologie*, 285–95.

40 The exception here is Lyotard, whom particular circumstances ally in this instance to the more philosophically conservative group of contributors. His article was written during the period when he was working on *Le Différend* (1983), which Lyotard presents as being more 'philosophical' than his other books. In *Le Différend* he shows greater respect for conventions of philosophical presentation and argument which elsewhere he brings into question. It is striking that in *Textes pour Emmanuel Levinas* only Wyschogrod's article approaches Lyotard's for the number of end-notes it contains; and in total the articles of Wyschogrod and Lyotard have eight times as many notes as the rest of the contributions added together.

41 Blanchot's article is translated by David B. Allison as 'Our Clandestine Companion', in Cohen (ed.), *Face to Face with Levinas*, 41–50.

42 Blanchot quotes *DVI*, 115 (quoted 86), where Levinas refers to the 'bustle [*remue-ménage*] of the *il y a*'; as Levinas indicates in the preface to the second edition of *Existence and Existents* (*EE*, 10; not translated in the English edition), the term *remue-ménage* is taken from Blanchot.

43 Derrida's essay is thoroughly examined in Critchley, *The Ethics of Deconstruction*, 107–44. Derrida's apocalyptic reading of Levinas is confirmed by his oration at Levinas's funeral on 28 December 1995, published as 'Adieu'. Derrida describes how Levinas's thought 'discreetly but irreversibly' disturbs 'the strongest and most self-assured philosophies of this end of millennium' (88); Levinas 'overturned [*bouleversa*] [. . .] the landscape without landscape of thought', bearing his immense responsibility with an awareness which was 'clear, confident, calm and modest, like that of a prophet' (90).

44 See Ricœur, *Soi-même comme un autre*; for discussion of Levinas, see in particular 387–93.

45 For examples of such accounts, see respectively Critchley, *The Ethics of Deconstruction*; Marion, *L'Idole et la distance*, 265–70; Chanter, 'Feminism and the Other', in Bernasconi and Wood (eds), *The Provocation of Levinas*, 32–56.

46 Bauman, *Postmodern Ethics*, 84.

47 Ouaknin, *Méditations érotiques*, 173–7.

48 De Beauvoir, *Le Deuxième Sexe I: Les Faits et les mythes*, 15; Derrida, 'En ce moment même dans cet ouvrage me voici', 54–5.

49 See Luce Irigaray, 'Questions to Emmanuel Levinas: On the Dignity of Love', translated by Margaret Whitford, in Bernasconi and Critchley (eds), *Re-Reading Levinas*, 109–18. See also 'The Fecundity of the Caress: A Reading of Levinas, *Totality and Infinity*, section IV, B, "The Phenomenology of Eros"', in Cohen (ed.), *Face to Face with Levinas*, 231–56; the French version of this article is published in Irigaray's *Éthique de la différence sexuelle*, 173–99.

50  Irigaray, 'Questions to Emmanuel Levinas', 110.
51  Irigaray, 'Questions to Emmanuel Levinas', 113.
52  Irigaray, 'Questions to Emmanuel Levinas', 113.
53  Derrida, 'En ce moment même dans cet ouvrage me voici', 54–5.
54  Le Dœuff, 'Ants and Women, or Philosophy without Borders', 49; ironically, Le Dœuff is specifically referring to Derrida's work here.
55  See, for example, Feron, who suggests that Levinas does not leave enough space for real dialogue with the Other (*De l'idée de transcendance à la question du langage*, 335), and Guibal, who describes him as too dependent on the structures of thought with which he wants to break (*. . . Et combien de dieux nouveaux II: Levinas*, 127–9).

## Conclusion

1  See, for example, Fish, *Is there a Text in this Class?*, 331–2.

# Bibliography

A comprehensive list of works by and on Levinas up to 1989 is given in Burggraeve, Roger, *Emmanuel Levinas: Une bibliographie primaire et secondaire (1929–1985), avec complément 1985–1989* (Leuven: Peeters, 1990). Works and editions used in this study are listed below.

## Works by Levinas in French

*Théorie de l'intuition dans la phénoménologie de Husserl* (Paris: Vrin, 1970; first edition 1930).

*De l'évasion* (Montpellier: Fata Morgana, 1982; first published as article, 1935).

*De l'existence à l'existant* (Paris: Vrin, 1978; first edition 1947).

*Le Temps et l'autre* (Montpellier: Fata Morgana, 1979; first edition 1947).

*En découvrant l'existence avec Husserl et Heidegger* (Paris: Vrin, 1974; first edition 1949, with additions in 1967).

*Totalité et infini: Essai sur l'extériorité* (Livre de Poche; The Hague: Martinus Nijhoff, 1971; first edition 1961).

*Difficile liberté: Essais sur le judaïsme* (Livre de Poche; Paris: Albin Michel, 1963 and 1976).

*Quatre lectures talmudiques* (Paris: Minuit, 1968).

*Humanisme de l'autre homme* (Livre de Poche; Montpellier: Fata Morgana, 1972).

*Autrement qu'être ou au-delà de l'essence* (Livre de Poche; The Hague: Martinus Nijhoff, 1974).

*Sur Maurice Blanchot* (Montpellier: Fata Morgana, 1975).

*Noms propres* (Livre de Poche; Montpellier: Fata Morgana, 1976).

*Du sacré au saint: Cinq nouvelles lectures talmudiques* (Paris: Minuit, 1977).

*De Dieu qui vient à l'idée* (Paris: Vrin, 1992; first edition 1982).

*L'Au-delà du verset: Lectures et discours talmudiques* (Paris: Minuit, 1982).

*Éthique et infini*, dialogues with Philippe Nemo (Livre de Poche; Paris: Librairie Arthème Fayard and Radio-France, 1982).

*Transcendance et intelligibilité* (Geneva: Labor et Fides, 1984).

*Hors sujet* (Montpellier: Fata Morgana, 1987).

*A l'heure des nations* (Paris: Minuit, 1988).

*La Mort et le temps* (Paris: L'Herne, 1991).

*Entre nous: Essais sur le penser-à-l'autre* (Paris: Grasset and Fasquelle, 1991).

*Dieu, la mort et le temps* (Paris: Grasset, 1993).

*Liberté et commandement* (Montpellier: Fata Morgana, 1994; two articles first published in 1953 and 1962).

*Les Imprévus de l'histoire* (Montpellier: Fata Morgana, 1994).

*Nouvelles lectures talmudiques* (Paris: Minuit, 1996).


**English translations of works by Levinas**

*The Theory of Intuition in Husserl's Phenomenology* (1930), translated by André Orianne (Evanston: Northwestern University Press, 1973).

*Existence and Existents* (1947), translated by Alphonso Lingis (Dordrecht, Boston and London: Kluwer Academic Publishers, 1978; reprinted in 1988 with minor corrections).

*Time and the Other* (1947), translated by Richard A. Cohen (Pittsburgh: Duquesne University Press, 1987).

*Discovering Existence with Husserl* (1949, 1967), translated by Richard A. Cohen (Bloomington: Indiana University Press, 1988).

*Totality and Infinity* (1961), translated by Alphonso Lingis (Pittsburgh: Duquesne University Press, 1969).

*Difficult Freedom: Essays on Judaism* (1963, 1976), translated by Seán Hand (London: The Athlone Press, 1990).

*Nine Talmudic Readings* (1968, 1977), translated by Annette Aronowicz (Bloomington: Indiana University Press, 1990).

*Otherwise than Being or Beyond Essence* (1974), translated by Alphonso Lingis (The Hague: Martinus Nijhoff, 1981).

*Beyond the Verse: Talmudic Readings and Lectures* (1982), translated by Gary D. Mole (London: The Athlone Press, 1994).

*Ethics and Infinity* (1982), translated by Richard A. Cohen (Pittsburgh: Duquesne University Press, 1985).

*Outside the Subject* (1987), translated by Michael B. Smith (London: The Athlone Press, 1993).

*Collected Philosophical Papers*, translated by Alphonso Lingis (The Hague: Martinus Nijhoff, 1987).

*The Levinas Reader*, edited by Seán Hand (Oxford: Blackwell, 1989).

*Emmanuel Levinas: Basic Writings*, edited by Robert Bernasconi, Simon Critchley and Adriaan Peperzak (Bloomington: Indiana University Press, 1996).


**Works on Levinas**

Aeschlimann, Jean-Christophe (ed.), *Répondre d'autrui: Emmanuel Levinas* (Neuchâtel: A la baconnière, 1989).

Aronowicz, Annette, 'Translator's Introduction', in *Nine Talmudic Readings by Emmanuel Levinas* (Bloomington: Indiana University Press, 1990), ix–xxix.

Bailhache, Gérard, *Le Sujet chez Emmanuel Levinas: Fragilité et subjectivité* (Paris: PUF, 1994).

Banon, David, *La Lecture infinie: Les Voies de l'interprétation midrachique* (Paris: Seuil, 1987).

Bauman, Zygmunt, *Postmodern Ethics* (Oxford: Blackwell, 1993).

Bernasconi, Robert, 'The Trace of Levinas in Derrida', in Robert Bernasconi and David Wood (eds), *Derrida and Différance* (Coventry: Parousia Press, 1985), 17–44.

Bernasconi, Robert, and Critchley, Simon (eds), *Re-Reading Levinas* (London: The Athlone Press, 1991).

Bernasconi, Robert, and Wood, David (eds), *The Provocation of Levinas: Rethinking the Other* (London and New York: Routledge, 1988).

Burggraeve, Roger, *From Self-Development to Solidarity: An Ethical Reading of Human Desire in its Socio-Political Relevance According to Emmanuel Levinas*, translated by C. Vanhove-Romanik (Leuven: Peeters, 1985).

Chalier, Catherine, *Figures du féminin: Lecture d'Emmanuel Levinas* (Paris: La Nuit surveillée, 1982; reprinted by Verdier).

Chalier, Catherine, *Judaïsme et altérité* (Lagrasse: Verdier, 1982).

Chalier, Catherine, *Levinas: L'Utopie de l'humain* (Paris: Albin Michel, 1993).

Ciaramelli, Fabio, *Transcendance et éthique: Essai sur Levinas* (Brussels: Ousia, 1989).

Cohen, Richard A. (ed.), *Face to Face with Levinas* (Albany: State University of New York Press, 1986).

Cohen, Richard A., 'The Face of Truth in Rosenzweig, Levinas, and Jewish Mysticism', in Daniel Guerrière (ed.), *Phenomenology of the Truth Proper to Religion* (Albany: State University of New York Press, 1990).

Critchley, Simon, *The Ethics of Deconstruction: Derrida and Levinas* (Blackwell: Oxford, 1992).

Derrida, Jacques, 'Violence et métaphysique: Essai sur la pensée d'Emmanuel Levinas' (1964), in *L'Écriture et la différence* (Points; Paris: Seuil, 1967), 117–228.

Derrida, Jacques, 'En ce moment même dans cet ouvrage me voici', in François Laruelle (ed.), *Textes pour Emmanuel Levinas* (Paris: Jean-Michel Place, 1980), 21–60, and in *Psyché: Inventions de l'autre* (Paris: Galilée, 1987), 159–202.

Derrida, Jacques, 'Adieu', in *L'Arche*, 459 (February 1996), 84–91.

Feron, Étienne, *De l'idée de transcendance à la question du langage: L'Itinéraire philosophique d'Emmanuel Levinas* (Grenoble: Jérôme Millon, 1992).

Finkielkraut, Alain, *La Sagesse de l'amour* (Folio; Paris: Gallimard, 1984).

Forthomme, Bernard, *Une philosophie de la transcendance: La Métaphysique d'Emmanuel Levinas* (Paris: Vrin, 1979).

Gibbs, Robert, *Correlations in Rosenzweig and Levinas* (Princeton: Princeton University Press, 1992).

Greisch, Jean, and Rolland, Jacques (eds), *Emmanuel Levinas: L'Éthique comme philosophie première* (Paris: Les Éditions du Cerf, 1993).

Guibal, Francis, . . . *Et combien de dieux nouveaux II: Levinas* (Paris: Aubier-Montaigne, 1980).

Handelman, Susan A., *Fragments of Redemption: Jewish Thought and Literary Theory in Benjamin, Scholem, and Levinas* (Bloomington and Indianapolis: Indiana University Press, 1991).

Huizing, Klaus, *Das Sein und der Andere: Levinas' Auseinandersetzung mit Heidegger* (Frankfurt am Main: Athenäum, 1988).

Irigaray, Luce, *Éthique de la différence sexuelle* (Paris: Minuit, 1984).
Laruelle, François (ed.), *Textes pour Emmanuel Levinas* (Paris: Jean-Michel Place, 1980).
Llewelyn, John, *The Middle Voice of Ecological Conscience: A Chiasmic Reading of Responsibility in the Neighbourhood of Levinas, Heidegger and Others* (London: Macmillan, 1991).
Llewelyn, John, *Emmanuel Levinas: The Genealogy of Ethics* (London: Routledge, 1995).
Malka, Salomon, *Lire Levinas* (Paris: Cerf, 1984).
Ouaknin, Marc-Alain, *Méditations érotiques: Essai sur Emmanuel Levinas* (Paris: Balland, 1992).
Peperzak, Adriaan, *To the Other: An Introduction to the Philosophy of Emmanuel Levinas* (West Lafayette: Purdue University Press, 1993).
Peperzak, Adriaan (ed.), *Ethics as First Philosophy* (New York: Routledge, 1995).
Petrosino, Silvano, and Rolland, Jacques, *La Vérité nomade: Introduction à Emmanuel Levinas* (Paris: La Découverte, 1984).
Poirié, François, *Emmanuel Levinas: Qui êtes-vous?* (Lyon: La Manufacture, 1987).
Ponet, James, 'Faces: A Meditation', *Orim: A Jewish Journal at Yale*, 1 (1985), 58–76.
Robbins, Jill, *Prodigal Son/Elder Brother: Interpretation and Alterity in Augustine, Petrarch, Kafka, Levinas* (Chicago and London: University of Chicago Press, 1991).
Rolland, Jacques, 'Sortir de l'être par une nouvelle voie', Introduction to Emmanuel Levinas, *De l'évasion* (Montpellier: Fata Morgana, 1982), 9–64.
Smith, Steven, *The Argument to the Other: Reason Beyond Reason in the Thought of Karl Barth and Emmanuel Levinas* (Chico, California: Scholars Press, 1983).
Vandevelde, Guy, *Expression de la cohérence du mystère de Dieu et du salut: La Réciprocité dans la 'Théologie' et l'Économie'* (Rome: Editrice Pontificia Università Gregoriana, 1993).
Vries, Hent de, *Theologie im Pianissimo und zwischen Rationalität und Dekonstruktion: Die Aktualität der Denkfiguren Adornos und Levinas'* (Kampen: Uitgeversmaatschappij J. H. Kok, 1989).
Wyschogrod, Edith, *Emmanuel Levinas: The Problem of Ethical Metaphysics* (The Hague: Martinus Nijhoff, 1974).
Ziarek, Ewa, 'Kristeva and Levinas: Mourning, Ethics, and the Feminine', in Kelly Oliver (ed.), *Ethics, Politics, and Difference in Julia Kristeva's Writing*, (New York and London: Routledge, 1993), 62–78.

**Other works cited**

Adorno, Theodor, *The Jargon of Authenticity*, translated by Knut Tarnowski and Frederic Will (London: Routledge and Kegan Paul, 1973; first published in German in 1964).
Althusser, Louis, *Lenin and Philosophy and Other Essays*, translated by Ben Brewster (London: NLB, 1971).
Beauvoir, Simone de, *Le Deuxième Sexe I: Les Faits et les mythes* (Paris: Gallimard, 1949).

Beauvoir, Simone de, *Le Deuxième Sexe II: L'Expérience vécue* (Paris: Gallimard, 1949).

Bell, David, *Husserl* (New York and London: Routledge, 1990).

Bennington, Geoffrey, *Legislations: The Politics of Deconstruction* (London and New York: Verso, 1994).

Bourgeois, Bernard, *Hegel à Francfort ou Judaïsme, Christianisme, Hégélianisme* (Paris: Vrin, 1970).

Bowie, Malcolm, *Lacan* (London: Fontana, 1991).

Buber, Martin, *Tales of the Hasidim: The Early Masters*, translated by Olga Marx (New York: Schocken, 1947).

Buber, Martin, *Tales of the Hasidim: The Later Masters*, translated by Olga Marx (New York: Schocken, 1948).

Deleuze, Gilles, and Guattari, Félix, *Capitalisme et schizophrénie: L'Anti-Œdipe* (Paris: Minuit, 1972).

Derrida, Jacques, *La Voix et le phénomène* (Paris: PUF, 1967).

Derrida, Jacques, *De la grammatologie* (Paris: Minuit, 1967).

Derrida, Jacques, *Marges de la philosophie* (Paris: Minuit, 1972).

Derrida, Jacques, *Force de loi* (Paris: Galilée, 1994).

Descartes, René, *Œuvres et lettres*, edited by André Bridoux (Paris: Gallimard, 1953).

Descombes, Vincent, *Le Même et l'autre: Quarante-cinq ans de philosophie française (1933–1978)* (Paris: Minuit, 1979); published in English as *Modern French Philosophy*, translated by L. Scott-Fox and J. M. Harding (Cambridge: Cambridge University Press, 1980).

Ferry, Luc, and Renaut, Alain, *La Pensée 68: Essai sur l'anti-humanisme contemporain* (Folio; Paris: Gallimard, 1988).

Fish, Stanley, *Is there a Text in this Class? The Authority of Interpretive Communities* (Cambridge: Harvard University Press, 1980).

Foucault, Michel, *Histoire de la sexualité, I: La Volonté de savoir* (Paris: Gallimard, 1976).

Foucault, Michel, *Histoire de la sexualité, II: L'Usage des plaisirs* (Paris: Gallimard, 1984).

Foucault, Michel, *Histoire de la sexualité, III: Le Souci de soi* (Paris: Gallimard, 1984).

Gadamer, Hans-Georg, *Hermeneutik 1: Wahrheit und Methode – Grundzüge einer philosophischen Hermeneutik* (Tübingen: J. C. B. Mohr (Paul Siebeck), 1986; first edition 1960).

Griffiths, A. Phillips (ed.), *Contemporary French Philosophy* (Cambridge: Cambridge University Press, 1987).

Haber, Honi Fern, *Beyond Postmodern Politics: Lyotard, Rorty, Foucault* (New York and London: Routledge, 1994).

Hammond, Michael, Howarth, Jane, and Keat, Russell, *Understanding Phenomenology* (Oxford: Blackwell, 1991).

Handelman, Susan, *The Slayers of Moses: The Emergence of Rabbinic Interpretation in Modern Literary Theory* (Albany: State University of New York Press, 1982).

Hartman, Geoffrey, and Budick, Sanford (eds), *Midrash and Literature* (New Haven and London: Yale University Press, 1986).

Heidegger, Martin, *Sein und Zeit* (fifth edition; Tübingen: Max Niemeyer Verlag, 1979; first published 1927); published in English as *Being and Time*, translated by John Macquarrie and Edward Robinson (Oxford: Blackwell, 1962).

Heidegger, Martin, *Lettre sur l'humanisme*, bilingual edition with French translation by Roger Munier (Paris: Aubier, 1964; letter first published 1947).

Hirsch, Jr, E. D., *Validity in Interpretation* (New Haven and London: Yale University Press, 1967).

Husserl, Edmund, *Logical Investigations*, translated by J. N. Findlay (London: Routledge and Kegan Paul, 1970; first published 1900–1).

Husserl, Edmund, *Méditations cartésiennes: Introduction à la phénoménologie*, translated by Gabrielle Peiffer and Emmanuel Levinas (Paris: Vrin, 1986; first edition 1931); published in English as *Cartesian Meditations: An Introduction to Phenomenology*, translated by Dorion Cairns (The Hague: Martinus Nijhoff, 1973).

Husserl, Edmund, *L'Origine de la géométrie*, translation and introduction by Jacques Derrida (Paris: PUF, 1962; first published 1939).

Husserl, Edmund, *The Crisis of European Sciences and Transcendental Phenomenology: An Introduction to Phenomenological Philosophy*, translated by David Carr (Evanston: Northwestern University Press, 1970; first published 1954).

Kristeva, Julia, *Pouvoirs de l'horreur: Essai sur l'abjection* (Paris: Seuil, 1980).

Lacoue-Labarthe, Philippe, *La Fiction du politique* (Paris: Christian Bourgeois, 1987).

Leibniz, Gottfried Wilhelm, *The Monadology and Other Philosophical Writings*, translated by Robert Latta (Oxford: OUP, 1898).

Lodge, David (ed.), *Modern Criticism and Theory: A Reader* (London and New York: Longman, 1988).

Lyotard, Jean-François, *La Phénoménologie* (Paris: PUF, 1954).

Lyotard, Jean-François, *Le Différend* (Paris: Minuit, 1983).

Lyotard, Jean-François, *Moralités postmodernes* (Paris: Galilée, 1993).

Marion, Jean-Luc, *L'Idole et la distance* (Paris: Grasset et Fasquelle, 1977).

Nancy, Jean-Luc, *L'Impératif catégorique* (Paris: Flammarion, 1983).

Norris, Christopher, *Deconstruction: Theory and Practice* (London: Methuen, 1982).

Pinto, Louis, *Les Philosophes entre le lycée et l'avant-garde: Les Métamorphoses de la philosophie dans la France d'aujourd'hui* (Paris: L'Harmattan, 1987).

Plato, *The Collected Dialogues*, edited by Edith Hamilton and Huntington Cairns (Princeton: Princeton University Press, 1961).

Ricœur, Paul, *Finitude et culpabilité II: La Symbolique du mal* (Paris: Aubier-Montaigne, 1960).

Ricœur, Paul, *Le Conflit des interprétations: Essais d'herméneutique* (Paris: Seuil, 1969).

Ricœur, Paul, *A l'école de la phénoménologie* (Paris: Vrin, 1986; essays originally published between 1949 and 1980).

Ricœur, Paul, *Soi-même comme un autre* (Paris: Seuil, 1990).

Rockmore, Tom, *Heidegger and French Philosophy: Humanism, Antihumanism and Being* (New York and London: Routledge, 1995).

Rorty, Richard, *Contingency, Irony, Solidarity* (Cambridge: CUP, 1989).

Sartre, Jean-Paul, *L'Être et le néant: Essai d'ontologie phénoménologique* (Paris: Gallimard, 1943).

Sartre, Jean-Paul, *Réflexions sur la question juive* (Paris: Gallimard, 1954; first published 1946).

Sartre, Jean-Paul, *L'Existentialisme est un humanisme* (Paris: Nagel, 1946).

Sartre, Jean-Paul, 'Merleau-Ponty vivant', in *Situations IV* (Paris: Gallimard, 1964), 189–287.

Scholem, Gershom, *Major Trends in Jewish Mysticism* (third edition; New York: Schocken Books, 1946).

Singer, Peter (ed.), *A Companion to Ethics* (Oxford: Blackwell, 1991).

Singer, Peter (ed.), *Ethics* (Oxford: OUP, 1994).

Spinoza, Benedict de, *Tractatus Theologico-Politicus*, in *The Chief Works of Benedict de Spinoza*, translated by R. H. M. Elwes (London: George Bell and Sons, 1887; first edition 1884).

Wiesel, Élie, *Le Chant des morts* (Paris: Seuil, 1966).

Wiesel, Élie, *Célébration hassidique* (Paris: Seuil, 1972).

Wiesel, Élie, *Paroles d'étranger* (Points; Paris: Seuil, 1982).

Wiesel, Élie, *Célébration talmudique: Portraits et légendes* (Paris: Seuil, 1991).

Williams, Bernard, *Ethics and the Limits of Philosophy* (London: Fontana, 1993).

# Index